Asian Medicine and Globalization

ENCOUNTERS WITH ASIA
Victor H. Mair, Series Editor

A complete list of books in the series is available from the publisher.

Asian Medicine and Globalization

EDITED BY JOSEPH S. ALTER

PENN

University of Pennsylvania Press

Philadelphia

10 9 8 7 6 5 4 3 2 1

Published by
University of Pennsylvania Press
Philadelphia, Pennsylvania 19104-4011

Library of Congress Cataloging-in-Publication Data

Asian medicine and globalization / edited by Joseph S. Alter.
    p.   cm.—(Encounters with Asia)
Includes bibliographical references and index.
    ISBN 0-8122-3866-4 (cloth : alk. paper)
    1. Traditional medicine—Asia.   2. Medicine, Ayurvedic—Asia.   3. Asia—Social life
and customs.   I. Alter, Joseph S.   II. Series.
GN625 .A744   2005
306.4′61′095—dc22   2004066109

Contents

vi   Contents

Chapter 1

Introduction: The Politics of Culture and Medicine

The chapters in this volume deal with the ways in which bodies of knowledge are manipulated to produce coherence and health, broadly defined. This book focuses on forms of medicine that tend to be linked, in practice and the imagination, to specific nations: India, China, England, and the United States most directly, but also Australia, Tibet, Japan, Singapore, and Germany. And yet the manipulation of health in any one of these places, borrowing ideas from any combination of the others—or from no clearly defined place at all—confounds the boundedness of these national entities. In other words, there is a powerful paradox manifest in the relationship between nationalism and transnationalism. This volume is designed to explore the nature of this paradox as it relates to medical practice and the development of medical knowledge.

Within the rubric of modernity it has become necessary, as Prasenjit Duara puts it, to "rescue history from the nation" (1995). The reason is that the legitimacy and power of nationalism is deeply vested in a particular construction of history. This construction is defined as an objective, authoritative, disinterested account of the past as such. It is, in part, the open-endedness and interpretability of the past that allows for it to be both captured and rescued, defined and redefined, according to different priorities. In this sense history is, simply, a more flexible medium than culture. As anthropologists have pointed out, culture can also be captured and rescued. However, by virtue of present tense, empirical temporality, the capture of culture—its strategic interpretation and manipulation—is often more covert than the capture of history. The heroic rescue of culture is championed overtly by those who claim value-free objectivity.

Culture and history come together at various points, and some of these points of convergence are much more prone to capture than others. Think of borders—what they mean, when they were drawn, and what the convergence of signification and demarcation means with regard to a whole spectrum of things for which the lines on a map are not particularly relevant but rather distort and disorient. If history must be rescued from the nation, the convergence of history and culture—as well as each of these unto itself—must be rescued from a world of partitioned and bracketed nation-states, and also from a worldview, reflected in academia as clearly as in business, that is predicated on the fractured and highly politicized nationalist perception that this entails. There are serious problems, in other words, in thinking about a large region of the world such as Asia—and where does that entity begin and end?—as though its history and culture could be subdivided according to geopolitical entities called China, India, Thailand, Korea, and Taiwan. This is a problem even for those whose topic of study—Buddhism in the tenth century, let us say—obviously crosscuts the borders of relatively old kingdoms and empires and modern states.

As more and more research is conducted on various medical systems in Asia by scholars from a range of disciplines, there is a tendency for the questions being asked to become more and more specific to the uniqueness of each particular case. This is good. We now know much more about medicine in China, Japan, Korea, Malaysia, Thailand, Sri Lanka, India, and Nepal—to string together a somewhat random list of countries—than we did even ten years ago. But it is also unfortunate. The structure of scholarship is invidiously and often invisibly structured by the priorities of the state: funding for research is linked to government interests and is often channeled through state bureaucracies. This can inadvertently produce the illusion that there is a "tradition" of medicine linked to each of these political entities, even when part of the illusion is that that "tradition" has undergone change through contact with other such traditions. So-called Traditional Chinese Medicine and Āyurveda provide the most striking examples. The fact that Āyurveda is the medical system of India goes almost without saying—and that is precisely the problem—even though the history of its development took place only in parts of what is now India, as well as what is now Pakistan, Afghanistan, Nepal, and Bangladesh, through an exchange of ideas that is probably more extensive than the borders of any one of these states or all of them put together.

Even a cursory overview shows that there is a tremendous amount of historical, theoretical, applied, and practical overlap between key concepts in the various medical systems of Asia. The similarity of such principles as *yin/yang* and *prakṛti/puruṣa*, *qi*, and *prāṇa*, the three *doṣa* and the four "Greek" humors, or the five evolutive phases and the five *mahābhūta* elements in the respective traditions of East and South Asia seem almost to demand a cross-cultural comparative analysis. Similarly, various forms of "Western" medicine have been integrated into the practice of medicine to the east of wherever it is that the West is thought to begin, and this dynamic process of exchange has been important from the time of Scythian nomadism through to modern colonialism and the peripatetic introduction of German, Dutch, French, English, and American medicine into various parts of Asia.

To date, however, the extensive and detailed analyses of Asian medical systems have tended to focus on the bounded regional form of practice within the framework of contemporary nation-states. On the one hand there are studies of the introduction of Western medicine into specific countries. On the other hand there are studies of Chinese traditional medicine, Tibetan medicine, Malay humoralism, Japanese Kanpo therapeutics, and Āyurveda in India, Sri Lanka, or Nepal, for example. Even Unani, or so-called Islamic humoral medicine, which in its span from the Middle East to Southeast Asia seems to resist narrow, regional demarcation, has tended to be studied within the confines of subregional local practice.

There is no question that the local, regional, and national appropriation of medical traditions is a common and important framework within which theoretical and practical innovation has occurred. In the scheme of historical time, however, centralized state demarcation—at least on a regional scale—is a relatively recent development, and tends to obscure the way in which Asia, however that entity might be defined, is characterized by an integrated history of practice and theoretical innovation as concerns the development of medicine. Stretching from the periods of "classical civilization" up to the advent of European colonialism in West, East, Southeast, and South Asia, history suggests extensive interregional contact and communication by way of trade, political conquest, and religious proselytization. Beyond this, the seemingly more hegemonic and seamless forms of medical practice in the colonial and postcolonial periods also crosscut regional and state boundaries in important ways.

This volume explores the nature of the tension between nationalism and transnationalism on a smaller, more geographically delimited scale. The focus is on the following key question: when, why, and how is medicine linked to the social, political, religious, and economic culture of a state, and when, why, and how does it extend beyond these delimited, bounded frameworks of legitimation? In many ways this question is framed by institutionalized state politics—that which, quite literally, is established to police the borders. However, reflecting current developments in social theory and cross-cultural comparative analysis, this volume focuses on the nationalistic politics of culture rather than the politics of governments as such, on transnationalism as a cultural process linked to globalization rather than on the formal structure of economic trade or international relations.

Apart from the relatively numerous works on medical knowledge and practice in various regions of Asia, there is a small but significant body of literature that has clearly laid the foundation for an examination of the relationship between nationalism, transnationalism, and medicine in Asia. First and most significant is the work of Charles Leslie, whose two volumes *Asian Medical Systems* (1976) and *Paths to Asian Medical Knowledge* (coedited with Allan Young, 1992) have implicitly if not explicitly defined the link between regional expressions of nationalism and health care. Both volumes are comparative and force a consideration of parallel and converging themes in the history and culture of medical systems that have become associated with different state entities. This theme, along with the question of medical syncretism—which foregrounds questions of transnationalism and globalization—is taken up by Waltraud Ernst in *Plural Medicine: Tradition and Modernity, 1800–2000* (2002). Although many contemporary anthropological and sociological studies of local practice situate medicine in the context of globalization, Connor and Samuel's *Healing Powers and Modernity: Traditional Medicine, Shamanism, and Science in Asian Societies* (2001) is particularly noteworthy for the way each chapter problematizes the relationship between local and global manifestations of medicine and medical knowledge, and how the volume as a whole engages with medicine in the context of state entities, without presuming that the states in question exclusively define the context of practice. By bringing together essays that focus on healing in the modern states of Korea, Malaysia, and India, healing on the margins of Malaysia, Indonesia, and China, and healing that involves Tibetan medicine as practiced in China, Tibet, and India—and by integrating a concern with both shamanic practice and institutionalized medicine—this volume clearly anticipates a direct and critical problematization of the link between medicine and nationalism.

Clearly colonialism and the study of medicine under imperial regimes force a consideration of the intersection of ideas about the body, health, and healing as these ideas intersect in the context of politicized culture. Beyond David Arnold's *Colonizing the Body* (1993), there is a rapidly growing literature in the field of colonial medicine and science studies (see, for example, Ernst and Harris 1999; A. Kumar 1998; D. Kumar 1991, 1995; Pati and Harrison 2001). Two other edited volumes, *Imperial Medicine and Indigenous Societies* (Arnold 1989) and *Disease, Medicine, and Empire* (MacLeod and Lewis 1988), situate medicine within colonialism, pointing out—implicitly if not always explicitly—the connection between the flow of knowledge through various parts of the empire and the resulting connection between nationalism and proto-transnationalism. As several scholars have pointed out (Chakrabarty 2000; Dirks 1998; Duara 1995; Kelly and Kaplan 2001; Prakash 1999) historians of colonialism must work against the logic of imperialism by refusing to let the trajectory of modern nationalism define the structure of history. By doing this it is possible to critically examine events that led up to the construction of state and cultural boundaries, without presuming where those boundaries are drawn, what they contain, or that the natural outcome was the formation of a thing called a state.

In his book *The Expressiveness of the Body and the Divergence of Greek and Chinese Medicine* (1999), Shigehisa Kuriyama directly takes on the question of how, when and on what terms it is possible to compare medical knowledge that is deceptively similar and linked both to the history of different regions and the history of contact between those regions. What is unique about Kuriyama's analysis, and why it is particularly significant here, is that it demonstrates how, apart from the sociology of practice—which is the primary concern of most anthropologists and historians of colonial medicine—medical theory is defined in the context of local practices that are influenced by the global flow of ideas and technology. As Kuriyama points out, what seems to be identical in fact—the pulse or a concept of vital breath—can be radically different in interpretation, and this disjuncture even crosscuts the "genetic kinship" between various theories and therapeutic techniques. For example, there may well be a direct developmental link between bloodletting and acupuncture (1999: 204)—a link that also connects Europe and Asia through an exchange of ideas about etiology and cure—but this does not at all mean that one place conceptualizes it in the same way as the other. There is, consequently, a critical tension, in terms of theory and practice, in the different ways "traditional" Asian medicine is conceptualized as either "nationalistic" or inherently transnational. Stretched to its extreme, this tension is reflected in questions that are probably impossible to answer, and thereby betray their own geopolitical bias—where does Greek medicine end and Chinese medicine begin? What sort of medicine does a physician practice when trained in the West—say Philadelphia—but gains experience that is integrated into practice while treating people in the East—say Beijing (see Brownell, this volume)? Building on the ideas developed by these and other scholars, this volume is designed to examine the relationship between medicine and the national and transnational politics of culture in terms of two sets of thematic questions.

The first set of questions concern the production of medical theory. How does theory reflect the political culture of its production, and does this political culture reflect a concern for containment and control or dissemination, teaching and "popularization"? When medical knowledge moves "across borders"—between India and China (Alter), between China and England (Lo and Schroer), between India and the

United States (Selby and Van Hollen), between British India and England (Habib and Raina), between England and British India and the Dutch East Indies and the Netherlands (Kumar), and between China and the United States (Brownell)—does it retain its character as the medicine of a particular region or state? If so, how and why?

The second set of questions focus on the modern transnational flow of knowledge, capital, and people. Within Asia how do states concern themselves with the modernization of "traditional" medicine? How does the transnational hegemony of science enable or limit the nationalist articulation of alternative medicine in the context of specific states? How do discourses of science and "New Age" spirituality facilitate the transnationalization of "Asian" medicine?

Alter focuses primarily on the first set of questions by looking at how a quintessentially Chinese mode of therapy—acupuncture—has been integrated, in both theory and practice, into an Āyurvedic framework. The modern development of a distinct theory of Āyurvedic acupuncture is in some sense motivated by a clear sense of nationalism. Claims are made that the original theory of vital points and the manipulation of vital energy was developed in India and taken to China by traveling scholar-monks in the late classical period. The basis for such a claim is thought to be a theory of *marma* (vital points) articulated in various South Asian medical texts; according to some, the link between *marma* and *nāḍī* physiology, and a tradition of healing based on the manipulation of various different kinds of vital points, includes *marma*.

Beyond this, there is the complex question of technology and the relationship between needles and cauterizing tools on the one hand and the distinction between surgery and needling on the other. To what extent are these things the same and to what extent are they different? And then, how does the inherent ambiguity imbedded in the answer to this question structure the dynamic between nationalistic claims and transnational processes? Clearly there was contact between practitioners of medicine in what is now China and what is now India, and it is probable that there was a dynamic exchange of knowledge between scholars at any number of locations between East and South Asia. However, modern articulations of theory both recognize and deny this contact, and the more refined and complex a modern theory of Āyurvedic acupuncture gets, the more clearly it reflects the paradox and irony of a nationalism that depends on but seeks to transcend—or elide—a transnationalism that makes it possible.

Lo and Schroer are also concerned with the first set of questions, focusing on shifts in theory and meaning in the development of ideas about *xie* in "traditional" Chinese medicine. How *xie* has been translated differently at different times in China and England provides for an analysis of the relationship between political culture and theory. In very broad terms *xie* can be translated as "evil, heteropathy or perversity"; it literally means "oblique, deviating," the opposite of *zheng*, that which is upright and straight. Although *xie* is linked to ideas about demonic possession and naturalistic illness, Lo and Schroer trace the earliest medical theories to social, political, and moral ideas on ritual and philosophy in general, and—striking a Pythagorean chord—to music in particular. They show how the link between music, mood, and behavior was problematized in the premodern period and how music and ritual served to subvert *xie* and promote harmony and balance.

Strikingly, a social and moral conceptualization of *xie* comes to inform medical theory as articulated in the Yellow Emperor's Inner Canon:

As deviant music causes counterflow *qi* that disturbs the emotions and disrupts the state, so *xie* in a medical context brings with it a way of talking about the body in moral terms, terms which associate parts of the body with socially disruptive behavior.

In this, the state and the body are conceptualized in much the same way, and the two domains are linked metaphorically. Thus purgation, exorcism, and exile are in some sense all theoretically connected. This linkage finds interesting expression in the Nationalist period as such, and also in the nationalism manifest in the Maoist regime. In the former, the principle of *xie* did not conform to ideas about the scientific modernization of Traditional Chinese Medicine, and was purged from the literature, so to speak. In the Communist period the idea of *xie*, as it was linked to superstition and the evil of demonic possession, was labeled feudal and disruptive and was exorcized from theoretical texts.

The link in *xie* between the body, the state, and political culture also finds expression and elaboration in the context of transnationalism. One dominant form of contemporary acupuncture therapy in England derives from a lineage of development—via Japan and Taiwan—wherein *xie* continued to be recognized as theoretically and practically important during the time when it was purged from practice in the PRC. In the context of modern England, the principle of *xie* tends to be interpreted not as evil per se, but as the malignant environment and, at least by extension, the "evil" of the state's environmental and economic policy, against which the body has to be protected.

Habib focuses on the history of Āyurveda and Unani in late nineteenth- and early twentieth-century India, when those involved in the nationalist movement were actively politicizing culture in general and the principle of *swadeshi*, or national self-reliance, in particular. In this context P. S. Varier, Hakim Ajmal Khan, and P. C. Ray came to be concerned with the modernization and revitalization of traditional Indian medical systems. Habib argues that early in the twentieth century Āyurveda and Unani came to be defined as traditional cultural systems, but also came to be identified as scientific systems that needed to be modernized. Verier, Khan, and Ray were involved in a complex process wherein the relationship between tradition and modernity was being worked out conceptually with reference to ideas about science and scientific theory. Thus, the key distinction between Āyurveda, Unani, and biomedicine was perceived to be one of relative progress and development rather than one of categorical ontological difference. What was perceived to be required was an epistemological shift rather than any kind of paradigmatic change. This allowed for tradition to be modernized in terms of science, with the essential Indianness of tradition being clearly preserved.

To preserve the "Indianness" of tradition, Habib and Raina argue, the cultural importance of science as a sign of Europe was played down in the discourse of modernization, using the logic of science itself: its claim to value-free, objective neutrality. At the beginning of the twentieth century the development of a discourse about the modernization of traditional medicine in terms of science helped to establish three critical axes that later in the century came to be recognized as the primary things that need to be changed in order to bring about reform and revitalization: the stagnation of knowledge, poor-quality education and training, and low-grade, poorly manufactured pharmaceuticals. While later in the century colonialism as such came to be blamed for the demise of traditional medicine along these axes, Habib and Raina point out that in the early part of the century the politics of culture was much more subtle. Although Verier, Khan, and Ray unselfconsciously looked to "Western" science, they did so in a context wherein there was at least a degree of parity, as reflected in Lord Hardinge's public recognition that modern medicine owed a debt to the medicines of India for "preserving knowledge" that was lost in Europe during the dark ages.

In general Habib and Raina clearly show how nationalism not only finds expression as ideology or dogmatic positionality but is deeply vested in broad, transnational exchanges of ideas and techniques, in particular, ideas about the nature of science. With regard to medicine in particular, elemental, practical concerns about quality define the parameters of a debate about modernization that involves tradition.

Kumar reinforces and builds on many of the key points made by Habib and Raina by developing a comparative analysis of colonialism and medicine in British India and the Dutch Indies. He points out that although colonialism can be understood as a pervasive discourse of power, historians must not lose sight of the fact that in specific instances the development of medical knowledge—as one facet of this discourse—reflects "insecurity, amazement, curiosity and frustration" rather than the clear-cut certainty that one might associate with the larger, authoritarian project of imperialism. Kumar focuses on what might be called the subtexts of specific forms of colonial practice and knowledge construction by comparing and contrasting Dutch and British experiences in South and Southeast Asia during the eighteenth and early nineteenth centuries.

He begins his analysis by pointing out that although the tendency now is to make a categorical distinction between Western and non-Western forms of medicine, this distinction was not that sharp until the relatively recent institutionalization of germ theory. Prior to 1880, one must focus as much if not more on the institutionalization of medicine as on ideological positionality regarding categorical differences in medical theory. Following from this, early in the nineteenth century there was a degree of curiosity and amazement on the part of scholar-surgeons concerning the possible effectiveness of new substances and novel forms of treatment.

One aspect of colonial practice that Kumar analyzes is medical training. He shows that in contrast to the Dutch, "the British in India had developed fine distinctions in terms of what to teach and whom to teach." In other words, the politics of health care administration was, in part, an issue of control over knowledge, and the proper transfer of knowledge between colonized and colonizer. In this context he points out that both the British and the Dutch very effectively exploited the hierarchical forms of social organization in their respective areas of rule.

At the fin de siècle the situation concerning medical theory had changed significantly with revolutionary advances in tropical medicine following germ theory and the epidemiology of epidemics. In both British India and the Dutch Indies this led to more hegemonic forms of public health administration and more intensive—and politicized—efforts in the institutionalization of medicine. Significantly, however, there was frustration on the part of colonial scientists studying tropical medicine, who felt as though their contextualized research was not being regarded as significant on account of being produced outside the centers of imperial authority, particularly London. As Kumar points out, there was also a degree of ambivalence on the part of colonial administrators regarding the role of philanthropic organizations. They provided much-needed funding for increased public health programs, but at the possible expense of the colonial government having to cede a degree of political and economic control.

In both Southeast and South Asia, a politicized, indigenous response developed in tandem with the expansion of colonial policy and practice. In British India a nationalist discourse was clearly articulated in the latter half of the nineteenth century as an issue that linked medicine to broader cultural concerns about self-rule and the value of tradition. This discourse took political form in the context of the Indian National Congress activism. In the Dutch Indies a nationalist discourse about medicine developed only after 1918 and did not have recourse to the same kind of "indigenous traditions" as Āyurveda and Unani. It was regard as a discreet problem of institutionalization linked to budgetary concerns and was debated in the People's Council that was established in 1918. Although this comparison would tend to place emphasis on the structural differences between the two articulations of nationalism, Kumar concludes his chapter with a discussion of the role of Dr. Soetomo who drew inspiration from Indian sources to negotiate the politics of culture defined by the circular intersection of colonial hegemony and the ideology of primordialism that it creates and recreates.

In her analysis of the use of "traditional" medicine for the treatment of HIV/AIDS in India, Van Hollen situates the contemporary nationalist debate within the context of colonial history. In the colonial context, Āyurveda in particular came to be constructed through a complex engagement with biomedicine and the colonial use of biomedicine as a "tool of empire." Although many proponents of Āyurveda argued for various ways in which it could be integrated with biomedicine, M. K. Gandhi articulated one of the most sustained and high profile critiques of biomedicine and a critique of the very idea of medicine as such. As Van Hollen points out, Gandhi's critique of biomedicine reverberates through the contemporary nationalist discourse concerning the value of Āyurveda. One of the issues that has become complicated in this discourse is that, largely as a consequence of Āyurveda's growing transnational appeal—and global market value—the terms of legitimacy are becoming more complicated, and the criteria for distinctiveness, such as spirituality, holism, and antimaterialism, less clearly reflected in theory and practice.

Contemporary nationalist debate centers on claims that Āyurvedic medicines can cure HIV/AIDS and revolves around defenses of this claim against challenges put forward by NGOs, the Indian government, and various international groups. Various individuals who claim to cure HIV/AIDS with "traditional" medicine defend their claims in terms of what they regard to be the proof of outcome—actual cures—as well as on the basis of cultural authenticity. In this context, transnationalism's confrontation with nationalism is paradoxical. To answer challenges from biomedicine, those who claim to cure people living with AIDS must accept the terms that give legitimacy to biomedicine. These terms "deconstruct" Āyurveda's primary link to the nation and national culture.

Following thematically directly on some of the points raised by Van Hollen and Lo and Schroer, Chen focuses on the discourse of science in contemporary China and the way in which the state and several different categories of *qigong* master engage in this discourse as it relates to theories about the nature of *qi* and claims to efficacy and power. Drawing on Donna Haraway's conceptualization of "invisible standards" encoded in science as a knowledge system, she focuses on how the Chinese government clearly has a nationalist interest in promoting science and scientific development in a broad range of fields. This is in part because science promotes development and progress, but also because science is both transparent and structured in such a way that it can be easily controlled and regulated. Conversely, the Chinese government is nervous about individuals who are able to claim power—physical, metaphysical, or social—by means that are thought to be supernatural. In this respect *qigong* masters present particular problems because their ability to heal people has the effect of making them very popular and therefore potentially powerful. As Chen argues, the response of the state has been to try and enforce, as policy, a cultural distinction between scientific and unscientific *qigong*. Masters who wish to practice must be licensed, ostensibly to protect common people from the influence of superstition and *xie* cults by formalizing scientific *qigong* as *zheng*.

In its effort to make *qigong* scientific, the state is confronted with a paradox. While it seeks to control the power associated with *qigong* and the charisma of popular masters, the very process of science undermines the power it is meant to control, which is based on abilities and techniques that are inherently mysterious. Thus, licenses authorize and empower in terms of a state-mandated nationalist discourse, but disempower on the level of popular discourse where cures are valued precisely because they are miraculous. Ironically, the discourse of science has, in effect, increased the popularity and power of some *qigong* masters whose refusal to be "scientized" is taken as proof of their authenticity. Furthermore, given the dynamics of globalization and the movement of people and information across national boarders, many charismatic *qigong* masters have left the country to build up larger, international followings. The development of a transnational discourse, intimately connected to "Chinese culture," undermines the state's nationalist intent.

In many ways transnational *qigong* masters fit into the discourse and commodified practice of so-called New Age health and healing. Selby examines this discourse with reference to Ayuryoga—a neologism of Āyurveda combined with yoga—in the context of the United States in general and its extreme localization in Austin, Texas, in particular. As with Lo and Schroer and Alter, she is concerned with transformation in the meaning of terms and the logic in theory in the context of transnational decontextualization. Using Arjun Appadurai's cultural analysis of commodities, and the "social life" of commodities in circulation, Selby examines the way in which women's health as articulated in the classical Āyurvedic texts has shifted from largely physiological concerns with pregnancy, childbirth, and the production of healthy male heirs to a loosely configured regimen of beauty and spa-based commodity consumption. As she points out, the merchandizing of Ayuryoga spa culture and the commodification of health and beauty products is very much a gendered enterprise, "where everything gains an equivalence, and all combinations seem infinitely possible."

This fetishistic and endlessly mimetic process is clearly reflected both in the English translation of the classical texts—where "egg" and "ovum" are problematically used to gloss the Sanskrit terms for menstrual blood and female semen—and in a large and growing number of popular self-help books that interpret and reinterpret the classical texts as well as one another. What gets articulated in these texts is a series of paradoxes where *doṣic* gynecology and obstetrics is interpreted in terms of self fulfillment, consumer-oriented individuality and the relative merits and beauty of different constitutional body types.

Topically following on the theme of how medicine is related to beauty, Brownell also focuses how meaning is grafted onto medical practice. She turns the tables on the direction of transnational flow, using John Mac-Aloon's notion of "empty form" to show how biomedicine, like modern sports, is what she calls an "empty frame": both are rigidly defined by the culture of science and yet very open to cultural interpretation of other kinds, particularly in the context of nationalist discourses. In this regard the development of plastic surgery as a distinctly Chinese form of medical practice reflects the same process as acupuncture being adapted to the conditions of Britain and Japan, or of its being analyzed and practiced with reference to Āyurvedic theory in South Asia.

Brownell situates plastic surgery in the context of modern Chinese history and the demand for reconstructive surgery during the war with Japan. Focusing on the career of Song Ruyao, who was sent to the University of Pennsylvania Medical School in 1943, she shows how plastic surgery shifted from a concern with the reconstruction and repair of wounds during the Korean War and the Cultural Revolution—when it was already considered bourgeois—to a concern after 1979 for cosmetic surgery, the double-eyelid procedure in particular. As Brownell points out, "More so than many other medical subfields, cosmetic surgery presents a challenge to the universalist assumptions of biomedicine." Concepts of beauty vary cross-culturally, and the techniques of surgery must be adapted to match these concepts within the context of variation in facial anatomy. Thus cosmetic surgery can be seen to be distinctly linked to cultural concerns, and, as Brownell shows, to a nationalist discourse in which it has become "plastic surgery with Chinese characteristics." Claims are made that certain Chinese techniques are better, that Chinese surgeons are better at certain procedures, and that the double eyelid is not an attempt to look more European but a procedure that enhances Chinese beauty.

In addressing the two sets of questions outlined above, each of the following chapters is framed by an overarching paradox: medicine is conceptualized in terms that are more directly linked to principles of nature—disease, physiology, and the technology of cure—than to principles of culture. Needless to say, the principles of nature are not organically natural; they are only constructed as such. But it is significant that medicine is, at base, a practical, pragmatic, and ultimately utilitarian endeavor. It is all about life and death, and most certainly not just in a metaphorical sense. This is what distinguishes it from art, music, literature and most other cultural things. And yet medicine is infused with culture and the politics of culture. The paradox is that as medicine is more deeply implicated in the politics of culture the act of politics often involves ever more elaborate claims about the organic, natural nature of medical truth and about the universal efficacy of one kind of medicine as against another.

What all the chapters in this volume clearly show is that power is neither simply institutionalized nor manifest as pure ideology, as can be the case with nationalism among a host of other cultural practices. In an important way the significance of medical knowledge is measured against the health of a specific person, manifesting specific symptoms, who is endowed with a rich and meaningful concept of self. This makes medicine a kind of social fact that mitigates against pure ideology, abstract theory, and formal policy. What I mean is that medicine is a social and cultural phenomenon wherein abstract theories—about acupuncture (Alter), Āyurvedic gynecology (Selby), the plastic manipulation of physical beauty (Brownell), qi (Chen), deviant airs (Lo and Schroer), the "cure" of AIDS with herbal drugs (Van Hollen)—are ultimately justified not by the integrity of culture, however that is defined, but by the integrity of the person upon whom medicine is practiced. The justification may not be direct and immediate, but medicine that is not effective in some way can ever develop into a system of medicine as such. In an important way this fundamental physiological materialism, and radical, reductive particularism, makes it impossible for medical systems to suffer the fate of other systems—economic ones, for example—wherein the product of social labor is fetishized as a thing apart from social labor as a thing of preeminent value.

An interesting angle to take on this is to "read backward," as it were, from the bodies of citizens, or the practices of specific physicians, to look at the way in which the state seeks to control bodies that it cannot quite control, either by institutionalizing laws or by developing ideologies. It is precisely because the embodied person is the ultimate object of medical treatment that the state is unable to fully control the body of the citizen in terms of medical knowledge and the production of knowledge by individuals.

All the chapters engage with the problem of modernity and specific, transnational transformations in the relationship between medicine and politics that can be linked to modernity. Transnationalism is a function of modernity, since it is the nation—rather than an empire, city state, or clan community—that must be "transed." Consider the case of a cosmetic surgeon in China who trained in the United States but practices medicine in China. Consider the popularization of Ayuryoga and Āyurvedic gynecology. Consider the case of Frank Ros in Australia inventing—or perhaps just reinventing—a theory of Āyurvedic acupuncture, and the example of Āyurvedic acupuncturists in India constructing their practice in relation to both ancient Indian texts and contemporary discourses about the nature and relative authority of ancient Chinese sources. Is all of this categorically and structurally different from what was going on when scholars from various parts of what is now China engaged with scholars at Nalanda, in what is now India, in the eighth century? Clearly "Science"—with a capital S—must factor into this, but the question is how and to what degree. With regard to the eighth century, the question is at least in part how and to what degree did Buddhism link Asia together, and to what extent it did not.

Clearly one thing which distinguishes transnationalism and globalization from the exchange of ideas between different parts of the world centuries ago is the rapidity of exchange, the sheer volume of things in circulation—with an emphasis on both volume and circularity. There is also probably both a degree of critical consciousness about the process itself and a certain looseness or flexibility in interpretation and creative synthesis, as well as a more pervasive sense of anxiety about authenticity, coherence, and the control of knowledge—which is, again, where the politics of culture comes most explicitly into play. Regardless, the uniqueness of transnationalism as a modern dynamic is primarily manifest in the way nationalism seeks to control culture. One can imagine an ancient chain of links in medical knowledge connecting what is now China to what is now Greece or India, with little concern for problems of "cultural integrity" but great concern and interest in what was new, innovative, and effective. Medical knowledge was, of course, jealously guarded. But it was probably not regarded as belonging to a place and "a people" so much as to a particular person with clearly manifest skills.

The premodern politics of medical knowledge seems largely to have been an issue of individual reputation and patronage. Consider that "Greek medicine" does not roll off the tongue very smoothly, or find its way into print as easily, as does the phrase Galenic or humoral medicine. References to the writings of Galen, Hippocrates, and Aristotle indicate a concern with the discrete delineation of knowledge rather than its abstract, impersonal, systemic homogenization. The classical texts of Āyurveda are known in terms of their authors, even though the level of agreement is such that one can, obviously, speak of an abstract system of medical knowledge overarching the specific contributions of Caraka, Suśruta, and Vāgbhata. The point is that systematicity takes on a life of its own, and becomes politicized as such, in the context of modernity.

The fact that nationalism promotes systemic medical insularity draws attention to a general question that has to do with a kind of hegemony that is built into transnationalism in general and the transnational dynamics of postcolonial academic scholarship in particular. It is a question that all of the chapters in this volume ask, but do not seek to directly answer. As such it is a question that opens the way to future scholarship.

The question is this: can we better engage with the forms of knowledge that are affected in modernity by suggesting that, at least on some level, one of the problems with modernity—colonialism and much more—is that it has imposed the whole category of medicine as such onto Asia? Most certainly this question must not lead back to a position of ethnocentric skepticism about the lack of efficacy and theoretical coherence manifest in Asian therapeutics. Rather, the point of posing the question is to think through what has come to be defined as medicine in Asia. The point is to destabilize the very idea of medicine, to dislocate it from what might be called axial status in the domain of culture-that-concerns-the-body. As many of the chapters show, what counts as medicine blurs into other things—martial arts, beauty regimens, alchemy, aesthetic surgery, diet, and yoga. Therefore, odd as it may sound, perhaps "medicine" does not provide the best framework for understanding the history of medicine or the cultural construction of medical knowledge.

This is not the same as saying that biomedicine does not provide the framework, for that is quite obvious. But the very idea of medicine—the category itself—might count as one of those "invisible standards" that Donna Haraway (1997) refers to in her critique of academic discourse in the history and philosophy of science.

The body and concepts of embodiment can serve as a way to think about medicine outside the strictures of medical logic. But in many cases things that relate directly to medicine extend beyond the body. Zoology, botany, cosmology, alchemy, and of course religion and philosophy come to mind. Common sense would dictate that medicine is the logical framework for contextualizing a history of medicine. But what is it that produces this sense of common sense? It is most certainly convenient to talk in terms of medicine, but convenience reflects a high degree of homogenization. Perhaps medicine—regardless of its utilitarian structure and function—is a derivative category of thought. And perhaps a problem with using the body as an alternative frame of reference is that it, too, poses the question of value in narrowly utilitarian and practical terms, or even in terms that place priority on the phenomenology of experience—being cured, for example—rather than on something which seeks to go beyond experience with regard to the problem of ordering and reordering the world.

With this in mind it is possible to think about the dynamics of medicine in the context of nationalism and transnationalism as animated by a more complex set of factors than the simple, structural opposition—or hybrid synthesis—of tradition and modernity. In this formulation, medicine in Asia can be understood to be defined, problematically, by the bracketing force of medicine itself—conceptualized across time as a naturally delimited system dealing with illness and disease—as against a history of health that encompasses much more than questions of disease etiology, diagnosis, and therapeutic cure. As historians have noted, medicine and the development of medical knowledge have often been very closely linked to philosophy. They also have close links to religion. There are links also between medicine and sport; medicine and war; medicine and botany—among a host of other things.

But another way of thinking about this is to see the "links" as diagnostic of a problem in modern delineation. Perhaps the links can be reconceptualized as shifting, discursive centers, rather than as fixed points of overlap or intersection. In any case, nationalism is, in some ways, concerned with the centering of medicine as medicine—be it Āyurveda, TCM, biomedicine, or some permutation of these plus others, and be it modernized or traditionalized—whereas transnationalism, in highlighting links or possible links, either destabilizes medicine as a category or complicates its structure, function, and meaning. Of course nationalism often "feeds off" transnational processes, just as transnationalism picks apart nationalist constructs. But what is involved here in questioning the commonsensical status of medicine as medicine is to shift attention away from the formal change in the nature of medicine as such and to focus on the structural change in the relationship of things that are thought to be linked to medicine, but are better conceptualized in terms of health, very broadly defined—including such things as wealth on the one hand, as well as practices that directly involve magic, spirituality and the supernatural, on the other.

The unfortunate situation has been that for decades, if not a century or more, medicine in Asia—and Asian medicine in particular—has struggled to gain legitimacy as medicine by excluding precisely these things. Arguably the methods of science, in both discourse and practice, have been used to make claims of legitimacy, even if one form of legitimacy is to claim for the medicine in question the status of an alternative science to the science that emerged out of the European Enlightenment. To question the status of Āyurveda or TCM as medical systems—not just to question their relative efficacy and systemic integrity—might be regarded as the ultimate postmodern insult added to the injury of colonial and postcolonial Orientalism.

However, in an important way the point of critique and cultural criticism is reversed, in the sense that the purpose of questioning the status of TCM and Āyurveda as medical systems is not to question their legitimacy or champion the cause of mysticism against rationalism—as some New Age advocates have done—but to point out the contingency of medicine itself as a disciplinary entailment of the Enlightenment that ineffectively captures, and ultimately distorts, the ways what have come to be called Āyurvedic medicine and Traditional Chinese Medicine define what should be counted as health and well-being.

With this in mind one can better appreciate the extent to which the cases analyzed by Brownell and Van Hollen—where biomedical categories loom largest—are those where the trenchantly disease-oriented, cure-driven, remedial structure of biomedicine fails to capture what gets counted as biomedicine: plastic surgery and a "cure" for AIDS. If plastic surgeons manipulate aesthetic ideals; if classical Āyurvedic texts describe regimens to produce immortality; if TCM and Āyurveda are as directly linked to sex as they are to pathology; and if the *zheng/xie* polarity involves but extends beyond the body, then perhaps it is necessary to theorize health in terms of truth, beauty, pleasure, wholesomeness, and supernatural power, rather than in terms of sickness, suffering, death, and disease.

Clearly this entails much more critical skepticism than uncritical New Age optimism. Although New Age practitioners have engaged in all manner of novel distortion and crass commercial exploitation—but so, to, have many others—the likes of Deepak Chopra and Vasant Lad are able to make their claims to better lives through healthy living precisely because the legitimization of Asian medicine through discourses of science has made it possible to transform discourses of health into commodified regimens of medicalized self-help. Most significantly, self-help is made relevant to public health in a context where stress, drug addiction, bad eating habits, and inadequate exercise are understood as medical problems of great importance. Whereas Deepak Chopra and others are, I think, completely wrong in terms of how various dimensions of Asian medicine are relevant to health in the New Age—since their concern is with self-help and is always incipiently remedial, their focus invariably on contingent problems to be overcome rather than possibilities as such, and their interpretations selective and rather superficial—they are absolutely right in seeing in these "medical systems" much more than counts as medicine.

But the point here is not so much to criticize the New Age paramedicalization of lifestyle as to suggest that a new critical perspective on what has been called Asian Medicine—and, indeed, the practice of medicine in Asia—shows how the development of biomedicine from Greek and medieval humoralism might be understood as progress by way of exclusion rather than progress through a shift in paradigm, the development of new theories, and a more refined understanding of how the body works in relation to nature. In essence the point is to show how medicine as a conceptual category produces and reproduces a narrow and rather unhealthy understanding of what counts as health, and not just with reference to the practice of medicine, but with reference to life as such. Given that medicine has subsumed the knowledge that produced it, it is difficult to appreciate the extent to which Galen, Caraka, Suśruta, and Chao Yuanfang might have conceptualized health in ways that were not strictly inhibited by the logic of healing. This is not at all to romanticize this conception of health, but to look at it from the vantage point of philosophy, in the original Pythagorean sense of that term.

What this allows for is to take seriously, in a new and more comprehensive way, such things as plastic surgery in China, Āyurvedic acupuncture, Ayuryogic cosmetics, attempts to find an Āyurvedic cure for AIDS, and attempts to give modern legitimacy to "traditional" medicine. Otherwise the conceptual framework of medicine makes serious cultural analysis impossible by forcing, in the final instance, the question of efficacy and proof. Instead of thinking about Asian medicine as the "Asian form of medicine," perhaps it is better to conceptualize what has come to be called Asian medicine as being various experimental techniques concerned with embodied life and longevity. Consider alchemy, and the embodiment of alchemy, that is found in yoga and *qigong*. With reference to this, medicine as a conceptual category can be thought of as a pragmatic, body-oriented copy of techniques designed to transform nature itself. It is a copy in the sense that clinic-based healing is a metaphorical instantiation, or fragmented mimetic reproduction, of immortality. It is, therefore, not so much that Asian medicine is not really medicine, as some Orientalist scholars evinced, or that it is ineffective quackery, as many practitioners of biomedicine continue to claim, but that medicine as such is a devolved form of alchemy. To the extent that science elides the mimetic relationship between alchemy and medicine, it has caused a profound transmutation in the logic of health all over the world.

This is not to make any historical argument about the developmental relationship of alchemy and medicine, but rather to focus on each in relation to the other as conceptual categories that involve health, the body, and the transformation of nature. To do so helps avoid the problematic conceptualization of Asian medicine—even in Asia—as alternative medicine. The question of difference, which remains important, is subsumed within difference itself: alchemy as different from medicine but applied to all medicine. In many respects an inclusive framework of alchemy also helps to get past the problematic of Science as the modern yardstick for measuring medical legitimacy—its gold standard or touchstone, so to speak. Even more significantly, this gets past a conceptualization of so-called "alternative sciences," which begs as many questions as does a theory of alternative modernities (Kelly 2002). To adapt John Kelly's recent formulation concerning modernity, alchemy provides a framework for medicine that is alternative to science itself. To be alternative to science, rather than simply "alternatively scientific," makes what has come to be called Asian medicine less affected by a sense of the sublime that seems to stick to the concept of science itself, despite—or perhaps on account of—its claim to reason, rationality and brute-fact empiricism.

Clearly many practitioners of medicine in Asia would disagree. But the formulation is designed less to challenge their claims than to shed light on the problems they confront in trying to modernize "traditional" medical systems within the culture of a state—the terminology itself signaling the logical contortions involved. Clearly practitioners of biomedicine would take issue with being called devolved alchemists, even on the level of conceptual categorization. But it is useful, I think, to think about major advances in medical science as indicative of a more meta-physical quest for immortality and perfection. There is "magic" in gene therapy, liver transplantation, and the methods used to find a cure for Alzheimer's. But it is a transnational perspective on real magic— what some *qigong* masters claim to be able to do; an herbal "cure" for AIDS; exorcism—that can help to make such as statement as this meaningful and interesting, as against letting it stand as a cliche, a metaphorical entailment to be subsumed within the reverential sublime of science-beyond-comprehension. Nationalism enforces difference—this medicine in relation to that—whereas transnationalism can be the articulation of difference itself.

The chapters in this volume clearly point in this direction by suggesting, either directly or indirectly, that there are limits to the way in which medicine can be understood as medicine or science understood as science. The politics of culture—manifest in both nationalism and transnationalism—has made it virtually impossible to talk about Asian medicine as anything but medicine, and as medical knowledge as anything other than science. To explore the various dimensions of this politics, as the contributors to this volume have done, makes it possible to take the next step: to question the hegemony of the conceptual category itself. Is there such a thing as medicine? To ask the question is—if I may use a term that falls somewhere between capture and rescue, the tropes with which I began—to chart a route of escape from a whole series of false or problematic dichotomies that have plagued the analysis of health, healing, and the body in Asia.

Chapter 2

Āyurvedic Acupuncture—Transnational Nationalism: Ambivalence About the Origin and Authenticity of Medical Knowledge

JOSEPH S. ALTER

Prelude: The Transnational Politics of Medical Theory

Few if any would argue that medicine is not politicized on a number of levels and that it is deeply permeated by culture and cultural values. Yet medical systems, like the sciences on which they are based, are usually founded on universalist principles of health and healing, defined in pan-human terms and in terms of natural laws that are thought to transcend culture. Quite apart from what happens in practice, on the level of theory medicine is usually imagined as objective and value-free or connected to pervasive forces of transcendent, spiritual, and metaphysical power. If not by any means always or even usually effective, in principle a medical system can be used to treat anyone, anywhere, under any set of conditions.

Considering this, one can imagine an Escheresque tableau wherein a biomedical physician at University of Pittsburgh Medical Center is taking the pulse of an Āyurvedic physician, who is taking the pulse of a Chinese physician, who is taking the pulse of a Greek physician, who, to complete the circle, is taking the pulse of the biomedical physician at the University of Pittsburgh Medical Center. Although they may disagree completely about what they are "feeling," they all think that what they know is true for the human condition that underlies their specific skills and training. They all think, unequivocally, that they could diagnose and treat each other.

Reflecting on this, I would like to consider here some of the dynamics involved when politics and culture—and more specifically the politics of culture—intrude more or less self-consciously into the domain of medical theorizing, and into the logic of scientific reasoning within medical theory. On the most basic level my argument is that the politics of nationalism does not just affect the practice of medicine—taking a pulse, for example—it has an effect on how practice is theorized. I will argue that medical theory is derived from the politics of transnational nationalism; that Chinese, Greek, American, and Indian physicians do not just feel what they feel, but are engaged in a complex process of somewhat nervously second-guessing each other's "feelings" and incorporating that into the sense of meaning and purpose that extends from the tips of their own fingers to the tips of their tongues, so to speak. My concern, however, is not with the pulse per se, but with the probing fingers and needles of acupressure and acupuncture. To this end I will somewhat arbitrarily close the circle, as it were, and leave the practitioners of Chinese medicine and Āyurveda in a "touchy" face off.

Introduction: Sleights of Mind

If all this is as you say, [the land of the sunrise] must indeed be the realm of Buddha, and I would like to be reborn there.[1]

In his book *Tantra in Practice* (2000), David White, scholar of religion and analyst of alchemy and embodied magic, suggests that if you look at Asia through the lens of medieval Tantric practice what you see is an area where national boundaries—and in some instances rituals of state unto themselves—seem to dissolve in the rich mixture of alchemy, Taoist philosophy, yogic breathing techniques, magic and various modes of meditation that are linked to powerful ideas about the body.[2] Within the broader sweep of a general history of Asia—if not also the world—that defines the prismatic of this lens, there is no doubt about the fact that a monk by the name of Nandi traveled round-trip from southern South Asia to central East Asia on several occasions in the seventh century C.E., once in search of medicinal herbs at the behest of the emperor (White 1996: 61), and that in the twelfth century scholars and travelers from what is now the People's Republic of China came and studied in centers of learning that are now located in the Republic of India. Quite obviously there is no doubt that contact between "China" and "India" set in motion the spread and transformation of what has come to be known as Buddhism throughout East and Southeast Asia.[3] The influence of this contact on medical knowledge is less well understood.[4] But it seems quite clear that ideas about physiology, anatomy, therapy, and diagnosis moved along the land and sea trade routes, and between the centers of learning and religious institutions located along these routes, particularly between the third and eighth centuries C.E.[5]

Significantly, Paul Unschuld points out that the exchange of ideas between China and India—often referred to as the Western lands—is difficult to explain. First the idea of *tridoṣa* was introduced to China from India in the late second and early third centuries, but it was almost as though the concept was impossible to translate into the Chinese conceptual framework of that time (1985: 142).[6] Although, as might be expected, medical ethics developed along with the introduction and spread of Buddhism (Unschuld 1978: 43–53), a Buddhist theory of physiology and etiology based on the character of the four elements, earth, air, fire and water had "a negligible impact on the secular-medical literature of China" (1985: 150). Unschuld goes on to state that "one can only guess" at why this was the case. "Perhaps the cultural gap was simply too great, or the attempts to bridge that gap to cursory, for genuine reception to have taken place" (1985: 15). Beyond this, Unschuld makes the following important observation:

As far as we know Buddhism only related its own "four-elements doctrine" to China; the "five-elements doctrine" of the Upanishads, generally identified as underlaying (ayurvedic) medical conceptions, does not appear in Buddhist texts translated into Chinese. (1985: 377 n. 14)

One can only guess why this was the cases, given the kind of numero-structural correspondences that are discussed below, and the way in which these correspondences signal a possible history of ideas. In any event there was clearly intellectual contact and an exchange of some medical ideas between the Western lands and the dynastic realm to the east into which Buddhism spread.

Far less clear is what more than a thousand years of cross-cultural contact—in whatever form and on whatever scale—can tell us about the inherent problem of thinking about this as contact between India and China, among other countries.[7] Clearly "China" and "India" are not now and never have been a single entity reflecting a seamless, homogeneous culture—although the appellation "Orient" and even "Asia" can lead to such radical conceptual blurring. But then China and India have never been single entities unto themselves until very recently. In some significant ways, to speak of Chinese culture or Indian culture—without being extremely careful about delimiting the historical and political frame of reference—does not really make any more sense than to speak about the Orient. Consider here, as a telling example, that no one is quite sure if one Bogar (or Pokar or Bhoga) was a southern Indian alchemist who studied in China—as well as northern South Asia, which is almost as far away—or a Chinese alchemist who studied in India (White 1996: 61).

Most scholars can avoid the issue by focusing on very specific, local, time-delimited topics. Thus within the field of medical anthropology one can study a specific feature of Āyurvedic practice, for example, and within medical history it is possible to focus on developments in Traditional Chinese Medicine at a given point in time. It is often with a sigh of relief—momentary to be sure, and with a nagging sense of chronic doubt—that I now settle into reading late twentieth-century popular treatises on Āyurvedic sexology, for example, with a concern for sorting out, without direct concern for nation or state, the relationship between hyperpotency and epidemics of impotency. Nevertheless, research on this micro scale and scope tends to get amalgamated, on a disciplinary and interdisciplinary level, into a more generalized discourse that is implicitly if not explicitly nationalistic—studies of "Chinese medicine," "Indian medicine," Middle Eastern, or "Greek medicine."[8] To a very great extent the discourse of nationalism and politics permeates modern conceptions of "traditional" medicine, perhaps even more so when speaking of Asian medical systems as a whole.[9] What does it mean, for example, to practice Chinese medicine in Japan or—even more problematically—what is suggested, in terms of the medical production of nationality, by the practice of Tibetan medicine anywhere, most of all in Tibet itself?

In some sense—and not to incense my colleagues who work in Japan!—India and China constitute the largest and "most powerful" national entities in Asia, at least as concerns medical knowledge. Thus the practice of Chinese medicine in India and the practice of Āyurveda in China might be regarded as most "problematic" with regard to questions of nationalism; problematic, that is, in terms of the question of how each system is understood—theoretically—within the context of its transplanted practice. The nationalistic dynamics involved are complicated by a range of competing and contradictory histories. Āyurveda can be conceptualized as "Hindu" medicine, anticolonial medicine, and the traditional medicine of modern India (Leslie 1976; Leslie and Young 1992)—with export revenues in millions of rupees (Bode 2000)—just as Traditional Chinese Medicine can be understood as Taoist medicine, the medicine of Imperial China (Unschuld 1992), or the traditional medicine of modern China (Farquhar 1994).[10] Alternatively both TCM and Āyurveda can be regarded as very loosely defined "systems of medical knowledge," each based on a series of binary, triadic, and pentadic structures of correlation common virtually to the whole of the Old World. The systemic insularity of each medical system can be regarded as less and less fixed at different points in time, and at different locations, and it is precisely this "fluid and flexible" history—as well as suggestive structural correlations on the level of theory—that can undermine those kinds of history that are based on the premise of various kinds of political and nationalistic insularity.

As an example of how these histories, despite their potential to contradict one another, are often woven together in curious ways, let me quote a passage from an edited volume published under the auspices of the All-India Institute of Medical Sciences, what is referred to as the "core book program" of the government of India:

The medicine of Tibet, untouched by wars until the Chinese occupation of this land, is based on Ayurveda. . . . The Chakpori Medical College at Lhasa was one of the oldest institutions of its kind. From Tibet, Ayurveda traveled to Mongolia and distant Northeast Siberia; and all the Buddhist monasteries in these areas became great centers of medical learning. The medical college of the Kumbum monastery in Sinkiang attained special renown, as it was the birth place of Tson-Kha-pa, the founder of the yellow sect. It has in its possession a vast array of charts illustrating ancient Hindu medical texts. Another famous Mongolian medical college was at the Yung-Ho-Kung monastery, a monument to a great era in Peking. . . . One of the most famous physicians from these Mongolian medical schools, known for his Ayurvedic practice and success in this therapy during the recent times in Leningrad, was a Siberian, N. N. Badmaev. He counted among his patients, some of the prominent Communist leaders, Bukharin and Rykov, the famous writer Alexei Tolstoy, and even Joseph Stalin. (Keswani 1974: 16–17)

On a more modest scale, and with fewer grand leaps and complex ellipses, this kind of discourse—what might be called transnational nationalist reification—is characteristic of a great deal of contemporary scholarship.

If not exactly involving a self-conscious sleight of hand, it requires a "sleight of mind" to recognize cross-cultural contact and then proceed to construct social and historical analyses that reproduce nationalist categories that are "destabilized" by that contact: In what sense is Tibetan medicine based on Āyurveda? In what sense are the medical texts in the Kumbum monastery "Hindu" texts? And in what sense is the Siberian N. N. Badmaev an Āyurvedic physician? For the time being—and to prevent total destabilization—we can simply take it at face value that Joseph Stalin was a Communist leader.

In any case, the unconscious "sleight of mind" which enables a conceptualization of Āyurveda going more or less directly—and in some sense intact—from seventh-century Nalanda to twentieth-century Stalingrad, via Lhasa, Sinkiang, Peking, and northeast Siberia, becomes a decidedly self-conscious and anxiety-provoking exercise when the perspective is slightly changed, and when the direction of "knowledge flow" is explicitly and unambiguously two-way.

This change of perspective is created by a somewhat unique case that I would like to focus on in this chapter—the popularity of acupressure and acupuncture therapy in modern India, and the construction of something called Āyurvedic acupuncture. Quite apart from whether or not Āyurvedic acupuncture is "authentic," the struggle to define it, and to define the significance of acupuncture as such within the context of modern Indian traditional medicine, transforms the unconscious sleight of mind involved in most considerations of Asian medical knowledge into a singularly nervous, self-conscious, and ambivalent exercise. In some instances this exercise provokes a strong nationalist response, particularly with regard to the question of origins—my medicine is older than yours. But it can also produce a synthetic discourse of theoretical innovation of the sort that probably characterized N. N. Badmaev's thinking, as well as the thinking of a whole range of characters in the history of medicine, ranging from Kumarajiva in the fourth century, to Hui-Seng, Fah Hian, and Sung Yun in the sixth (see Beal 1869), Hsuan Chung and I-Ching (1896) in the seventh, up to P. H. Kulkarni (n.d.), D. G. Thatte (1988) and Frank Ros (1995) in the twentieth.

The Discourse of Origin and Authenticity

It is difficult to imagine anything more distinctively "Chinese" about Traditional Chinese Medicine than acupuncture therapy. According to most sources it has been "in constant use throughout the Chinese culture-area" for at least 2,500 years (Lu and Needham 1980; Needham, Lu, and Sivin 2000).[11] This is true not only on the level of public awareness, but also on the level of theory and practice, where the logic of "needling" loci points known as *hsueh* is dependent on *qi* and a theory of meridian structure and function that is linked to both the principle of *yin/yang* complementarity and the five evolutive phases—to state it rather baldly.[12] In other words, acupuncture makes sense in terms that invoke a great deal more about China than is captured within the sphere of medicine as such.[13] This has meant that acupuncture and acupressure therapy in India—and the "shift" from needles to fingers is very important with regard to popularization[14]—is theorized and practiced in a specific way with reference to a particular kind of politicized discourse. Let me begin with the politicized discourse and then consider theory and practice.

In a speech made in the Rajyasabha of the Government of India on July 2, 1982, Dr. Ashima Chatterjee, a former MP, proclaimed that acupuncture was not invented in China but was, rather, an Indian innovation. Subsequently, during a government-sponsored conference on the question of acupuncture's connection to China, held on August 10, 1984, the president of the Indian Acupuncture Association, Dr. P. K. Singh, provided data and analysis showing that acupuncture had originated in India. Following on this the Indian Acupuncture Association has expanded, and a number of independent practitioners, with various degrees of training and experience, have established clinics and health centers across the country. These practitioners, and others more directly involved in research, have continued to make claims concerning the Indian origin of acupuncture and acupressure.

Dr. Attar Singh, a retired research officer and deputy director in the Punjab government, established the Acupressure Health Center in Chandigarh in 1984. His articles on health and self-help regularly appear in newspapers, but he has also published, in Hindi, what is proclaimed to be an extremely popular book entitled *Akyūpreśur: Prakṛtic Upchār* (*Acupressure: A Natural Therapy*) (1999; first published in 1984). Here is his account of the origin of acupuncture.

There are differences of opinion about how long ago and in which country acupuncture originated. One view is that acupressure, upon which acupuncture is based, originated in India approximately 6000 years ago. There is proof of this in the classical texts of Ayurveda. In ancient times, travelers from China came to India, learned the techniques and knowledge of acupressure and took it back with them to China, where it was put into practice and became very popular. Practitioners of medicine in China recognized the wonderful advantages of this therapy and appropriated it. They have made great efforts to make it both popular and profitable. It is for this reason that today it is known the world over as a Chinese medical therapy. (1999: 34)

A similar—but in fact historically very different—version is provided by Dr. Harjit Singh, the founder of Health Care Systems and author of the Hindi text (with English subtitle) *Akyūpreśur: Siddhānth āwñ Cikitsā: Health and Divine Life Through Acupressure* (1998). After providing the Latin etymology for the root "acu"—and stating that proof of acupressure therapy is found in the classical medical texts of India—he points out that knowledge of nerves (*nāḍi*),[15] upon which the therapy is based, is integral to the common practice of massage as a home remedy, and thus part of the basic cultural knowledge and heritage of Indian peasants. Dr. Singh continues:

According to scholars of Indian medicine, acupressure therapy was popular throughout the country at the same time that Buddhism was the dominant and pervasive religion. Just as Buddhism spread to China, Japan and Korea, so did acupressure therapy. Once it was integrated into common practice it became known as acupuncture. This is because the vital points are the same. Modern texts report that knowledge of acupressure originated in India approximately 4000 years ago, from where it spread to other countries all over the world. Integrated into modern practice it has become known as acupuncture. (1999: 1)

Thus China's "traditional" therapy is defined as a modern innovation based on "truly" ancient knowledge located in India.

Having cited two modern Indian authors who are concerned primarily with popularization and the development of their own client base, it is now possible to look at what more established scholars have said about the question of the most ancient origins of Asian medical knowledge and—at least by extension—authenticity. For reasons that will become clear, it is difficult to do this with respect to acupuncture as such, but there has been considerable speculation on related issues of medicine, physiology, and therapy. Remember, here the issue is not a question of historical accuracy, so much as the nationalist tone and implications of scholarship. Here is Mircea Eliade, in his classic *Yoga: Immortality and Freedom* (1990, first published in 1936 but significantly revised in 1954), referencing an eminent French scholar.

It is probable that, at least in its neo-Taoist form, this discipline of the breaths was influenced by tantric Yoga; certain simultaneously respiratory and sexual practices reached China as early as the seventh century of our era. Dr. Jean Filliozat definitely concludes in favor of a borrowing from India: "Taoism could not borrow a notion of the physiological role of the breath in this systematized form from ancient Chinese medicine, for ancient Chinese medicine includes no such notion." (1990: 61)[16]

Since the time when Filliozat ([1949] 1964), Needham (1962, 1965) and others (see Porkert 1974) produced their seminal works, an understanding of the history of medicine has become more detailed and refined. This is reflected in the scholarship of Paul Unschuld (1978, 1985, 1989), Nathan Sivin (1987), and Charlotte Furth (1998) on the one hand and Kenneth Zysk (1991), Jan Meulenbeld (2002), and Dominik Wujastyk (1998) on the other. But in some ways it is precisely the historical quest for more accurate and complete details—the search for the physiological role of breath in ancient Chinese medicine, for example—that reinforces a nationalist discourse.[17] Relative to the significant research being done on specific "traditions" of medicine within the geopolitical boundaries of modern states—and most directly to the point, the ancient history of medicine as bracketed by modernity—there is very little work being done that self-consciously problematizes the mind-set of modernity, a mind-set which tends to be nationalistic by default.[18] After all, who among us can claim any sort of expertise beyond the limits of our own field, as our field is defined by increasingly bounded geopolitical interests? And these interests are both purely academic as well as much more than that. Granted most scholars would probably be very skeptical about the claim made by Ashima Chatterjee on the floor of the Rajyasabha, but scholarship that produces and reproduces a history of medicine on nationalist terms—even terms that are "benignly" nationalistic—make overtly political claims both possible and meaningful.

Theory: Background, Context, and Orientation

Based on my reading of the Āyurvedic literature, both primary and secondary, I think it is safe to say that most scholars would not understand, at first blush at least, what was meant by Āyurvedic acupuncture.[19] Which is not at all to say that they would not be able to construct—in the manner of one presented with a riddle—a plausible scenario for practice. But they would not be able to locate a theory of practice as such in the standard classical literature.

The authenticity of Āyurvedic acupuncture is based on two somewhat contradictory claims: the existence of a text called the *Sūchi Veda*, which Chandrashekkar Thakkur translates as "the art of piercing with a needle" (see Ros 1995: 3), as well as several other ambiguously dated and extremely rare texts,[20] and the claim that a great deal of Āyurvedic knowledge is not contained in texts at all, but has been jealously guarded and passed down secretly by word of mouth from one generation of practitioners to the next. The latter discourse explains why the knowledge was "lost," and the former how it has been found but also never really "lost" in the first place! The secret nature of transmission—a kind of history of undocumentable continuity, wherein the lack of documentation is what produces authenticity—is also what enables a plausible theory of practice.

On one level a theory of Āyurvedic acupuncture is as complex and detailed as Āyurveda itself. I will not attempt to go into all possible details here—since my own tendency would be to get deeply enmeshed in the construction of a plausible theory of practice!—and restrict the discussion to several key points. I will begin with a kind of theoretical contextualization.

To begin with it is of fundamental importance to be as clear as possible about what it is that we are referring to. This may seem obvious, but with respect to the ancient history of Āyurvedic acupuncture—and perhaps the Chinese variant as well—one is immediately confronted with a host of technologies that are relatively more or less like "needles."[21] (And are needles a single thing in any case?)[22] Similarly, there are a range of different procedures that can be construed as more or less like "needling," that involve generalized surgical instruments, blades, tubes, rods, chisels, cauterizing tools, and miniature saws.[23] And then there are leeches of many different species that can be used to suck on specific "points" rather than to somewhat indiscriminately suck blood.[24] Terminology is a vexing problem, since it cannot be analyzed independently of either theory or practice. Apart from a theory of cause and effect based on a structural theory of anatomy and a functional theory of physiology, the terms puncturing, poking, pressing, cutting, and slitting, for example, can mean very different things in different languages, and even different things in the same language depending on the specific context of use.[25] And yet, when translating from one language to the next, puncturing is puncturing, sucking is sucking, and poking is poking.[26] Is it legitimate to translate the Sanskrit term *sūchi* for the Chinese term *bien*—or even the respective terms used for surgery, wind, heat, and energy—even though it is obviously possible to do so since both mean "needle"? The space between "possible" and "legitimate" is almost completely under the control of nationalism.

In some respects, Āyurvedic acupuncture—whatever it is—is enabled by a theory of *marma* or vital points. References to *marma* are found in the classical medical texts, but are far more clearly defined and elaborated in the literature associated with martial arts, most specifically Kalarippayattu (Zarrilli 1998). In the context of Kalarippayattu, *marma* mark vital points on the body which, if struck, can cause injury (Thatte 1988: 23). Skill in the martial art is defined—at least in part—by one's knowledge of these spots and ability to strike them.[27] In the Āyurvedic literature as well the *marma* are regard as vital points, but they figure almost exclusively in discussions of surgery. The extent to which a person has been wounded is determined by the degree of injury to the vital points. In other words, it is not so much a question of manipulating these points in the context of healing as being aware of their significance with regard to questions of diagnosis and emergency medical assessment. S. K. Ramachandra Rao summarizes Suśruta as follows:

[*Marma* are] vital points or spots on the body which are sensitive and vulnerable ("mortal spots" "mārayantīti," from the root *mṛ*, "to die"). The are described [in the *Suśruta Saṃhitā*, *śarīra*, 6, 15 and by Vāgbhata in the *Ashtānga-samgraha*] as places where flesh (*māṃsa*), veins (*sirā*), arteries (*dhamanī*), ligaments (*snāyu*), joints (*sandhi*), and muscles (*peśī*) unite or are intimately associated (*sanipāta*): and, therefore, life abides there especially. An injury to this spot (by a cut, incision, blow, burn, or puncture) would result in permanent deformity of that organ or death.

It is also defined [in the *Rāja-nighantu*] as *jīva-sthānaṁ*, the spot where the vital forces are concentrated, and [in the *Śārngadhara-samhitā 1, 5, 39*] as *jīva-dhāraṇī*, that which sustains life. The reason why they are mortal spots is that they are the primary seats of the activating air (*vāyu*), the cooling moon (*soma*) and the warmth-endowing heat (*tejas*); and also of the three fundamental aspects of all existence, viz. sattva, rajas, and tamas. The five sensory faculties are also located there; these are called twelve *prāṇas*. It is natural, therefore, [as indicated in the *Suśruta Saṃhitā*, *śarīra*, 85) that the "embodied self" (*bhutatma*) resides in these spots. (1987: 118–19)

According to the classical texts, there are a total of 107 *marma*,[28] and these are distributed on the body based on two different schemes. But to say "on the body" and to think of these points as markers of something at a location defined exclusively by spatial coordinates is somewhat misleading. It is better to think of *marma* as spatio-substantive nodes or loci keyed to the body's subtle metabolic transubstantiation. One scheme defines their location with reference to the dominant material aspect of the body at any given point: 11 of muscle, 41 of veins, 27 of ligament, 8 of bone, 20 of joints. The term "of" rather than "at" is used purposefully since each point—located with reference to the surface of the body, where it is "at"—is an intersection of the six aspects of gross physiology.[29] Since no points are defined as being "of flesh," it is also possible to conceptualize flesh as the "location specific" common denominator of all points.[30] In other words, their flesh component enables them to be located, whereas their primary attribute is to be a vital intersection of things—both gross and subtle—that characterize the body as whole.

The second scheme of classification is more location specific: 11 on each extremity, 12 on the chest and abdomen, 14 on the back, and—interestingly—37 on the head and neck. Although at specific locations, each point is still regarded as being an intersection of the six aspects of physiology, with the one aspect that predominates corresponding to the name of the point. Most significantly, irrespective of the scheme of location-classification, all 107 *marma* are grouped into the following categories of risk based on injury: (1) those that cause immediate death; (2) those that cause death after a short time; (3) those that cause death when the thing causing injury is extracted; (4) those that do not cause death but cause deformity; and (5) those that cause intense pain (see Dharmalingam 1991: 5; Thatte 1988: 1–33). Risk corresponds to the element associated with each category: 1 is fire, 2 is a combination of fire and "moon," 3 is air, 4 is "moon," and 5 is a combination of air and fire.

If "moon" is interpreted as water—since it has the character of cool liquidity, just as the sun has a hot and fiery attribute[31]—then it is possible to classify all the points with reference to various combinations of the three basic "humors" that are integral to Āyurveda as a whole, *vāta*, *pitta*, and *kapha*.[32] Based on this classification one can produce a theory of acupuncture treatment that is cognate with and congruent to almost all aspects of Āyurveda—although one is confronted with a range of complex problems, risk and injury being only the most obvious.

Before considering treatment and practice, it is necessary to look at one other key point with respect to Āyurvedic theory: *prāṇa* (see Zysk 1993). Having said "Āyurvedic theory," I must immediately add a significant qualification, for *prāṇa* is integral to the practice of yoga, and a general theory of *prāṇa* as the vital force of life—which is very much like the principle of *pneuma* in Greek medicine and philosophy—derives from Sāṃkhya philosophy. It is important to note that in the Āyurvedic literature as such, *prāṇa* can be said to be movement and energy itself, rather than a material substance that moves. S. K. Ramchandra Rao points out the basic Sāṃkhyan understanding of *prāṇa* in Āyurveda, explaining that it

is an evolute of *prakṛti*, and is identical with the *mahat* category. In its cognitive and assimilative aspect, it is called *buddhi*, while in its aspect as activity it is known as *prāṇa*: it is the power to initiate movements. It is referred to as *vāyu*, only because it shares with air the power to initiate movement. (1987: 167)

Significantly, there are five subdivisions of *prāṇa*. Together they are linked to the three so-called inner instruments—consciousness, ego and mind—and the interaction of these support the body as a functioning whole. In a sense, the relationship between *prāṇa* and the inner instruments, reflects the cosmic relationship between *prakṛti* and *puruṣa*, as this relationship defines creation as a dynamic ongoing process. In any case, that *prāṇa* is vital energy that is subtle and pervasive, and that there are five *prāṇa*, is significant for the development of a theory of Āyurvedic acupuncture. Each of the five *prāṇa* is associated with a specific part of the body and body function. It is important to note, however, that in Āyurveda, as distinct from yoga, *prāṇa* is not of great significance with regard to therapy.

Prāṇa causes the flow of substances through *nāḍī*, and there are both subtle and gross *nāḍī* as well as subtle and gross substances that flow through them, including blood, semen, air, and other things.

There are said to be three [and a half-crore] of *nāḍīs*, gross and subtle, in the human body, all rooted in the region of the umbilicus and spreading upward, downward and across. Among them 72, 000 are gross, and carry the properties of the five sense-functions. The subtle ones (called *sirā*, in the *Suśrata Saṃhitā*, *śarīra* 7, 3) are 700 in number; and they carry uninterruptedly the food juice (*anna-rasa*) prompted by the body wind to all parts and satiate the entire body, "like a hundred rivers that flow into the sea." (Rao 1987: 129)

In his book *Moola Bandha: The Master Key*, which contains a chapter on acupuncture and a yogic theory of internal "locks" placed on the flow of *prāṇa*, Swami Buddhananda quotes an almost identical metaphor found in *The Yellow Emperor's Classic of Internal Medicine.* "Man possesses four seas and twelve main meridians, which are like rivers that flow into the sea" (1996: 114).

It is interesting to note that in the physiology of Āyurveda the most "subtle" *nāḍī* are conduits for a substance that is, in and of itself, not so much subtle as highly refined. *Anna-rasa* is the most basic and primary of the body's seven constituents and is regarded as "the source of all vital functions" (Rao 1987: 172). Unlike *prāṇa*, however, *anna-rasa* is linked, directly and materially, to a process of metabolic transformation involving the production, in sequence, of blood, flesh, fat, bone, marrow, and semen. Once *anna-rasa* has been digested or "cooked" it is transformed into *sāra* and channeled to the heart: "From there it is circulated to all parts of the body through twenty-four channels (*dhamanī*, 10 going upward, 10 downward and 4 across), prompted by the forms of the wind in the body (*vāta*)" (Rao 1987: 172). The *dhamanī*—a term synonymous with *nāḍī*—are integral to the process of the metabolic transformation of *sāra* into the six other constituent substances.

In yogic theory and practice, as quite distinct from Āyurveda, there is a clear tendency to conceptualize all of the *nāḍī*, and the three axial *nāḍī* in particular, as carrying *prāṇa* as a generalized subtle force. Here it is not possible to go into a complete discussion of the importance of *nāḍī* to the practice of yoga.[33] However, *nāḍī* are directly related to the practice of *prāṇāyāma* breathing exercises, as these exercises are said to purify the *nāḍī* and, most significantly, promote the channeled flow of *prāṇa* through and to various key points in the body. To understand and appreciate the logic of Āyurvedic acupuncture—as quite different from believing that it is authentic—it is necessary to keep in mind both an Āyurvedic and yogic understanding of *nāḍī* and *prāṇic* flow.[34]

Having set the stage, by way of a discussion of *marma*, *prāṇa*, and *nāḍī*, the focus may now be shifted to a consideration of acupuncture as such in South Asia.

Points, Counterpoints, and the Needling of Humors

Based out of Coimbator with an office in Chennai, the Lok Swaasthya Parampara Samvardhan Samhithi (LSPSS) is an organization committed to the advancement of indigenous systems of health care. More specifically it is concerned with the "reconstruction of local health traditions" so as to promote self-reliance in primary health care within India (Dharmalingam, Radhika, and Balasubramian 1991: ii). It is, therefore, nationalistic on a programmatic level. Under the auspices of this organization, Vaidya V. Dharmalingam, Vaidya M. Radhika, and A. V. Balasubramanian have published a book entitled *Marma Chikitsa in Traditional Medicine* (1991), which provides a clear point of entry into Āyurvedic acupuncture as it is conceptualized and practiced in a specific form.

The Tamil term for the Malayalam term *marmam*, which is derived from the Sanskrit *marma*, is *varmam*. According to a number of sources there is a South Indian therapy, practiced in Tamil Nadu and Kerala, called *varma cikitsā* (see Rajamony 1988; Pillai 1993; Shastri 1964; Subramanian and Madhavan 1983; Thatte 1988: 22–33). *Varma cikitsā* is closely linked to the martial arts of this region (see Rosu 1981; Zarrilli 1989, 1998, 2001b; also Tilak 1982), and although it primarily involves pressure point massage—and massage in general (Zarrilli 1995)—there are also, according to at least some sources, quite specific techniques for needling *varma* points (Dharmalingam 1991: 22). Interestingly, Dharmalingam points out in a published interview that the ritualized practice of *vel*—piercing the skin with "spears"—to perform penance in the context of Lord Subrahmanya worship is also based on a knowledge of *varma* points (1991: 22).

What are referred to as *varma* points and *varma kalai* or *varma cikitsa* by Dharmalingam seem to fit directly into what is referred to as *adankal* or *adangal* therapy by a number of other authors (Thatte 1988; see also Zarrilli 2001b: 650). According to most sources there are fifty-one *adangal* points, twelve of which are of greater significance than the others.[35] Clearly the *adangal* points are defined in some relationship to *varma*, and there is a tendency in some texts to speak of them synonymously. But as Zarrilli points out, *adangal* may be thought of as points of "counter-application," so as to revive the injured person by counter-acting the effect of a *varma* being hit or injured (2001b: 650).[36] Here Thatte's work is most instructive for he points out that *adangal* therapy is based, at least in part, on striking points on the body that are "on the opposite side" of the *marma* (1988: 24–26).[37] In any case, it seems that *adangal* therapy is most clearly developed as a branch of emergency medicine to restore consciousness, as the restoration of consciousness is conceptualized as the free and unobstructed flow of the inner wind (Zarrilli 2001b: 650).[38]

In this regard one of the most interesting treatments of the subject is Thatte's attempt to explicitly compare the position of *marma* and Chinese acupuncture points. Although Thatte's method of comparison is perhaps not as rigorous or transparent as it could be—he uses a scale of similar, approximately similar and dissimilar—what is striking is the extent to which there is a high degree of dissimilarity between the location of *marma* and acupuncture points.[39] If acupuncture points are *marma*, this raises serious questions and problems, but if *adangal* points and, as we will see below, so-called *nila* points are in fact more like acupuncture points than are *marma*, then the dissimilarity is not surprising at all. In fact, what becomes problematic is that there is any point-on-point correlation at all between *marma* and acupuncture points.

Perhaps the most compelling evidence for applied Āyurvedic acupuncture in South Asia is found in Devasena's extremely detailed account of the ethnomedical history of southern Sri Lanka from about the sixteenth century to the present. Through an analysis of texts dating to the seventeenth and eighteenth centuries, and through interviews with an impressive array of practitioners, Devasena shows how a late medieval tradition of practice, recorded on palm-leaf texts, was translated into modern practice through the experimentation and the manufacture of medical implements modeled on early descriptions and drawings (1981: 33).[40] Of particular interest in this regard is the way in which *salya cikitsā* is used to "puncture and pressurize *nila* points" (1981: 15, 25, 27). It is not at all clear if these *nila* points are the same as *marma/varma* points, but Devasena suggests that they are not, and that the confusion of *nila* points with *varma* is a profound confusion indeed.[41] In any event, there is clear if very limited evidence that some Sri Lankan physicians in the eighteenth and nineteenth centuries needled patients in order to treat various ailments.

Apart from this, however, there is far more evidence that the *Salla Vidya* and all other late medieval and early modern Sinhala and Tamil texts were directly concerned with cauterization and bloodletting, and concerned with what might be called "acupuncture" only to a relatively minor degree.[42] In some ways the "confused" relationship between cauterizing and needling can be graphically illustrated with reference to a common kind of medical implement called a *bottam katuva*.[43] These are three- to four-inch-long "spike"-shaped metal tools. Although it would seem as though the pointed end is used in therapy, in fact it is the blunt end that is heated and used to cauterize a fairly large area on the surface of the patient's body, whereas the sharp end is hafted on a wooden handle (Devasena 1981: 20). Even so, it is interesting to note that cauterization and bloodletting may well have become "fashionable" as a result of the way in which early European exploration of the Far East caused a revival of interest in these modalities of treatment.[44] Speaking of southern Sri Lanka and the possible communication of medical knowledge between inland monasteries and physicians located on the coast, Devasena writes,

In the fourteenth, fifteenth, and sixteenth centuries there was constant contact between South Indian culture as well as with Islamic culture. Their influence on traditional medicine continued in subsequent periods. With the arrival of the European powers, eastern medical techniques came under closer observation and in some instances gave much-needed publicity to eastern methods of healing. For instance, the *Geschichte und Beschreibung von Japan* by Engelbert Kaempfer (1651–1716) gives a Japanese chart of cauterization points which correspond broadly to some of the points mentioned in our *Salla Vidya*. (1981: 50)

Beyond the question of the transnational communication of medical knowledge, what is significant about the emphasis placed on cauterization and bloodletting is that the application of these therapies must avoid the *marma* rather than puncture or cauterize them. Thus Devasena points out that many texts on "acupuncture therapy" produced after the sixteenth century make reference to the *marma sthāns*, only to point out that these points cannot be punctured. Many authors, he points out circumspectly, were more concerned with "maintaining a record of traditional practice" than with "putting forward consistent theses" (1981: 50). Therefore, the importance of the Samararatne manuscript is in the fact that it makes *no* reference to *marma* in its delineation of techniques for cauterizing so-called acupuncture points (1981: 50).

Devasena's work directs attention to a specific collection of Sri Lankan historical documents, and it is possible to recognize the relationship between theories expounded in these documents and a range of therapies that are put into practice now in various contexts, most notably the institutions of Kalarippayattu that are organized within the framework of the state of Kerala, and now, at least to a degree, the Republic of India (Zarrilli 2001a: 227). They are also put into practice through organizations like the Lok Swaasthya Parampara Samvardhan Samhithi. In what remains of this chapter I would like build on this discussion, but also to shift back to a consideration of Āyurveda with a capital A, as this capital A invokes the politics of transnational nationalism.

Drawing on the work of P. H. Kulkarni at the Institute of Indian Medicine in Pune and on D. G. Thatte's *Acupuncture Marma and Other Asian Therapeutic Techniques*, Dr. Frank Ros, director of the Australian Institute of Ayurvedic Medicine, has published a book entitled *The Lost Secrets of Ayurvedic Acupuncture: An Ayurvedic Guide to Acupuncture* (1995). Kulkarni, Thatte, and Ros are involved in a project wherein a theory of acupuncture is discovered in the classical literature and a plausible scenario of practice is constructed. What remains ambiguous is the way "Chinese" medicine factors into this project. Although virtually no reference is made to China and acupuncture in China beyond the Foreword, by David Frawley,[45] there can be little doubt that Ros has based his book on Chinese medical theory. Among many other things, the meridians are named and classified with reference to *yin* and *yang* organ systems, the organs are classified as either hollow or solid, the vital points are labeled using standardized Chinese medical terminology, and there is a lengthy discussion of the supporting and restraining sequences of the five evolutive phases.[46]

In terms of politicized discourse, of course, Chinese medicine is the motive force—the reason why it is necessary to define "Indian" acupuncture as such. But comparability on the level of theory presents very complex problems. Without detailed sources and documented proof, it is all too easy to be accused of cultural piracy and plagiarism—of deriving a plausible scenario of practice in ancient India based on a theory of traditional Chinese medicine; a theory that is documented and elaborated with incredible sophistication and detail in publications from around the world, most particularly China, but also India. For example, it is instructive to contrast Ros's book, in which China is elided, with one written by Dr. A. K. Mehta entitled *Acupuncture for Everyone: A Home Guide.*[47] Trained in Āyurvedic medicine and surgery as well as acupuncture, Mehta makes absolutely no reference to anything Āyurvedic in his discussion of acupuncture. Although designed for popular consumption in India, his characterization of acupuncture is based exclusively and explicitly on TCM.

On one level, what all this suggests is that what is needed more than anything else is documentary historical evidence to prove, once and for all, that contemporary accounts of theory can be linked to authentic Sanskrit texts, or that they cannot—something on the order of the famous Bower manuscript discovered near Bamian in Afghanistan that deals with needles and "*marma* meridians" rather than garlic and humors. My concern, however, is more with a theoretical discourse that emerges precisely as a consequence of the fact that documentary evidence can always be challenged. Beyond this, my concern is with the way in which ambiguity and ambivalence in a nationalist discourse of practice can, in a sense, deconstruct nationalism by reconstructing a plausible history of transnational or transregional theoretical innovation. This reconstruction can be based on more or less solid "facts" of history, or else on pure imagination based on structural symmetry and correspondences of theoretical comparability.

To examine this ambiguity and ambivalence let me quote the key point of articulation between "Āyurveda" and "Chinese" medicine as expressed by Dr. Peeyush Trivedi, a graduate of the Rashtriya Ayurveda Sansthan, Jaipur.

There is a continuous flow of bioenergy or Prana in the human body. This energy flowing internally and externally has been maintaining an inter-connection between each and every organ of the body. Particularly, on the outer skin the flow of bioenergy takes place through the nervous system and is found on the body in the form of points on the skin. Numerous bioenergy points found on the skin of human body keep the structure of body bound together.

Every system of bioenergy is connected to all the organs in the body in the form of circuits, known as channel system. Each channel or meridian has a pillar like structure which provides stability to the body. When energy flows through the system of these channels, bioenergy reaches each and every organ through the respective course or channel, and keeps the various cells of the body free from disease. Bioenergy flow through 12 regular meridians (in Chinese these are called *Tying*) and 8 subsidiary meridians (known as *chi* in Chinese).

Energy flow in regular meridians helps in keeping the internal organs of the body active and alive. The 12 meridians are present in the form of 6 pairs in the body. These have their own polar energy. (1998: 13)

Trivadi then provides a chart that identifies six organ systems, the location on the body of the meridian that corresponds to each system, and the "polar energy" that characterizes each meridian. He then continues:

In Ayurved, these 6 meridians are known as *marm* or vital organs. Acharya Sushrut has shown the number of vital sensitive points to be 107. Even he has said that if there is a loss of energy in any of these vital points or it is hurt, it results in the destruction of bioenergy.

Extent or the area of a vital (sensitive) point is expressed in *Tsun*. *Tsun* is a special standard unit for this purpose. The breadth of the thumb is 1 *Tsun*. The width of four fingers turned inside is 3 *Tsun*. (1998: 14)

Following on this Trivadi delineates a list of what appear to be the most important *marma* identified by Suśruta using a unit of measure that is specific to acupuncture in China.

For the moment we should not be in the least concerned with the accuracy, legitimacy, or authenticity of Trivadi's discussion. Clearly it introduces an enormous range of theoretical and practical issues for possible elaboration and clarification, and it is precisely the point that one can turn to treatises on Chinese medicine to most effectively elaborate and clarify—if not also "correct"—all of the points that Trivadi is trying to make.

To state the problem in overly simplistic terms, those who seek to articulate a theory of Āyurvedic acupuncture are in some way, forced to make it make sense in terms of traditional Chinese medical theory, as this theory is innovatively and ambiguously translated into an Āyurvedic theoretical framework. In doing so, several key problems arise. First, as noted above, *marma* are vital points but not needling points. Second, the Āyurvedic scheme of three humors does not easily accommodate the logic of *yin/yang* duality. Third, the pentadic scheme of *pañcabhūta* elemental structure is not itself configured as a cycle of transmutation, as are the five phases in TCM. Equally important, the five elements are different in each case. Although water, fire, and earth are the same—at least nominally—metal and wood in the "Chinese" scheme are counted as air and ether in Āyurvedic texts. Fourth, Āyurvedic physiology is based on the idea that the body continually remakes itself through a metabolic process of transmutation. In this scheme the organs are relatively unimportant in comparison to both *dhātu* (substance) and *doṣa* (humor) Moreover, in Āyurveda there are of two types of "organs," those for action and those for cognition, and neither of these sets include things like the heart, lungs, kidneys, and gallbladder, nor do they correspond to the idea of organ systems as theorized in TCM.

These "problems," however, are problems of a peculiar kind, for in precluding direct one-to-one translation, so to speak, they necessitate creative innovation. The basis of creativity, enabled by a theory of *marma, nāḍī* and the energized flow of *prāṇa*, is encoded in the problems themselves. For example, although the idea of organs is completely different in Āyurveda and TCM, it is quite possible to graft, if not directly transplant, one onto the other by finding a correspondence between *jñā-nendriya* and *karmendriya* categorization on the one hand and the classification of *yin* and *yang* organ systems on the other (see H. Singh 1998: 93). Similarly, the important principle of *dhātu* transmutation is very different from the evolutive phases of elemental transmutation, but the process of transmutation in both Āyurveda and TCM—be it blood into muscle, fat, bone, marrow, semen, and vital energy or fire into earth, metal, water, wood, and fire again—makes it possible to conceptualize their structural relationship to one another. This structural relationship produces what might be called a logic of intellectual history that invokes the possible and probable history of cross-cultural contact in fact. Here is a clear example, albeit with a distinctly yogic twist, drawn from Swami Buddhananda's attempt to make sense of the lowest *mūla bandh* or "perineum lock" in the practice of *prāṇāyāma*, wherein the structure of *nāḍī* physiology corresponds to meridian structure in the *Tai Chin Hua Tzang Chih*:

It is interesting to note that both the conception vessel and the governor vessel seem to correspond to the arohan and awarohan psychic passages visualized in kriya yoga. Kriya yoga seems to have been known in China, for a system which possesses many similarities are in a scripture called *The Secret of the Golden Flowers*. The conception and governor vessels are imagined to run end to end to form an unbroken ellipse, and chi was visualized to travel in an anticlockwise fashion beginning at Gv1, circulating the body and ending at Cv1 in the perineum. . . . It is not surprising that the pathways of the conception and governor vessels correspond exactly to the psychic pathways in yoga meditation. But it is interesting to note that not only is Cv1 the meeting point of the conception and governor vessels and the site for moola bandha, but in acupuncture theory it is also known as General Lo point, through which the disequilibrium of yin and yang in the whole body (in particular the small intestines, heart, lungs, colon, bladder, kidneys, circulation, and three heaters) can be rectified. (1996: 112)

Although the range of specific details and possible points of correspondence between Indian and Chinese systems of medicine is almost limitless, it is possible to distill the logic of Āyurvedic acupuncture down to two problems, one metamathematical (how to divide three into two while maintaining the integrity of both three and two) and the other alchemical (how to change metal and wood into air and ether). Quite apart from alchemy, the transubstantiation of two into three is unto itself fundamental to Āyurveda, insofar as the cosmic union of *puruṣa* and *prakṛti* produces the five elements of the natural world. In a 2-1-2 combination, which is one of the structural foundations on which Āyurveda physiology is based, the five elements produce the three *doṣa*. In Āyurveda *tridoṣa* is the dynamic basis of all life. A problem with respect to theorizing Āyurvedic acupuncture is that in classical Āyurvedic texts the dualistic agency of *puruṣa* and *prakṛti* as a complementary opposition is primarily of philosophical significance—insofar as it derives from Sāṃkhya—and does not function like the complementary opposition of *yin* and *yang*. In any case, attempts to fit a system of three humors into a system of binary opposition—and to diagrammatically if not alchemically change metal and wood into ether and air—can be a rather disorienting exercise; as disorienting and anxiety-provoking as trying to prove, in the complex calculus of transnational nationalism, that India is where Chinese acupuncture originated. This disorientation is not expressed as such, for what is expressed is creativity based on cultural essentialism and the discovery of ancient truths. The disorientation is reflected in dislocated, unstable theories, at once nationalistic and transnational.

Drawing, it seems clear, on a theory of meridian structure and function linked to twelve organs divided into two sets of six organs each, one hollow the other solid, Ros points out that the twelve meridians in Āyurvedic acupuncture are conceptualized in subsets of three types. These three types correspond, at least in part, to sets of six meridians on each limb, three on the inside and three on the outside. Thus, for example, a diagram of the three inside arm channels, showing the location of a series of vital points, is labeled in accordance with the *yang* solid organ that defines their primary character—spleen, liver and kidney. However, the organ system, thus subdivided into a triptych scheme based on binary classification—and thereby linked to principles of etiology, nosology, and therapy—is made to correspond to the key classificatory schema in Āyurveda: *vāta, pitta,* and *kapha*. What this allows for is to think through the indexical problems of *marma, nāḍī,* and *prāṇa* and conceptualize a whole therapeutic system wherein humoral balance and flow can be directly and systematically manipulated.

A very interesting example of this general process is found in the delineation of organs. Ros's categorization of the organs follows the Chinese system exactly, except with respect to the triple warmer. He refers to this organ as *Tridosha*, and points out that it

is not a physiological organ per se, but in Ayurved it is considered as such. Tridosha is a generalization of the three areas of the trunk which relate to the three humors (dosha). These are *Vata, Pitta,* and *Kapha*.

As the trunk can be considered a hollow pipe, the Tridosha is a hollow organ.
. . . The flow of fluids through these three areas of the trunk can be affected by
an imbalance in one or more of the three humors, so that the mutual balance
of all is reflected in the Tridosha and its pranic channel. The Tridosha (3D and
the pericardium are therefore related and their pranic channels interconnect.
(1995: 73–74)

As might be expected, needling the *tridoṣa* is precisely what Āyurvedic
acupuncture is primarily concerned with, and so this "hollow organ
channel" of the whole body is particularly important.

[It] connects with the Tridosha area of the body, which is a generalization of the
three humors and its three sections of the trunk: Kapha (thorax) Pitta (below
thorax and above navel) and Vata (below navel). The 3D channel therefore
affects the mutual harmony of these three, and the flow of fluids through these
three area. The 3D channel connects with he back of the ring finger and has
twenty-three *marma*s or needling points. (1995:128)

Related to this is a further—and not completely consistent—
delineation of what Ros calls "*Chakra* points." Based on yogic theory,
cakra points are said to be the points through which *prāṇa* flows.
Although there are seven primary *cakra*s situated on the trunk, there are
also said to be a whole range of minor *cakra* points located on the limbs
and extremities. These are not the same as *marma*. Rather, in Ros's formulation, they are linked together as a bio-energy channel configured
in terms of the five elements, plus *prāṇa*. *Prāṇa* is most directly associated with the two "highest" and most subtle *cakra*s on and above the
head, where as the five "elemental" *cakra*s are located along the axis of
the trunk. Having theorized physiology in these "yogic" terms, Ros then
seems to use a Chinese understanding of phase transubstantiation to
make sense of bio-energy flow in the body. He refers to two cycles, or
"wheels": the "Alamba Chakra," wherein fire, earth, wind, water, and
ether support one another, and the "Vinaya Chakra," wherein the control sequence is earth, water, fire, wind, ether. As indicated above, the
Āyurvedic five-phase system includes ether and wind and does not
include metal and wood. Following classical Āyurvedic theory, these five
elements combine to configure the three humors, although in Ros's formulation of Āyurvedic acupuncture they are configured differently
depending on the character of the wheel. In other words, in the control-
ling sequence earth and water constitute *kapha*, fire alone constitutes
pitta, and wind and ether constitute *vāta*. In the supporting sequence,
on the other hand, wind and water make up *vāta*, ether and fire make
up *pitta*, and earth alone makes up *kapha*. In this way Ros clearly inte-
grates a theory of *tridoṣa*, with a theory of phase transubstantiation.
    A clearly related, but in many ways completely different conceptualiza-

tion of the connection between *prāṇa*, acupuncture and *cakra* physiology is developed by Swami Buddhananda, who, as pointed out above, makes an explicit attempt to link yoga and Traditional Chinese Medicine. Buddhananda's book is, in essence about the key value of one specific *cakra*, the *mūlādhāra cakra*, and its manipulation through *mūla bandha*, wherein a person seated in *padmāsana* places the heel of one foot firmly against the perineum, seeking to channel the downward flowing *prāṇa* upward. Buddhananda goes into great detail on many important issues, but in some sense the whole appendix of his book is concerned with defining and explaining the value of the *mūlādhāra cakra* as a key acupuncture point that can be stimulated to promote the flow of *prāṇa* through yogic acupressure (1996: 111–18)

Conclusion

There can be little doubt about the efficacy of acupuncture and Āyurveda, and in some sense the growing global popularity of Āyurveda and the proven effectiveness of acupuncture in particular renders the whole question of nationalism moot. In effect all forms of medicine are theorized as transcultural systems. Sickness and death, as symptomatic of our species as a whole, frames medical knowledge in the most universal of universal terms—and beyond speciocentrism it is worth noting that both Āyurveda and TCM include a veterinary component.[48] Nevertheless, there can be endless debate and disagreement about why a particular kind of medicine is effective, what sort of medicine is most effective, and how any given sort of medicine works. There can also be endless debate about how to delimit a "medical system" as such. It is these questions that get framed by nationalism and the politics of culture, even as the pragmatic and practical search to find cures and promote health and fitness, renders boarders and boundaries—both intellectual and political—rather porous.

In this sense, Dr. Frank Ros in Australia, Dr. Attar Singh in Haryana, and Dr. Peeyush Trivedi in Jaipur, as well as Dr. Harjit Singh, Dr. P. H. Kulkarni, Dr. D. G. Thatte, and Ram Lal Sah, Binod Kumar Joshi, and Geeta Joshi[49]—the primary theoreticians of Āyurvedic acupuncture—are trying to refine medical knowledge in general so as to provide better, more effective treatment, in any way and on any terms. Whatever else they may doing—making money and gaining notoriety—healing and the desire to heal is the fundamental justification for their various interrelated projects. But whereas some doctors in some parts of the world can just practice medicine, without a great deal of concern for the way in which history and culture links their practice to politics and nationalism, Dr. Attar Singh—as one prominent example—must struggle through and manipulate the politics of culture when trying to establish himself as a doctor who practices acupressure therapy in Chandigarh.

However, it is not so much this that makes him unique as the fact that he must self-consciously address the problem that unless he nationalistically theorizes the system of medicine he practices he runs the constant risk of being an Indian practitioner of Chinese medicine. And for various reasons this seems to be much more problematic than being an Australian practitioner of Āyurveda, a Pakistani-born Malay practitioner of "Greek" medicine—to use labels that help force the issue—or an American practitioner of naturopathy, for example.[50] It is problematic, at least in part, because of the "categorical" difference between India and China as world civilizations—construed as different from the vantage point of modernity—and the residual traces of an ancient history of locally graded, intraregional, pan-Asian communication. In terms of this communication there is the possibility that *prāṇa* flowed east and *qi* flowed west, the twain meeting—with silken ease, so to speak—and many other ideas getting mixed up in the process.

It is this ancient history of communication, factual and imaginary, documented and textualized, that frames the problem of modern nationalism less as a problem of history and more as a problem of medical theorizing and the production of theoretical texts. In this light, and with what I hope is an obvious degree of irony, let me simply end with two quotes. The first is Hsuan-Chuang's pointed response to the monks at Nalanda. The second is from I-Ching, an eighth-century resident of Hopei,[51] an "enemy of onions" and outspoken critic of the use of excreta in medical treatment as well as one of the most famous and prolific of all Buddhist monks, who, in search of knowledge, came south and spent a good portion of twenty-four years studying at Nalanda—or so we are told by Needham, who had a wonderful sense of the importance of details.

The Monks of Nalanda to Hsuan-Chuang: Why then do you wish to leave, having come so far? Moreover, China is a country of *mlecchas,* of unimportant barbarians, who despise the religious and the Faith. That is why the Buddha was not born there.

Hsuan-Chuang's Response: Buddha established the doctrine so that it might be diffused to all lands. Who would wish to enjoy it alone, and to forget those who are not yet enlightened? Besides, in my country the magistrates are clothed with dignity, and the laws are everywhere respected. . . . [O]ld men and sages are held in honor. Moreover, how deep and mysterious is their knowledge. . . . [T]hey have been able to calm the contrary influences of the yin and the yang, thus procuring peace and happiness for all beings. . . . How then can you say that Buddha did not go to my country because of its insignificance? (English translation based on Stanislas Julien's 1853 French translation of Hui Li's biography of Hsuan-Chuang; quoted in Needham 1965: 210)

In the healing arts of acupuncture and cautery, and skill of feeling the pulse, China has never been surpassed by any country of *Jambudvipa* (*oikoumene*); the drug for prolonging life is found only in China. . . . Is there anyone, in the five parts of India, who does not admire China. (Takakusu 1896; quoted in Needham 1965: 211)

Chapter 3
Deviant Airs in "Traditional" Chinese Medicine

VIVIENNE LO AND SYLVIA SCHROER

Difficulties in rendering into English the Chinese term *xie* have dogged historians of Chinese medicine working in different historical periods and social/religious contexts. A core meaning of *xie* is "oblique" or "deviating," not *zheng*, "physically upright," an opposition frequently invoked in Chinese discourses on morality and early Chinese medical classics. Common translations of the term in a medical context include "evil," "heteropathy," or "perversity"; it refers to invading agents, both conscious entities and manifestations of naturalistic phenomenon like wind or damp, that enter the body and cause varying degrees of devastation. Related treatments range from draining toxic agents to acupuncture exorcism. Given the historical and geographical range of this chapter (from early imperial times in China to present-day Europe), our aim is not to seek definitive translation, but to examine changing medical interpretations. Classical Chinese medical terminology is unusually adaptable to different cultural contexts: its inherent flexibility has underpinned the survival of many practices styled "traditional" into, and beyond, the boundaries of modern China.

Medical ideas about demonic possession and invasion by entities associated with climatic conditions come together under the rubric of *xie zhu* (lit. *xie* pours in) in Chao Yuanfang's encyclopedic *Chaoshi zhubing yuanhou lun* (601) (Mr. Chao's origins and symptoms of medical disorders, completed 610 C.E.), which provides the following definition:

When we speak of *xie* it is *qi* that is not *zheng* (upright, proper). The *qi* and blood of the viscera and bowels is *zheng*. Wind, cold, summer heat, damp, and goblins, are all *xie*. When *xie* pours in it is as a result of a person's body becoming deficient and weak, so it can be damaged by the *xie qi*, which pierces and pours through the *jingluo* (channels/tracts/conduits/vessels), remaining in the organs, and causing the human spirit and will to become unsettled. Some become mournful, others afraid, and so we call it *xie zhu* "pouring in."

The concept of *xie zhu* (*xie* pouring in) is inextricably tied up with belief about the body weakening and becoming vulnerable to contamination and epidemic, often to corpses (Li 1996; Sivin 1987: 100–104). Here the *xie* itself can be a goblin or heat, but it is the *qi* arising from these factors that damages. Scholarly practitioners and commoners alike sustained such ideas of disease caused by demonic influences throughout the Song dynasty (960–1127) (Hinrichs 2003: 61–75). Indeed, elite medical theory, as well as state-sponsored medical compilations, continued to implicate demonic infestation of the body right through the Ming and Qing periods. Some writers, such as Xu Dachun (1693–1771), attempted to naturalize explanations of demonic influence, but as Chen Hsiu-fen states, "the triumph of a completely 'iconoclastic' medical view over a 'superstitious' one did not happen until the late imperial period" if indeed it happened then, or has even now (Chen Hsiu-fen 2002: 196; Unschuld 1998: 127). But perhaps we should also question the rigid distinction between natural and supernatural: in ancient China natural phenomenon, the rivers and mountains and the heavenly bodies were by extension also the spirits of those phenomenon (Lo 2004).

Our research began with a simple question about continuity and change in ideas and practices related to *xie*. The intention was to combine the skills and experience of both authors in a study that would align fresh historical research with an ethnographic study using participant observation.[1] Had the concept of *xie* been excised from contemporary European practice of traditional Asian medicine? If not, to what degree do modern practitioners acknowledge, teach, translate, interpret, and actively use it? As we set about framing the questions, and interviewing some fifteen European practitioners of Chinese medicine in an informal setting, our focus was drawn to the metaphors emerging through their narratives, and in particular the moral dimension of their discourse.

Varying from one culture to another, and by explaining one domain in terms of another, metaphors are pervasive in thought and action (Lakoff and Johnson 1980: 3). They provide a symbolic bridge across social, cognitive and biological domains, ordering experience (Kleinman 1980: 41–42; Lyon 1990). As pattern-making devices, metaphors take a central position in the development of theory inasmuch as they provide conceptual *significance* to experience (Miles and Huberman 1994: 250–51). In medicine they are particularly powerful in establishing coherence between contemporary moral discourse and theories about the body (Turner 1985: 21). Given the moral discourse embedded in *xie* polarities from the very earliest times, metaphors associated with *xie* provide an excellent opportunity to study the changing negotiation of moral concerns through the medium of the body in Chinese medicine.

Medical anthropologists working in the 1980s taught that each culture generates a multiplicity of bodies (Scheper-Hughes and Lock 1987). In the period of its conception the acupuncture body, for example, was a microcosm of the known universe, a metaphor for structures that early Chinese found in heaven and earth (Sivin 1987: 72). Li Jianmin characterizes the acupuncture and moxibustion channels as "a field of temporal spaces" that act as a pivot of many different worlds; at once analogous to the rivers of China, to astronomical movements, to rivers of blood and channels of communication, patterns against which human disharmony with different environments could be judged (Li 2000). Others compare the flowing channels in the body to the conduits of empire, enabling the free passage of troops, provisions, the thoroughfares of bureaucratic administration—and obstructions with the loci of disorder and illness (Unschuld 1985: 99–100). And in the imagination of *qi* flooding through the body, strengthening it against attack from *xie* influences, we can find a physiological mirror of the exercise of executive power and the unifying principle of imperial authority, with its dual action of construction and defense.

Especially pertinent to understanding the body as vulnerable to external attack is a historical consideration of the environments within which that attack takes place. What defined its inner and outer dimensions, the self to cultivate and the alien to eject (Lo 2000). As early Chinese medical theory aligned the geographical, political and social hierarchies with seasonal and biological cycles, it provided complex analytical tools to determine the boundaries and relationships of individuals with their environment—what Hsu might term the early Chinese "body ecologic" (Hsu 1999: 80). Since the body was conceived in the broadest of terms it not only reflected the physical health and welfare of each individual, but also social and moral condition and responsibilities. Consider the social construction of illness inherent in the following quotation from *Yinshu* (The pulling book), an early self-cultivation manual. *Yinshu* points out that a person's class is distinguished by the way he or she gets ill and the knowledge or ability to cultivate good health: a common person is subject to external elements beyond control: the vicissitudes of their labor and the weather, but the *guiren* (nobility) do not harmonize their inner bodies. Through extremes of emotion they tend to disrupt Yin or Yang *qi* and must normalize the thermostatic environment through breath control:

If they [nobility] are joyful then the *yang qi* is in excess. If they are angry then the *yin qi* is in excess. On account of this, if those that follow the Way are joyful then they quickly exhale [warm breath], and if they become angry they increasingly puff out [moist breath], in order to harmonize it. If they breathe in the quintessential *qi* of heaven and earth to make *yin* substantial then they will be able to avoid illness. The reason that lowly people become ill is exhaustion from their labor, hunger, and thirst; when the hundred sweats cease, they plunge themselves into water and then lie down in a cold and empty place. They don't know to put on more clothes and so they become ill from it. Also they do not know to expel air and breathe out (dry breath) to get rid of it. On account of this they have many illnesses and die easily. (*Yinshu*, 299)

It is the special qualities that the *xie/zheng* analysis brings to the construction and boundaries of these bodily environments that sustains its relevance through both ancient and modern worlds of medical practice.

Our overall intention, then, is to explore some dynamics between streams of medical history in China and the creation of contemporary medical cultures in Europe. The study is by definition interdisciplinary: we have a survey of Chinese textual sources, mostly selected from a period two thousand years ago, and we follow this with a qualitative treatment of the stories of fifteen individual subjects in our local European environment. The voices they represent are remote from each other and any search for shared meaning would be fanciful: the first are likely to represent a medley of anonymous authors, whose thoughts are blended at different times in different contexts, the second are individuals speaking in our common idiom in contemporary Europe.

At the point of practice, medical texts (and the concepts and techniques they convey) take on culturally specific meaning and should not be taken as authoritative rendering of abstract bodies of knowledge (Farquhar 1992: 72). Yet the circumstances of their historical production and of the development of related techniques continue to bear upon the various entities that constitute the ever-emerging and changing practice of traditional medicine (Pickering 1995; Scheid 2002: 43–47). Examining metaphors applied to and inspired by the body in the different times under consideration provides us with a way of bridging some of the difficulties encountered in combining anthropological and historical approaches.

Metaphor analysis allows us to transcend the simple observation that even without geographic removal the "tradition" of a traditional medicine is only tenuously connected to past cultures and practices—and that when severed from those elements of culture that provide some semblance of continuity (lineages of aural and textual transmission), it is largely a contemporary construction. Instead, rather than becoming sidetracked by intricate details of ethnoscience, we can focus on how the particular virtues of the framework of analysis embedded in early Chinese medical theory have contributed to the continuing relevance of Asian medical ideas in modern settings worldwide.

On Deviant Airs and Public Morality: Conceptions of *xie* in Early Chinese Literature

Our approach to the historical records began with a general search through the concordances to pre- and early imperial Chinese literature, aiming to build a basis for interpreting several significant treatises in the canon of Chinese acupuncture theory, *Huangdi neijing suwen* and *Lingshu* (the Yellow Emperor's Inner Canon, hereafter *Suwen* and *Lingshu*). It is now thought by most European and American scholars that the earliest texts of the canon were set down during or after the first century B.C.E. Collectively, they represent the kind of debate through which classical medical concepts matured and therefore provide us with a range of references to research *xie* as it was developing in early imperial times (Sivin 1993: 199–201).

Numerous studies have argued that perceptions of *xie* embrace both demonic and more naturalistic constructions of illness (Unschuld 1985: 68; Sivin 1987: 102–6; Li 1996; Hinrichs 2003). One might conclude that these two conceptions of *xie* illness developed in parallel, perhaps representing a division between more popular and scholarly forms of medical knowledge, or that the naturalistic views of *xie* were an abstraction of early themes in popular religious healing. Yet there are only a few references in the transmitted or excavated literature from the late Warring States and early imperial period that associate *xie* with demons. In *Guoyu* (Sayings of the States), there is one record of a lord who dreams of a yellow bear in the room and refers to it as the *xie* of a *mo gui* "malignant spirit and ghost" (*Guoyu* 4.105).

In contrast, many premodern medical theories about *xie* are grounded in social and moral ideas developed in earlier treatises on ritual and philosophy. Our survey therefore begins with the "Record of Music" *Yueji* in the *Liji* (Record of Rites), a "ritualist's anthology of ancient usages, prescriptions, definitions and anecdotes" (Knoblock and Riegel 2000: 293–96). The dating of the *Liji* remains controversial, and how many of the 49 sections originated at the same time, or indeed relate to the 23 said to have been studied and edited by Liu Xiang (78–8 B.C.E.) has yet to be established. But the ideas expressed generally accord with literature that is more accurately dated to the early period, such as *Lushi chunqiu* (The annals of Lu Buwei 239).

The combined institutions of music and ritual are promoted in *Liji* as a form of social control, ensuring peaceful relations and filial piety: music moderates inner feelings and ritual is the external regulation and expression of harmony:

Therefore the instruction and transforming power of ceremonies is subtle; they stop (*xie*) depravity before it has taken form, causing man daily to move towards what is good. (*Liji* 27.6, tr. Legge 1885: 239)

In the manner in which different qualities of music constitute an agency that emanates from outside and influences the inner emotional body, and consequently human behavior we will find a model for the naturalistic constructions of *xie* as a cause of illness:

This is the reason that when the early rulers formed the rituals and music, their purpose was not to satisfy the mouth, stomach, ear and eye, but rather to teach the people to moderate their likes and hates, and bring them back to the correct direction in life. (*Yueji* 1, tr. Thrasher 1980: 25)

In the polarity between *xie* and *zheng* "physically upright," *xie* refers to a slanting or deviating shape:

Red greaves on their legs, *xie fu xai xia* "cross-laced" below. (*Shijing* 222, tr. Waley 1937, 186–87)

And this gives us the metaphor for not being upstanding in a moral sense, that is, crooked, deviant, or perverse. The responsibility for maintaining control and respect among his subjects fell to the ruler whose personal behavior must always be *zheng* "upright" and generous. *Guoyu* charges the lord with being the moral shepherd of his people: *mu min yi zheng qi xie* (shepherd the people to correct their *xie*). For, with the exception of the Mencian doctrines of the goodness of human nature, there was a common belief in Warring States literature that ordinary folk had a natural tendency toward *xie* (deviant or perverse) behavior. *Xie* in early Chinese texts tends to describe aberrant behaviors, and in association with *qi* anticipates later medical conceptions: the lord is said to act with "*zheng* upright/correct *qi*," lesser people, on the other hand, act with "*xie qi*," a condition brought on by the stimulation of the senses with flavors, licentious music, sensuous colors, lust, and the expression of extreme emotion (*Guoyu*).

Extreme emotion was to be avoided. In the following translations of *Liji* from James Legge (1885), *Sacred Books of the East*, we can see the profound effect of music on the emotions:

The blending together without any mutual injuriousness (of the sentiments and the airs on the different instruments) forms the essence of music; and the exhilaration of joy and the glow of affection are its business. (*Zhongzheng*) Exactitude and correctness, (*wuxie*) without any inflection or deviation, form the substance of ceremonies, while gravity, respectfulness, and a humble consideration are the rules for their discharge. (*Liji* 19, tr. Legge 1885: 101)

Both *Xunzi* and *Mengzi* also refer to *xieshuo* (*xie* persuasions or theories) with which one might mislead the people.[2] When the lord, himself, does not deport himself in a *zheng* "upright" or "correct" manner, and is "*liu pi*, careless disorderly, *xie san*, perverse and dissipated" then widespread chaos will ensue (*Guoyu* 2.15). With the inclusion of the term *qi* here, we can begin to understand that the lord is not simply modeling behavior for his subjects. The nature of his influence on the people springs from a pervasive worldview in which there is a developing notion of *ganying*, a kind of syncretic resonance, mediated by an almost physiologically conceived influence, namely *qi*. The following passage from "Record of Music" describes the process:

Whenever notes that are evil and depraved (*jian*) affect men, a corresponding (*ni qi*) evil spirit responds to them (from within); and when this evil spirit accomplishes its manifestations, licentious music is the result. Whenever notes that are correct affect men, a corresponding correct spirit responds to them (from within) and when this correct spirit accomplishes its manifestations, harmonious music is the result. The initiating cause and the result correspond to each other. The round and the (*xie*) deflected, the crooked and the straight, have each its own category; and such is the character of all things, that they affect one another severally according to their class. (*Liji* 19, tr. Legge 1885: 110)

The good Reverend Mr. Legge, first professor of Chinese at Oxford, is much concerned with evil, which he uses to translate both *jian* (the character pictures three women together and is generally rendered "adultery," "fornication," "debauchery"), the description of musical notes, and *ni qi* "evil spirit" (more literally "reversing" or "counterflow" *qi*). We have deliberately not provided new translations of these quotations from *Liji*, since Legge's interpretation serves to emphasize important changes that occur in the process of translation. Moreover, despite superimposing a Christian ethic, Legge's translation has the effect of bringing out the inherent moral dimension of this protophysiology of the body's relationship with its environment. *Xie* in this passage is an abstract quality that is the opposite of round, as crooked is the opposite of straight, but by association gathers to itself all the connotations of the other terms. The significance of the description to our topic is that we can see how deviant music inspires *ni qi*, a form of *qi* that moves in a retroverse or "deviant" direction. In contrast, correct, modulated music automatically embodies in harmonious physical action a process which seems to occur without passing through the consciousness of the subjects concerned.

Now music produces pleasure;—what the nature of man cannot be without. That pleasure must arise from the modulation of the sounds, and have its embodiment in the movements (of the body);—such is the rule of humanity. . . .

The ancient kings, feeling that they would feel ashamed (in the event of such disorder arising), appointed the tunes and words of the Ya and the Sung to guide (in the music), so that its notes should give sufficient pleasure, without any intermixture of what was bad, while the words should afford sufficient material for consideration without causing weariness; and the bends and straight courses, the swell and diminution, the sharp angles, and soft melody throughout all its parts, should be sufficient to stir up in the minds of the hearers what was good in them, without inducing any looseness of thought or (*xie*) depraved air to be suggested. Such as the plan of the ancient kings when they framed their music. (*Liji* 26.6, tr. Legge 1885: 127)

The ancient kings used *zheng* music to reinforce political control: modulated music moderated physical pleasures and manifested in harmonious behavior mitigating against social deviance and political disorder.

Guo feng (Airs of the States), the first book of *Shijing* (The Book of Songs, 1,000–600 B.C.E., contains 160 folk songs from fifteen different kingdoms). It is a lyrical description of the daily lives, emotions, and festivals of ordinary people (Loewe 1993: 417). *Feng* the "airs" is the same term used to designate "wind." From the Shang era (ca. 1600–1045), wind was conceived as a demonic entity, a cause of disease (Kuriyama 1999: 233–70). Abstracted as a natural climatic influence like heat or cold, in imperial medicine wind was responsible for acute and rapidly changing illnesses and could stir the passions. Ultimately it became significant to the etiology of different types of madness. In modern Chinese the term *fengkuang*, which incorporates the graph for wind, still translates as "madness." Here, then, we have two types of *feng*, the "winds" and the "airs," which influence the inner workings of the body and potentially arouse the passions. Both can become deviant: in the physiology of *xie* music and other deviant stimulants on the senses, we can find a model for *xie* wind, or *xie qi*, as they are construed as causing sudden or dramatic emotional turmoil in the diverse medical treatises of the *Huangdi neijing*.

Huangdi neijing (the Yellow Emperor's Inner Canon)

In early Han ritual treatises we have found a metaphor that pervades later medical theory about *xie* in treatises of the *Huangdi neijing*: as the lord instructs and shapes the bodily passions of his subjects with proper ritual music so the Han dynasty practitioner manipulates the *qi* of his patient, strengthening *zheng* and draining away *xie*. Disorders of the inner body are "primarily a result of the inability—or willful negligence—of man to adapt his behavior to the influences of his environment. At rest and at work, in eating and drinking, in their senses and desires, so criticizes a passage in *Huangdi neijing*, men violate the *zheng* 'correct' course of things thus providing an open invitation to the influences of *xie* 'evil'" (Unschuld 1985: 83). Here the description of the dangers of excess and the inherent weakness of human nature to environmental influences is barely different from that which we have seen in the *Liji* discourse warning of the effects of the wrong kind of music.

In *Suwen* 13 we find the Yellow Emperor interrogating his minister, Qibo, about changes in medical techniques:

The Yellow Emperor asked saying: "I have heard that in ancient times when treating illness, in moving *jing* 'essence' and transforming *qi*, all they had to do was make spells. In modern times when treating illness, poisons and herbs treat the inside (of the body), needle and stone treat its outside—why do some promote recovery and some do not promote recovery?" Qi Bo answered: "in former times the ancients dwelled among the birds and beasts. In their movements they avoided the cold, they stayed in the shade and avoided the summer heat; inside they did not harbor envy and outside they did not have the appearance of reporting to an official. In a quiet and peaceful world, '*xie* influences' could not penetrate deeply inside, poisons and herbs were unable to treat the inside, needle and stone were unable to treat the outside, so spells for removal alone were able to move the essence."[3]

Here we find the authors pontificating about a golden and morally pure age when *xie* was not a serious problem that invaded the interior of the body, when it could be easily eliminated with spells. The implication was that a deterioration in lifestyle and a loss of alignment with the natural rhythms of the universe have brought about a new form of vulnerability that requires more sophisticated medical intervention.

Xie is one of the most common terms in Han medical literature. Different theories about the nature of vulnerability to and strategies for dealing with *xie* are specifically set out in a number of treatises of the *Lingshu*, primarily *Lingshu* 43, *Yin xie fa meng* (Overflowing [this term has an alternative meaning of immorality] *Xie* and Dreaming),[4] which describe the physiological process through which people become vulnerable to dream disturbed sleep; *Lingshu* 7,: *Xie ke* (*Xie* lodges),[5] which is more generally concerned with the theory of forms of health and vulnerability to *xie*; *Lingshu* 4: *Xie qi zangfu bing xing* (The shape of illness of *Xie Qi* in the viscera and bowels),[6] which distinguishes the physical areas of the body vulnerable to invasion by *xie* and the conditions under which it moves into the channels, bowels, and viscera; *Lingshu* 20, *Wu xie* (Five *Xie*),[7] which is concerned with techniques for treatment of *xie* illnesses with acupuncture; and *Suwen* 27: *Li he zhen xie lun* (Theory of the Separation and Coming Together of *Zhen* [the true] and *Xie*),[8] which adds specific elements of diagnosis and treatment. It is in these medical treatises that we find the *xie/zheng* polarity achieving full maturity.

Lingshu 4 sets out a pathophysiology of *xie* as it attacks the upper part of the body and enters specific channels in the form of dampness. Vulnerability to *xie* increases when the *couli* (a superficial gateway structure at the surface of the body, often referring to the pores) are open. Failures of lifestyle apparently cause this condition: the effects of drinking and eating, sex or bathing directly after the sweating of sexual activity following a hard day's work, the accumulation of excessive anger, or the sadness and anxieties of the heart. Here there is evidence of the well-established hygienic tradition of medicine that we know dates to before the second century B.C.E. (*Yinshu*; Lo 2000).

Yet in the *Huangdi* treatises these theories gain much greater technical detail, and are appropriated into the domain of the professional physician and medical theorist. Each behavioral transgression is differentiated according to which of the viscera might be invaded by *xie qi*.

Lingshu 43 (Overflowing *xie* and dreaming) describes how both *xie* and *zheng* enter the body and influence the *qi* in the organs, stimulating dreams. Here *xie* influences stimulate bodily passions:

when the liver *qi* flourishes, then one dreams of rage; when the lung *qi* flourishes, then one dreams of fear and weeping, and flying; when the heart *qi* flourishes, then one dreams of tending to laugh and tremble; when the spleen *qi* flourishes, then one dreams of singing and music.

When *xie* causes pathological counterflow *qi* (the same *ni qi* that we met in the ritual texts responding to licentious music), people dream of weird physical experiences such as not being able to move forward, sinking, or flying. Equally *ni qi* in the body causes dreams of social disorder: random killing; taking and giving; flying gold and iron; thoroughfares; quarrels and litigation; cutting open one's own body; decapitation; disorders of the natural environment; great fires; rain and storm damaging the house.

In working out how the quality of state ceremonial musical "airs" affect the passions and civility of imperial subjects, the ritual texts model a physiology of the body—a physiology developed in medical treatises in the succeeding centuries. As deviant music causes counterflow *qi* that disturbs the emotions and disrupts the state, so *xie* in a medical context brings with it a way of talking about the body in moral terms, terms which associate parts of the body with socially disruptive behavior. Although these are only dream scenarios of social and physical disruption, in the long-standing relationship between *xie* and mad, passionate behavior we find medical techniques to normalize emotional and social relationships with the environment.

Treatment of *Xie* in the *Huangdi* Corpus

Xie lodging within the viscera is clearly inauspicious, and according to *Lingshu* 71, fatal when it reaches the heart. *Lingshu* 71 argues that "the heart is the great ruler of the five viscera and six bowels, where the quint-essential spirits lodges, its viscera is firm and solid and it cannot contain xie. If it contains it then the heart will be harmed; and when the heart is harmed the spirit will leave and when the spirit is gone then the [patient] will die." There is no remedy for *xie* in the heart. Here we have the music/state metaphor encountered in *Liji* brought to a physiology of the body: as the ruler must not play *xie* music for fear of a revolt among the people, so the spirit will leave the body if the practitioner allows *xie* to accumulate in the Heart.

Suwen 27 then provides a variety of information about diagnosing and treating *xie* in other parts of the body. Apart from identifying innumerable physical signs of its presence, a big pulse felt at the *cun kou* (the radial edge of the wrist) is consistent with the "arrival" of *xie* in the body.[9] Several of the *Suwen* and *Lingshu* treatises describe different, sometimes contradictory techniques to disperse *xie*: draining or stimulating, bloodletting, or decoctions are all variously recommended.

Needle techniques to remove *xie* are very specific about the quality of attention needed, for "the crude (physician) . . . does not know the comings and goings of blood and *qi*, of *zheng* and *xie*":

How to get rid of the *xie qi*: use the left hand to hold the muscles and the right hand to follow it, do not fill/bunch the flesh (?) . . . in draining you must have the tip on the perpendicular, in supplementing you must close the pores, support the needle, and lead the *qi*, then *xie qi* will overflow and the true *qi* will remain.

The passage goes on to say that it is important to practice the correct needle technique to ensure that you do not disperse the spirit. Where healthy *qi* flourishes the *xie qi* cannot get a grip. These techniques are reminiscent of the way the spirit itself is handled:

The sophisticated practitioner needles at the three hundred and sixty five places where the *jie* (nodes) cross, "where the *qi* of the *shen* 'spirit' (or alternatively *qi* and *shen*') travels in and out, not the skin, flesh, tendons and bone."

Even though *xie* and *qi* might seem to be featureless medical terms, as targets of medical practice they take on the quality of spirits and souls as they move in and out of the human body at its joints and junctures. This becomes even more clear when we see the physiological dance of *qi* and *xie*:

Qi Bo said: when the lung and heart have *xie*, the *qi* stays in both elbows. When the liver has *xie* the *qi* flows in the two armpits. When the spleen has *xie*, the *qi* stays in the two hamstrings.

Rather than filling the body as if with the quality of fluid, *qi* and *xie* seem to be individual bounded entities that move discretely around the body, and this is an idea that we find recurring frequently in early and medieval acupuncture literature. *Hamajing* (Toad canon) charts the course of *qi* and the spirits of the body as they moves from site to site, around the body, according to temporal cycles such as the waxing and waning of the moon (Lo 2001).

Early Chinese techniques aimed at purging *xie* invasion developed in the context of a worldview where many discrete entities moved freely in, out, and around the body and its environment. Medical purging is an extension of the kind of exorcism that was at the heart of Han ritual practice (Harper 1998: 162 ; Bodde 1975: 75–138). It is well attested in later styles of acupuncture exorcism, beginning with Xu Qiufu (*Nanshi* [*History of the Southern dynasty*]: presented in 659, but covering the period 420–589) and immortalized in Sun Simiao's (581–682) *Qianjin yaofang* (Essential prescriptions worth a thousand), where the thirteen acupuncture "ghost" locations for treating the "one-hundred *xie*" are attributed to the mythical patron of the acupuncture arts, Bian Que (Sun: 261). Ghost- and demon-related illness manifest in aberrant behaviors such as elective mutism, wild talking, singing, crying, and laughing. Working in the same period Wang Tao's *Waitai biyao* (Arcane essentials from the imperial library, 752) picks up on the *Huangdi Neijing* themes of how *xie* affects the passions in dream life. He is particularly concerned about differentiating the causal factors when women dream about sex with human partners (*xu lao*, "depletion and exhaustion") or demons (*feng xie*, "wind *xie*"), the latter the result of invasion by fox, ghost, and goblin spirits (Chen Hsiu-fen 2002). As scholarly medical theory ranks naturalistic and demonic conceptions of disease causation in the same categories, embracing worldviews pervasive in popular religion, it simultaneously denies transcendence to the world of gods and spirits.

Acupuncture exorcism is a fascinating topic that deserves in-depth study, and this brief introduction is only a précis of our original survey. Central influences on the history of *xie* illnesses, such as the relationship with wind, have also been casually brushed past and deserve much more detailed analysis. We do not have the space for an analysis of the features of *xie* in Taoist histories or popular martial arts culture. At this juncture, for fear of losing ourselves and the reader in multiple narratives about demons, deviation, and perversity, we must attend to the main themes that emerged as our research moved back and forward between historical and anthropological approaches to deviance in Chinese medicine.

In the next section we will see that in a modern European context, practitioners of "traditional" Chinese medicine remain aware of *xie* as a medical phenomenon causally related to a wide range of illness and dis-

ease. But they almost universally demonstrate discomfort with ideas
about demonological causation in Chinese medical culture, preferring
to attribute damaging agents to an environment constructed in a recog-
nizably contemporary way. Our analysis of the music/state metaphor in
the construction of medical theories of deviance will allow us to bridge
ancient and modern, Chinese and European medical cultures.

Xie in a Modern European Context

Were it not that various forms of medical exorcism are enjoying a revival
in China today, we might have deemed that the coming of Western biomedical culture, compounded by Chinese Marxist theories of dialectical
materialism, dealt the medical ideas of demonic infestation a fatal blow.
In the construction of a new Traditional Chinese Medicine (TCM) consistent with modern political and medical discourse, notions of evil
(along with many other concepts of Chinese medicine) were exorcized
from the top down in successive political campaigns to scientize medicine and against the "feudal" and "superstitious" from the 1940s
onward (Taylor 2001: 136–243). Textbooks played down or further
abstracted notions of *xie*, emphasizing the innocuous such as the invasion of wind or damp in the etiology of the common cold, or the psychi-
atric in wind-related illnesses such as madness.

Modeled, for the most part, on mainland Chinese textbooks, European and American TCM texts and articles tend to relate the concept of
xie to "invasion by wind or dampness" or refer to it as "pathogenic *qi*,"
thereby avoiding having to deal with the notion of "evil" or "deviance"
in the abstract or concrete (Deadman, Al-Khafaji, and Baker 1998: 626;
Scott 2002). Widely used teaching texts exclude all references (Maciocia
1989: 435–36; 1994; 905–6). Practitioners of Chinese medicine in
Europe have recently been given access to information about Ghost
Points (Deadman, Al-Khafaji, and Baker 1998: 50–51), and there is some
evidence that methods of acupuncture and herbal medicine are being
used to help individuals troubled by phenomena commonly described
as paranormal (Chace 1993; Hicks 1997; Young 1997). But these are
exceptional traces of medical ideas of demonic infestation that for the
most part relied on complex lines of medical transmission outside of
China that were not quite so effectively interrupted by the instruments
of state (Eckman 1996).

Thus in the various phases of transmission to Europe the practice of
acupuncture became severed from its native Chinese theories and
adapted to the local environment (Bivins 2000). Familiarity defined how
easily each theory or technique gained acceptance: Chinese conceptions
of sphygmology were found marvelous yet "obscure" and "phantasti-

cal" (Kuriyama 2000); *yin* and *yang* are translated into Western anatomical language; Wilhelm Ten Rhynne's insistence on *flatus* as the cause of disease in his 1683 treatise seems to underpin a translation of the Chinese physiological essence *qi* as wind; moxibustion is chosen over needling as a gentler and more familiar form of local cautery techniques.

In the first part of this chapter we have seen how *xie* "deviant" music invading the body and inciting rebellion in preimperial China provided a metaphor for medical constructions of *xie* attacking the inner realms and causing a breakdown of bodily harmony and health. The metaphors that emerge in practitioner narratives in the modern context about *xie* are hardly less rich and complex and similarly reveal fundamental patterns through which we, as patients and citizens, commonly negotiate our places in society and the world around us through the medium of the body.

The study of contemporary *xie* practice was conducted by Schroer, who interviewed fifteen of her colleagues whom she knew through working alongside them in a clinic in central London or had met in postgraduate training courses in Chinese medicine. Schroer's own background in Chinese medicine included initial training in Worsley-style acupuncture; training in TCM in both China and the UK; training in Kanpo, a Japanese approach to Chinese herbal medicine; postgraduate courses in Vietnam and in Japanese acupuncture approaches including Toyohari, meridian therapy, and Manaka style, which she learned in Amsterdam with Stephen Birch and Junko Ida. Her conventional medical experience had been in the area of mental health and depression and after gaining a degree in psychology she cofacilitated a psychotherapy group in early 1980s. She has also completed a metaphysical training with Gill Edwards and as a result is conversant with New Age concepts and language.

Practitioner Sample and Background

With the exception of one practitioner whom we chose to give the TCM perspective, we interviewed practitioners who had trained to some degree in Worsley and Toyohari styles of practice. Both these styles pass on forms of acupuncture that have evolved through Taiwan or Japanese acupuncture lineages and interpret teachings from pre-Communist China (Eckman 1996; Birch and Felt 1999: 56) and we felt they were more relevant to our theme of *xie*. Our practitioner sample is therefore not representative, since the dominating model for "traditional" acupuncture practice in Europe since the mid-1990s has been shaped by the principles of the form of mainland Chinese TCM that was modernized and standardized in the 1950s (Taylor 2000).

We will briefly outline how we as authors and practitioners see the concept of *xie* in relation to Worsley and Tohohari styles of practice as we have already discussed it in relation to TCM. Two techniques taught by Worsley were arguably related to the concept of *xie*. First, there was a treatment taught as "internal /external devils (IDs/EDs)," a kind of possession lyrically described as "the seven dragons to chase away the seven demons" and related to various states of emotional distress, including "madness" and depression (Worsley 1990: 170–74; Hicks 1997). Second, although *xie* was not an explicit part of common medical discourse at the college, the *xie/zheng* discourse emerges in a treatment known as "aggressive energy," something external to be drained away, unlike "healthy energy," which was to be strengthened (Worsley 1990: 175–78; Shifrin 1997). Japanese Toyohari explanations of pathology frequently refer to *jia ki*, the Japanese term for *xie qi*, associating it with abnormalities of the pulse (Fixler and Kivity 2000: 11); however, in the training course teachers frequently used the term "evil" *qi* to describe it.

In order to protect the identities of the practitioners we will present them as a group. Eleven practitioners worked in the UK and were members of the British Acupuncture Council, currently the largest representative professional organization for traditional acupuncturists. Two worked in Holland, one in Germany, and one in Switzerland. Four, two doctors and two nurses, had a background in conventional medicine. The two doctors and one of the nurses continued to practice conventional medicine with acupuncture as a part-time profession. Several practitioners had a background in biology; one of these worked with the effects of air pollution on plants and ecology, another had gone on to working in a corporate environment not related to biology. One practitioner had worked in the construction industry and another had worked as a translator and interpreter. Several had been professional counselors. The professional background of three was unknown. The practitioners varied in how long they had been working as acupuncturists; two had been practicing for over twenty years and two for two years, with the rest somewhere in between. Two-thirds of the practitioners were female and although we did not ask their ages, most were between thirty and fifty. A full ethnography of the practitioners would demand a thesis-length study in itself. Suffice it to say that their ethnicity reflects the multicultural urban environment of modern Europe with several practitioners being second generation Asians. Most have at least college degrees, if not postgraduate training.

Our focus was on practitioners rather than patients, but some brief details about the practice and funding of acupuncture in the countries where the practitioners in our study worked in may be useful to the reader. In the UK the National Health Service (NHS) does not usually provide traditional acupuncture; patients have to pay for treatment themselves and find their own practitioner. Practitioners usually work in private clinics, possibly with other complementary therapists, or their own homes. A relatively small number of insurance companies fund acupuncture treatment in the UK (compared with Germany, Holland, and Switzerland, where funding by insurance companies is much more common, so patient demographics may be slightly different). As far as a patient profile is concerned we are able to have a reasonably accurate impression of the client base from our own experience of working in the same or similar practice contexts. Our impression agrees with earlier UK research into the patients of complementary therapists, which suggests that, in comparison to general practice, there is proportionately a greater number of women than men, of all social classes, but with a tendency to be wealthier and to have a tertiary education (Vincent and Furnham 1997; Fulder and Munro 1985).

CONTENT AND SETTING OF THE INTERVIEWS

The interviews were conducted informally in three settings. The first setting was a course in Toyohari, which took place in Amsterdam and in which Schroer was a teaching assistant. Here she interviewed five postgraduate students in two groups and four course teaching assistants in pairs and individually. An acupuncture center in central London at which Schroer and Lo are practitioners formed the second setting for five individual interviews. The final interviewee was one of Schroer's colleagues who practices and teaches TCM and was interviewed in her own home. Only this last interview was tape-recorded.

Practitioners were specifically asked about the term *xie*, which was translated as evil. Schroer asked them what they understood by the term; how they would translate it; whether they used the concept in their clinical work; under what circumstances they might use it and what specific treatment would be given. They were also asked how they might explain it or describe it to patients. If a practitioner had trained in Worsley style and did not specifically mention Possession treatments or Aggressive Energy drains they were asked whether they considered these treatments worked on *xie*.

ANALYSIS OF THE PRACTITIONER NARRATIVES

Notes were made from the interviews and a narrative account was created which retained all the metaphorical descriptions that had originally been used in the interview. With the exception of the final interview, which had been recorded, the narrative accounts were sent back to the practitioners by e-mail for verification to ensure that their views had been correctly represented by Schroer. Ten of these fourteen narratives were verified. Schroer coded the narratives and identified metaphors and constructs used by practitioners to describe *xie*. This process enabled her to get close to the data and make comparisons between different narratives.

Polluted Bodies and Private Morality: The Ecology Ethic

In a modern European context, practitioners of "traditional" Chinese medicine remain aware of *xie* as a medical phenomenon causally related to a wide range of illness and disease. They are less comfortable with ideas about demonological causation in Chinese medical culture: although "evil" is the most common translation in European acupuncture, texts eight out of fifteen explicitly rejected it, particularly as a term for explaining treatment to their patients. One even stated that she would not speak of "evil" for fear of attracting it to her work. For others "evil" has an emotive force apparently too rooted in religious belief. Typical statements include "I don't like it, I would use the word polluted" or "I prefer the word excess to explain it as the word evil has implications which you don't mean in the sense of implying a judgment, this creates a framework of morality which is not appropriate and not something I feel comfortable with in the context of my therapeutic work."

Most practitioners preferred to implicate damaging agents in an environment constructed in a familiar, contemporary way. They used metaphors relating to ecology, military attack, or information systems, where *xie* might cause a "breakdown of the body's defenses" or "system overload." *Xie* or *xie*-related causes of illness were most frequently conceived as external and in need of elimination, transformation, or dissolution: "it is something that isn't good for you which originates from outside the body." Some thought it was a violent invasion "an attack from outside" that directly influenced the channels: "external pathogens have invaded the person's body and lodged in the channels." Others were more neutral, imagining "an exterior attack such as catching a cold, the result of climactic environmental influences, or incorrect diet."

Metaphors infused with the ecological ethic pervaded practitioners' accounts. Patients' bodies might be polluted, contaminated, murky with toxins; their channels might become irritated with blockages and stagnation. Symptoms associated with these pollutions ranged from the common cold to severe mental and emotional disturbances that entered the body as a result of weakness following physical or emotional trauma.

One practitioner imagined *xie* as "the scum floating in the corner or the Tesco [supermarket] trolleys beneath the surface of the canal." Another visualized "black mist or polluted water . . . something hidden but polluted." Another echoed "I think of *xie* as being a sort of polluted *qi*, something that is disturbing the channels . . . someone's energy is contaminated."

When negotiating causes, manifestations, and treatment of illness and suffering with their patients, practitioners generally privileged environmental or ecological discourse as more effective than constructs of pathology rooted in biomedicine or demonic infestation. Illness was "something murky . . . the result of climactic, environmental influences." One practitioner would tell patients that he was "going to do a clearing, detoxifying treatment to remove *qi* which gets stuck in the channels." Another thought the best way to communicate about the nature of their practice to patients was to tell them "that I'm going to give them a general detox-type treatment to clear their system a bit before I start to balance their energy. Most people seem to be able to relate to this and think it's a good idea." What works in communicating over matters of health is to invoke priorities in a contemporary environment. The *New Fontana Dictionary of Modern Thought* defines

Ecology (2): a growing awareness of environmental problems during the 1960's and 1970's led to the formation of activist groups, particularly in the USA and Western Europe, with the result that governments increasingly introduced legislation to control the release of toxic substances into the environment. Major environmental disasters . . . Union Carbide (1984) . . . Chernobyl . . . (1986) . . . have placed ecological issues firmly on the political agenda of most countries. (Bullock and Trombley 1999: 247)

Indeed, the Rio and Johannesburg earth summits of recent years have made sustainable development strategy essential to states who want status in the international community (www.earthsummit2002.org).

Strengthening Oneself or Eliminating the Other?

Negotiating Therapy

By analogy the practitioners style themselves as overseeing a process of purification and cleansing. Specific techniques are used to drain pollution from the channels: "I think of it as letting in the light, turning something that is dark, black, or gray into something light, white, or pure. . . . I usually use the word polluted or say something needs to be drained or strengthened . . . these treatments (AE, IDs/EDs) are releasing treatments and once done the energy flow is corrected." One practitioner described her main therapeutic concern as the removal of "stagnation"; another stated that "My therapeutic work engages with this concept of eliminating this imaginary pollution . . . It is a clearing treatment" (AE).

The practitioners' belief in a dynamic between building up their patients' bodies and strengthening them against external invasion echoes the concerns of the early Chinese state metaphor of construction and defense in terms of a modern environment. Xie, however, is still associated with disordered emotional states, with a buildup of stress and passions that threaten to become out of control. "It [xie illness] can be brought on by outside things entering but also by tension building up inside . . . the result of emotional factors which are difficult to deal with." At the level of practice this dynamic between theories of internal or external cause plays out in techniques of removal and draining away xie illness factors, or "tonification" and strengthening of the body's defensive mechanism so that the body performs the expelling itself. Toyahari acupuncture provided one practitioner with "new skills to specifically work with clearing the evil or pollution . . . not only in terms of my intention but in the action of needling itself." These are specific techniques to drain this evil from the channels. With "draining" and "clearing" techniques responsibility for removing the xie factor is located in the practitioner's agency. Where strengthening the patient's body is implied in the technique the onus of removal rests in the dynamic between the practitioner and the patient's own resources.

In my own therapeutic work I try to be caring and strengthen or tonify the person, I see tonification as opening a door for things to leave. . . . I don't consider that I am removing something from the body of my patient but that I am stimulating their own wei qi [defensive qi], I am encouraging their own wei qi to fight whatever it is that is there, it is their body that does the work. . . . I need to decide if the person is weak and needs to be strengthened or whether the evil can simply be eliminated.

Part of strengthening a patient no doubt resides in lifestyle reeducation. Just like the Han dynasty elite had to know how to deport themselves after bathing, or used breath control to moderate their passions, so modern patients of "alternative health care" are taught to distinguish themselves in their attitudes to work, diet, stress, exercise, and relaxation.

MODERN DEMONS: PERSONAL BLAME

The one practitioner who claimed her treatment was based entirely on the TCM model condemned the morality implicit in medical constructs of *xie*. "Evil" too easily implies the interference of a malevolent consciousness:

I don't use the term *xie* or evil. I don't like it because it can make the patient feel guilty about their illness. This is particularly the case in illnesses such as cancer, ME, or multiple sclerosis, and it's very destructive for the patient to feel blamed in this way. That they have somehow brought their illness upon themselves. They haven't because they had no awareness about it. The term *evil* implies that something has a mind, so even bacteria are not evil.

This statement needs to be understood in relation to the growing culture of blame upon individuals for their inability to maintain a healthy "body, mind and spirit." To many, biomedical models of health care delivered in a context where we shared collective responsibility for the health of the nation (NHS) had the effect of disempowering the individual, absolving the patient of personal responsibility. It is surely not coincidental that the two decades of Margaret Thatcher's "spirit of free enterprise," when the notion of responsible citizenship was explicitly divorced from the concept of "society" with the dissolution of unions, state-run rail networks, industries and free higher education, were the years when the domain of alternative therapies and their emphasis on individual responsibility shifted from a minority fringe resistance to the *dominant* cultural norm. Coward identified the same shift: "alternative therapies came to be viewed as something more than complementing or supplementing the failures of allopathic medicine. They became the place for a new philosophy of personal responsibility" (Coward 1989: 201–2).

With late twentieth-century secularization of Western European society, the emphasis in individual morality moved away from religious sin to "bad parenting, bad diet, bad posture, and the abuse of food and nature. The solutions to these are rarely political. They are individual. It is up to individuals to transform themselves, to deal with the pain and suffering imposed by modern life" (Coward 1989: 203). Our study has demonstrated how practitioners have adapted the moral concerns inherent in the concept of *xie* to the ecological debate that has increasingly taken center stage since the 1960s and 1970s. One practitioner identifies modern demons in "abuse or self-abuse," the *xie* agent being the abuser, in this case either the patient or some other individual:

I'm not currently comfortable with the role of clinician, being mixed up with some sort of psychospiritual perspective (which was part of my original training) which can extrapolate into "exorcist-type" treatment . . . I find myself both ill-equipped and ill-informed to perform. I do, however, find that the "Leamington possession treatment [IDs/EDs]" is occasionally helpful when treating people who have a history of abuse or self-abuse. I remain unsure, however, whether this type of "block" (if this is what it is) is *xie qi* in the sense it is described in the *Neijing*.

Surely what we are seeing in the reinterpretation of possession treatment is the modern-day demonizing of aberrant behavior. Other modern-day demons for practitioners of Chinese medicine are illnesses such as cancer or even the effects of biomedical interventions: "after chemotherapy or general anaesthetic I might test for it" (AE).

Our practitioners have effectively adapted their metaphors about health and sickness to mediate their patients' bodies with the hazards of a contemporary environment. With the focus on patient lifestyle choices, a certain morality accumulates around the body. In this case the discourse of "polluted bodies" is instrumental in the negotiation of a shift in the larger sociopolitical context from a public to a private political morality—a morality keyed to an international multicultural environment where practitioners and patients construct responsibility for themselves as global citizens within an international community. The *zheng/xie* polarity (much more than *yin* and *yang*, the more neutral construction of polar oppositions in Chinese medicine) once again focuses attention on the body as a site for negotiating propriety, excluding what is deemed improper, and strengthening the wholesome, and on the physician's role as a mediator of social process.

Conclusion

We chose this topic because we knew it would prove controversial, and that it would be less inclined to inspire the subjects to monolithic historical narratives aimed to legitimate their modern practice. We might have chosen to detail continuities we found in the theories and techniques associated with the physiology of *xie*—to mark up how *xie* still relates to symptoms of madness and emotional distress, or to point out the effective transmission of ancient medical needling—but it has not been our intention to emphasize similarities from one time to another. What "invasion by damp" might mean to a practitioner or patient working through London's gray winters is likely to be very different to those up against the climatic conditions and agrarian lifestyle of Han dynasty China.

Comparing metaphor provides us with a way of getting up and over the particulars of ethnoscience to the varied meanings that different practitioners impute into medical concepts and terminology. What we have found is that the *xie/zheng* polarity in medicine conditions practitioners' engagement with the metaphors specific to the culture they work in. It provides a tool to determine the boundaries of the body, to identify what is alien and other, what is to be supported and what is to be expelled. Most importantly, it allows both practitioner and patient to negotiate individual social and moral responsibilities in relation to the environment through the medium of the body and its health and illness. The nature of that environment then is absolutely culture-specific.

Undoubtedly what we see manifest in the deliberate excising of *xie* and notions of demonic infestation from TCM is one dimension of the complete intolerance of the PRC to any manifestation of social deviance. Modern Chinese and European received versions of TCM completely subsume the concept of *xie* under the rubric of environmental illness, and any traces of "dreaming sex with demons," madness, or other potential perversity is neutered into the etiology of wind and the common cold. Despite state support and consequent flourishing of Traditional Chinese Medicine in contemporary China, the transmission of theory and techniques of Chinese medicine considered here have not come to us directly from the mainland but through roundabout routes in Southeast Asia. Just as we owe the survival of the *Taisu* recension of the *Huangdi* corpus to its preservation within the Ninnaji temple, so we may owe a lively reconstruction of one ancient Chinese medical tradition to a revival of the study of Chinese medical canons in early twentieth-century Japan.

We began with the dissonance of musical notes and their subversive effect on the mood and passions of early Chinese imperial subjects and ended with the detoxification of our polluted and sick bodies. In the concept of *xie* as a simple medical notion of "deviance" or "perversity," in polar opposition to *zheng* "propriety" and "correctness," we find continuing relevance to the moral definition of the landscape of our bodies—with the subjugation of ghosts, ghouls, goblins and demons to the confines of cinematic and TV nightmares, a process of decongesting and expurgation demonstrates that environmentally friendly "cleanliness has finally taken the place of godliness" in the everyday negotiation of health and well-being.

Chapter 4
Reinventing Traditional Medicine: Method, Institutional Change, and the Manufacture of Drugs and Medication in Late Colonial India

S. Irfan Habib and Dhruv Raina

Several themes resurface in accounts of the encounter between so-called traditional systems of Indian medicine and modern allopathic medicine, each of which focuses differently on the politics of knowledge, science, and empire (Petitjean, Jami, and Moulin 1992). In each of these themes, the nation-state most visibly confers an identity on traditional knowledge systems and often frames the encounter between these knowledge systems in terms of conflict or dialogue (Raina and Habib 1999; Chakrabarty 1998). The history of science as a discipline retreated from its original Enlightenment ideal of the late eighteenth century to a phase where regional or continental essentialisms or national centrisms explicitly or implicitly shaped the topos of the discipline (Bernal 1987; F. Cohen 1994; Raina and Habib 1999). The founding conflict of the eighteenth century that shaped the history of science as a discipline was that of the "ancients and moderns" (Crombie 1994). This European contest between the ancients and the moderns reappears in the history of science of the non-Western world as a dichotomy that distinguishes tradition and modernity. Historians who have internalized this distinction have more often than not assumed a static view of both culture and knowledge—wherein that designated traditional is unchanging, threatened, and fighting a pitched battle against a modernity that would like to see it buried (Leslie 1976). This assumption, it could be safely suggested, is common to both traditionalists and modernists who view the prevalence of the premodern as an obstacle to the realization of an authentic modernity (Wittrock 1998).

Another perspective, probably more problematic but closer to the actual practice of the different systems of medicine, would frame the encounter in terms of the mutual shaping of knowledge systems that are designated "traditional" and "modern." This does not discount the political nature of the encounter between different knowledge systems and does not reduce knowledge to power. This mutual shaping or transformation is occasionally reflected in the historical narrativization of this encounter, as different kinds of national centrisms that frame these narratives usually seek to structure the circulation or flow of knowledge in terms of transmissions that flow in one direction only. In this manner historical priority accords prestige to the imagined nation (Adas 1990; Harding 1998), and in the day of intellectual property rights, history confers or denies rights upon possible communities wishing to access this knowledge.

The history of the encounter between modern allopathic medicine and so-called traditional medicine is one such field of cultural debate. However, it appears that the interlocutors for, or gatekeepers of, traditional medicine did not always entertain this perspective of the encounter between the modern and traditional. Recent research on some seventeenth-century Āyurvedic texts suggests that they are scattered with appeals to novelty as a "literary and intellectual virtue." However, the most widely distributed of these texts were more circumspect in their appeal to novelty, while the less successful proclaimed it more stridently (Wujastyk forthcoming). It could be suggested then that the response during the period of late colonial rule was quite a varied one, often inspired by very pragmatic considerations that guided medical practice (Alter this volume). The chemist P. C. Ray, discussing the future of the Āyurvedic pharmacopoeia, was quite forthright in asserting: "All that was needed was that [the] active principles (of Āyurvedic formulations) should be extracted according to scientific up-to-date methods and they should receive the imprimatur of the practitioners" (Ray 1932: 104). He appeared to have been convinced that Āyurvedic medicine had to be reconfigured along modern lines (Raina 1997a). The main drawback of the system, as perceived by some of its practitioners, was that its knowledge had become dated. Āyurveda failed to keep pace with the times and labored within the parameters of knowledge developed centuries before (Panikkar 1993: 292). Hakim Ajmal Khan, a leading Unani hakim and very closely associated with the Indian Congress party at the turn of the twentieth century, also attempted to revitalize indigenous medical systems in the light of modern medical developments, stating that these systems could benefit from modern anatomy and surgery. He was convinced that the modern innovations in the organization of medical practice and pedagogy in Europe were worth emulating (Habib 2000: 258–59).

In any case, political struggles for decolonization or cultural transformation have evoked traditional knowledge, values, and norms in order to establish parity with the hegemon (Habib and Raina 1989). This counterhegemonic ideology in each case evoked the traditional in a language that was more or less shaped by the idea of the modern. The traditional that was evoked was epistemically reconceived in the light of the modern (Raina 1997b). The theoretical vocabulary of this evocation is modern. This itself is a reflection of the conceptual engagement of the traditional with modern allopathic medicine. In the historical discourse this side of the engagement is invisible to the participants in a combat; just as the modernizers are unaware of how the "traditional" seeps into their own discourse, transforming it in ways not yet evident to us.

This chapter addresses the transformation of Āyurvedic and Unani Tibb medical practice in the late nineteenth and early twentieth centuries, through the efforts initiated by three iconic figures: P. S. Varier, Hakim Ajmal Khan, and P. C. Ray. The latter two were closely associated with the nationalist struggle, and P. C. Ray of course was a practicing chemist and is considered the father of modern chemical research in India. It will be argued that the trope of decline of the traditional systems of medicine is employed by the three of them to press for the modernization/revitalization of traditional systems of medicine. Revitalization in their eyes required an epistemological revision, a reform of institutional practices related to the former and revamping of the manufacturing and distribution system of drugs and medicaments. All three components of the revitalization were informed by the practices of modern science and adapted within the frame of the existing medical systems. Inasmuch as the colonial system was also one of economic expropriation, the manufacturing and distribution of Āyurvedic and Unani pharmacopiea aligned with the early twentieth-century politics of Swadeshi.[1] The Indian nationalist movement, unlike the contemporary incarnation of ultra-Hindu nationalism, was based on a theory that sought not merely to liberate India of the yoke of colonial rule but to liberate the English of the idea of imperialism (Nandy 1983; Visvanathan 1997). In order to do so new identities were often forged—and this is reflected in the creation of institutions such as the Āyurvedic and Unani Medical College in 1916 (Nizami 1988).

Perceptions of Decline

The encounter with Europe produced among sections of India's intelligentsia in the nineteenth century the feeling that Europe had leaped ahead economically and politically. The other face of this perception was the prevailing feeling of the decline of the sciences in India as consecutive waves of modernization swept the Indian subcontinent. This produced a diversity of responses among the intelligentsia in the nineteenth century (Habib and Raina 1989; Kaviraj 1988; Kopf 1970; Sarkar 1975), particularly among those drawn to modern science, there arose a reflection on India's underdevelopment. This reflection broke with the continental essentialism of Occidental discourse and found its moorings in social and economic history (Pandey 1990). Thus in the writings of Varier, Ajmal Khan, and Ray we reckon with several utterances concerning the state of decline of the traditional systems of medicine. Hakim Ajmal Khan expressed his concern regarding the woeful neglect of the ancient works of medicine, and its inadequacy for the times: "we have lost much ground by avoiding a thoughtful study of ancient works of medicine. Our syllabus has a limited number of textbooks, which are insufficient for the requirements of our times" (Khan n.d.: 16). Thus Ibn Sina's *al-Qanun fi'l tibb* was not adequate as a textbook, since "Ibn Sina himself laid stress on continuous growth of knowledge." Reflecting a longue durée perspective on the decline of the sciences, Ajmal Khan turned despondency into optimism by setting out the possibility of revitalization. In 1901 he wrote:

Although the sun of Eastern arts and sciences kept rising in its own times and many *qaums* (communities) drew benefits from its light, now that sun has declined and the age, as is its habit, has given birth to a new sun that fulfils the needs of the people of the age. . . . The results of this reversal, which previous nations have already endured will happen to us: we will see our former greatness and glory in the hand of oblivion, if we do not take thought to preserve it. (Khan, quoted in Metcalf 1986: 311)

In a similar vein P. S. Varier dwelled upon the loss of ancient knowledge that had resulted from the nonavailability of texts as well as their distortion in actual practice (Panikkar 1992: 298). As a chemist P. C. Ray mined Indian *materia medica* for its rich medicaments and in the process went on to write his well-known *History of Hindu Chemistry,* the purport of which was not so much historical revival but to join the mainstream of science. He wrote, "if the perusal of these lines will have the effect of stimulating my countrymen to strive for regaining their own position, in the intellectual hierarchy of nations, I shall not have laboured in vain" (Ray 1902).

This reckoning is more or less contiguous with the utterances about the general state of decline within Indian society and Indian underdevelopment. The confrontation with this pathology prompted a diagnosis of the malaise itself. The analysis into the causes of the decline of the traditional systems of knowledge or of economic underdevelopment were consequently of prime importance for the rejuvenation of the

country and hence the salience of this project for the nationalist struggle whose goal was decolonization. The attempt to reconstruct historically Indian science or Indian medicine was meant to achieve cognitive
justice that had been violated within the pedagogy instituted by colonialism (Raina 1997b)—colonialism had produced forms of self-validation
that Harding would refer to as institutional Eurocentrism (Harding
1998). Burgeoning struggles for national liberation would turn to
"indigenous" knowledge systems in this political combat to recover what
was salvageable through the optic of modern science (Raina 2003). The
colonial confrontation thus launched a program that sought to relate
the cultural antiquity of Indian thought (its achievements in science
included) to the prevailing context, and in the process signaled the transcendence from that ancient context (Habib and Raina 1989: 53). If the
decline were to be reversed, the light of science must shine again. In
so reframing the argument, Ray was neutralizing the cultural import of
science as Western, and thereby instituting the possibility of dialogue,
rather than be preempted into a program of hegemonic erasure of traditional knowledge by modern knowledge (Raina 1997a: 13).

There were two critical elements of this diagnosis into the causes of
decline, one directed outward to the proponents of colonial rule, the
other directed as self-criticism of the prevailing social conditions and
knowledge-related practices. The decline of Āyurveda for Varier could
be traced back to the interdictions imposed on the dissection of corpses;
the reproduction of a system of Āyurvedic practitioners that could not
check the spread of quackery; and finally the production of poor-quality
drugs that in turn told upon the reputation of the system itself. We can
already see a prefiguration of three dimensions of revitalization that will
be focused on below. Tarashankar Bandapodhyaya, another Āyurvedic
practitioner, pointed out that the steady decline of Āyurveda was trig-
gered by factors both external and internal. This decline was to be
understood in terms of the currency of the idea among the exponents
of the system that Āyurveda was a perfected science, and this blind belief
had curtailed its further development (Panikkar 1992: 290). Panikkar
suggests that this blind belief among some Āyurvedic practitioners
related to the origins of medical knowledge and espoused the view that
ancient Āyurveda was the "janani . . . of all medical knowledge" (291).
Nevertheless, the perception of decline and its analysis prompted the
project of revitalization. The internal causes of decline related to the
"stagnation of knowledge," poor quality practitioners and the poor
quality of medication (292). These we suggest become the axes for revitalization. The axes of revitalization could as well be interpreted as the
axes for another kind of modernization. The first of these is a critique
of Indian scholasticism from the frame of novelty. The second and third

critiques finally transmute into prescriptions for standardization in terms of pedagogy and the preparation of Unani Tibb and Āyurvedic drugs and medication.

The external critique is often construed as a purely political one, but implicit within it is an understanding of medical institutions. The declining patronage of the state for traditional medicine was seen as the primary cause behind the descent of traditional medicine. The loss of political sovereignty had precipitated this turn of events (Panikkar 1992: 293). The implicit argument, also a very modern one, is that the support of the state for institutions of education and the provision of suitable employment were imperative for the survival of a system of medication that reached out to a larger community.

Ajmal Khan's efforts at institution building for Unani medicine are quite similar. The Tibbi Madarsa was founded by his brother and had graduated as many as 65 hakims by the end of 1901. In 1909 when education for girls was generally neglected, Ajmal Khan decided to include women in his scheme of Unani medical education. Finally, he was convinced that indigenous medicine had no hope of progress unless it undertook scientific researches to meet the exigencies of the times. For this he set up a research unit and participated in its programs. He was to remark that:

It is urgently needed that *we should stand by the progress medicine has achieved in the present age*. Much time has already passed. Knowledge is on the increase, but we are stagnant. We have made no progress, rather we have gone down and followed the path of backwardness. (Ghaffar n.d: 323; emphasis ours)

We do not see here any sense of competition with the modern; the lament is restricted to the decline of Unani Tibb itself. He felt that the cause of revitalization would not be served merely by an institution such as the Tibbi Madarsa and a trip to Europe in 1911 further convinced him of this fact. On his return he expressed the dire necessity of a larger institution at a meeting in 1912:

The Madarsa Tibbia cannot fulfill the aims and objectives which we have resolved to achieve; what is needed is a big institution which could impart complete education, theoretical as well as practical in Indian medicine. We want to produce indigenous doctors who along with theoretical knowledge in Unani and Ayurvedic systems may become good surgeons. (Khan n.d.: 73)

Hakim Ajmal Khan strived hard to mobilize funds for the proposed college and finally convinced the Viceroy to inaugurate it on March 29, 1916. His address on the occasion is worth quoting, as it highlights the permeability of the boundaries between the traditional and the modern:

the Ayurvedic and Unani systems of medicine are very good. From time immemorial the people of India—rich and poor, literate and illiterate, townsmen and villagers—all benefited from these systems and are still deriving benefits from them. . . . However, the Ayurvedic and Unani systems are taught mostly in the clinics of the vaids and hakims of India. . . . *We should, therefore, not feel reluctant to get benefits from modern system of medicine so as to update our own.* It is for this reason that we need a college for imparting education in Ayurvedic and Unani systems of medicine as also in subjects like surgery. (Memorandum 1916; emphasis ours)

Lord Hardinge, the viceroy, despite his reluctance to open the college and his continued hostility to nonallopathic systems, said in response, "I came to the conclusion that our Western system, however much it may strive after perfection, has not attained it yet. Its theories are constantly undergoing change and development. . . . I may add that it has borrowed some of its best known drugs from the East where the study of medicine was kept alive through the dark ages" (Memorandum 1916). It is important here to note that while the college was set up through contributions coming in from private donors, the hakim found it essential to have the college symbolically blessed by a representative of the state.

Axes of Modernization

Approaching the Threshold of Modern Scientificity

It has been discussed in great detail that Raja Rammohun Roy in his *Tuhfat-ul-Muvahidin* produced one of the foremost legitimations of modern science toward the end of the eighteenth and early decades of the nineteenth century. Roy attempted a classical recovery of elements of empirical and rational thought from the resources of the Indo-Persian and Hindu traditions. In establishing a quasi-continuity between the past of an Indian science and the present he was creating a bridge for the transition to modernity (Sarkar 1975; Seal 1933; Tagore 1975). Consequently, Indians writing on the history of Indian medicine recuperated those epistemic elements from these traditions that concurred with the received epistemic tenets of modern medical practice. Thus the *pramana sastra* underpinning Āyurvedic practice received attention in the writings of Seal, Ray, and Varier (Panikkar 1992; Ray 1902; Raina and Habib 1996; Seal 1985). In Seal's methodological preface to *The Positive Sciences of the Ancient Hindus* the shadow of Mill's *Systems of Logic* is evident (Habib and Raina 1989; Seal 1985). Ray was both a professional scientist and a historian of chemistry, but he was more careful about the intrusion of presentism into the history of science than were his chemist colleagues. For him, then, alchemy was not a lower grade chemistry whose memory was to be expunged from its history. In his lectures he seeks to recuperate those elements in Indian alchemical practice that were epistemically homologous with modern empirical practice (Raina 1997a). This new predilection with method had a Baconian inspiration and set the terms for the modernization of these traditions.

P. S. Varier was introduced to modern medicine through Dr. V. Verghese, an assistant surgeon of the government hospital, through whom he became acquainted with surgery and modern anatomy. It could be suggested that this acquaintanceship opened up the avenues for realizing his desire to contribute to the advancement of the frontiers of Āyurveda rather than promote the mere textual transmission of an ancient science—this departure from scholasticism was part of the changing landscape of Indian intellectual thought (Panikkar 1992). This attempt at revitalization was not as self-conscious as is the subsequent Āyurveda movement that Paul Brass labels revivalist (Brass 1972). Varier was not perplexed at the prospect of borrowing ideas or theories from modern medicine, having translated a number of books on physiology and anatomy from English into Malayalam. The readership of these textbooks included students of Āyurveda (Panikkar 1992).

INSTITUTIONAL CHANGE

The transformation of Āyurveda on modernist lines did not require merely grounding Āyurvedic practice in a new theoretical setting but also routinizing a new set of institutional practices that were elements of the modern research system. Thus the Arya Vaidya Samajam Conference was founded in 1902 on the lines of any modern scientific society. This society became the forum for the exchange of Āyurvedic knowledge. The Samajam conferences also sought to institutionalize modern transparency that would in turn stimulate not just the transmission of Āyurvedic knowledge but its development as well. As mentioned earlier the institutionalization of the new practice was preceded by an analysis of the perceived decline of Āyurveda as a science. In addition to the causes mentioned above, two more were part of the combinatory that had resulted in the decline of the tradition. The oral tradition and the mechanism of oral transference of knowledge were perceived as a barrier to the authentic multiplication of expertise—the code of secrecy that enjoined various practitioners was in that age perceived as an impediment to the effective growth and dissemination of Āyurveda. Furthermore, though this argument is not encountered frequently at a later date, there existed a feeling that the practitioners had distanced themselves from the health concerns of society at large (Panikkar 1992). In this manner the new norms for the open exchange of ideas associated with the institutionalization of modern science were being employed as a template for redefining Āyurvedic practice. When Varier's efforts are placed against this larger institutional and epistemic context, revitalization of traditional medicine at this juncture does not correspond with Brass's characterization of the Āyurvedic movement as a revivalist one.[2] Later movements would acquire this color, but the period discussed here reveals a little more catholicity among the so-called traditional interlocutors.

However, it could well be conjectured that the Bombay Medical Registration Act of 1912 catalyzed the process of institutional reform in the traditional systems of medicine. The process of institutional reform of the traditional systems predated the promulgation of the act by at least twenty years. But one of the many outcomes of the act was that it relegated the two fields of traditional medicine to an inferior status; the colonial state frowned upon them and had initiated steps whose outcome would be the delegitimization of this knowledge (Panikkar 1992: 287–88). These fields of medicine were found wanting in their knowledge of medicine and surgery—cognitive inadequacy; the quality of the medication administered was poor—lack of standardization; the practitioners lacked the ability to establish a relationship of cause and effect—epistemic drawback, but also one of poor training. This critique was voiced by colonial administrators at the inauguration of new institutes being founded for the revitalization of the traditional medical sciences.

THE NEW MANUFACTURING AND DISTRIBUTION SYSTEM

Similarly, in order to compete with the modern pharmacy, a new manufacturing and distribution system was to be instituted. Here it is of relevance to discern two different responses and a third that could be considered a combination of the two. The Arya Vaidya Sala, founded by Varier, was an establishment dedicated to the bulk production of specialized and standardized Āyurvedic formulations. While this system of manufacturing and standardization sought to legitimize Āyurvedic therapeutic regimes by weeding out quack formulations, it could as well be suggested that bulk manufacture and distribution of these formulations would enhance the outreach of the system that was fast being effaced by the financial successes of pharmaceutical and industrial chemistry. This takes us to the other response, that of P. C. Ray, who completed a doctorate in chemistry from Edinburgh in the last decades of the nineteenth century. He then returned to Calcutta and commenced an exploration of Indian *materia medica*, and went on to salvage those formulations that were compatible with developments in modern pharmacology. This involved extracting the active ingredient of each of these formulations and then employing the principles of modern industrial chemistry to develop a manufacturing process locally. Between these two responses we could locate Hakim Ajmal Khan's Tibbiya College and Hindustani Dawakhana at Ballimaran in Delhi. Ajmal Khan's discovery of the effects of a medicinal plant commonly known as *asrol* or *pagal booti* led to sustained researches establishing the unique efficacy of the plant known as *Rauwolfia serpentina*. The discovery of the formulation named after him as Ajmaline and related formulations stand out as an exemplar of the potential for novelty resulting from such hybrid projects.

Revisiting Old Questions: Traditional and Modern Medicine

A number of questions still need to be addressed. For example, studies on the interaction between Āyurveda and Unani medicine during the late medieval and early modern periods reveal that the tension or animosity between the two fields of medicine was negligible if not nonexistent (Wujastyk forthcoming). In fact, the encounter between the two involved a trading in pharmacopoeia (Panikkar 1992: 284). We must then ask of colonial historiography how it produced an image of Indian science resisting foreign influence. This image is shared by both Hindu ultranationalist and colonial historiography. For other histories inform us that "indigenous" medical practitioners incorporated "foreign" pharmacopoeia into Āyurveda and vice versa. Arab medicine had a longstanding record of such internalization while remaining loyal to the theories of Galenic medicine (Bagchi 1997). What was it about colonial rule that produced this "turning inward" as far as medical practice was concerned?

This chapter suggests that this turning inward was probably not as marked in the late nineteenth century it has been over the last four decades of the twentieth and into the twenty-first centuries. In other words, what factors metamorphosed the pragmatism of the "traditional" healer into the dogmatism of contemporary practitioners' traditional medicine? When and how did this closure to foreign influence in the retrospective reconstruction of these fields take place? The period under discussion was certainly one when it possibly did not occur. The issue here is to disentangle the play between the positionality of the storyteller and the lifeworld within which Āyurvedic practice, probably more than Unani, is today embedded.

The second issue that requires attention is the need to comprehend the long-term impact of these efforts at reform in different regions of the country. In some of these regions the traditional survived in the zones unoccupied by modern allopathic medicine. In addition to the cognitive and cultural aspects, there is a need to interrogate their relationship with the new political economy. Thus at the end of the nineteenth century it was felt that the indigenous systems still had an outreach to nine-tenths of the Indian population—a section that was still beyond the reach of "official medical aid" (Panikkar 1992: 289). A combination of factors were thus responsible for the ascendancy of the one and the "marginalization" of the other, whereby the changing perceptions of local elites to modern medicine and the detours of the nationalist struggle en route to independence would have to be brought into focus.

Chapter 5

Health and Medicine in British India and Dutch Indies: A Comparative Study

DEEPAK KUMAR

India and Indonesia provide a striking example of similarity and contrast. In both countries, their famed tropical riches attracted foreign intervention and both fell to colonization. Health was considered crucial in both countries and both had a medical tradition of their own. Western medicine, on the other hand, moved overseas riding the colonial wave. It became an integral part of the colonial project. Recent scholarship considers Western medicine "imperialist" both metaphorically and literally, and "as a form of knowledge and as a practice" (Cunningham and Andrews 1997; D. Kumar 1995, 2001; MacLeod and Lewis 1988).

There is, however, a note of caution. Colonial medical discourse as a "discourse of power" may not leave sufficient room for the many discursive elements which are present in the colonial medical writings and represent insecurity, amazement, curiosity and frustration (Van Heteran 1996). Heterogeneity must be properly acknowledged and differences be explored. A medical practitioner in a colony had to perform a variety of functions: surgeon, military man, explorer, naturalist, or teacher as exigencies demanded. The practitioner had to work for or address to colleagues, administrators, and patients simultaneously or separately. The scope of intervention was enormous and the methods not fixed. The objectives were predominantly political (extension and consolidation of the empire), yet not always so. They could at the same time be partially evangelical, philanthropic, or economic. Colonial practices did differ in different politico-cultural theaters. But was this true for colonial medical practices as well? What attempts were made outside Europe to reconcile the older discourse of body humors and environmental miasmas with the new language of microbes and germs? What role did the "peripherals" play? Could a synergetic relationship between the core and periphery develop? Some explanations may be found in the evolution of medical structures, patterns of medical education and research, and in their interactions with the local and the traditional.

The Beginnings

During the seventeenth and eighteenth centuries, almost every ship that sailed under the European East India companies had a surgeon-naturalist on board. They were products of scientific institutions and represented an emerging cosmopolitan medical system which stressed scientific causality. Epistemologically they were Galenic and not radically different from the Asian systems. The Indian Āyurvedic system was based on three humors instead of the Galenic four and the six in Chinese medicine. Herbal healers and shamans were found in every society. But the medico-religious side of Asian medical practices, such as incantations and amulets, attracted Western derision. Pearson makes a forceful plea not to ridicule the folk medical practices of the East. He finds not only healthy interaction in early Portuguese Goa but considerable European dependence on indigenous medical practitioners in certain kinds of ailments (Pearson 1989: 33).

Garcia de Orta, for example, was the first major naturalist to study the medicinal plants and drugs used in the East. But he could not build a new syncretic medical paradigm based on his Asian experiences, thus falling short of making a dent into the age-old Hippocratic-Galenic foundations of Western medicine. Similarly, the Dutch incursions in East Asia helped create a "Dutch School" of physicians as opposed to the traditional "Chinese school." Peter Boomgaard lists a number of Dutch physicians in the employment of the Japanese, Siamese, and Bolivian ruling classes (Boomgaard 1996: 42–64). There did occur a give and take. In South Asia the traditional healers had learned bleeding and phlebotomy from the Europeans, while the latter borrowed rhinoplasty from India. In East Asia, the Europeans learned moxibustion and acupuncture whereas Asians received modern anatomy, surgery, and hospitals. The two had similar magical/humoral pasts, but Western medicine moved toward specialty and "superiority" with the discoveries of Vesalius and Harvey. The ultimate separation was accomplished by the germ theory of disease in the 1880s. Until then, Europeans believed in "invisible miasmata" as causing diseases whereas the Asian folk-healers held invisible "evil spirits" responsible. It was the microscope which could finally drive away both the invisible spirits and the invisible miasmas. But in the process any possibility of a "syncretic" medicine was lost.

The Two Cultures

From the Indian point of view, the first half of the nineteenth century was a period of looking for fresh opportunities and acquiring new knowledge. Syncretism, not revivalism, was the agenda. Even among the British officials there were some who wanted the government to attempt a fusion of "both exotic principles and local practices, European theory and Indian experience," and thereby "revive, invigorate, enlighten and liberalise the native medical profession in the mofussil [interior]") (Adams 1868: 322–23). Similar views were echoed by the emerging Indian intelligentsia. The ruler of Tanjore, Raja Serfoji (1798–1832), assembled leading physicians from Āyurvedic, Unani, Siddha, and Western systems. He had procured hundreds of European medical books and surgical instruments (S. G. Rao 1977: 1–4). In Bombay, B. G. Jambhekar (1802–46) translated the nosology of Madhav and anatomy of Suśruta into English and advocated the dissemination of new medical knowledge through the means of local language (1835).[1] All this must have induced the traditional physicians to take cognizance of the new therapies and methods. The effort was to blend the indigenous culture with the intellectual tools acquired from the West.

In the Dutch Indies, the indigenous population were usually regarded as barbaric or depraved and little or no attempt was made to understand or appreciate the Indonesians' cultural background. Unlike India, change came much later (in the twentieth century) under the Ethical Policy. It was nonetheless a curious situation. The Europeans were willing to admit the worth and beauty of indigenous institutions, but not to the point of forgetting their own antecedents. The Indonesians strove to master Western techniques without making the thought process behind the technique their own (van der Knoef 1980).

Exchange in medical ideas may not have been vigorous, but the early colonial medical men did produce a number of medical-ethnographic, climatological, and topographical descriptions. Some of these were of outstanding scientific value, while some reinforced or even created myths about racial and physiological differences. The "natives" had no means to defend themselves; there was (perhaps still is) no level field, much less level pegging (D. Kumar 1997: 172–90). In shamanistic healing the human body is thought of as a microcosm that is constantly influenced by the macrocosm. And what happens within this microcosm is believed to affect the macrocosm. Thus, breaches of *adat* (customary rules) may cause natural disasters or epidemics. This etiology raised doubts and invited derision. Yet some recognized the time-honored curing devices of traditional Javanese and Indian health care. The meridians used in acupuncture are real links in the nervous system and the main *cakra* (energy centers) along the *suṣumna* (spinal column) in yoga theory do correspond to the main glands of the body (Slamet-Velsink 1996: 65–80).

In British India, such understanding was rare. Dr. John Tytler, the first principal of the Calcutta Medical School, argued that though the indigenous systems were medieval, they did contain some grains of truth. He would allow the students to draw comparisons, sort out errors, and then work toward the improvement of their own system (Tytler 1935: 7–9). He was promptly criticized by those who sincerely believed that the whole literature of Asia was not worth a single shelf of a European library.[2] Tytler found himself in trouble when he started preparing Arabic translations of a few European textbooks. The problem of vocabulary was most serious, for in order to translate an English word he spent hours in searching through Arabic lexicons, only to find that its counterpart did not exist. He concluded that translations were unprofitable, and that many years would elapse before the Indians rejected the "crude fallacies" their medical system upheld. The result was that in early 1835 the medical classes at Calcutta Sanskrit College and Madrasa were abolished along with the medical school itself, and a new college was established wherein all pupils were required to learn the principles and practice of medical science in strict accordance with the mode adopted in Europe.[3] This was an important event, for henceforth, through syllabi and language, a "dependent science" was to be fostered and Indians were made to look for Western models in every field of medical science. And the traditional Kavirajas and Vaidyas, who were confident of getting no encouragement from a foreign government, kept themselves aloof from the modern scientific world (Mukhopadhyay 1923: 18).

New Institutions

Around this time in Java very little was happening except cash-crop exploitation. A botanic garden had been established at Buitenzorg. When the British took over the Indies in the wake of the Napoleonic wars in 1811, the new governor, Thomas Stanford Raffles, established a medical service in accordance to the Bengal medical regulations. A civil medical service was organized in 1820, but only seven years later it was merged with the military medical service. The Indian Medical Service (IMS) was the guiding star. Similarly the example of medical education in India led to the establishment of the Dokter Djawa School in 1851. Like the medical schools in India, its purpose was to find and train local intermediaries. Importing physicians and surgeons was too expensive. Europeans' health was looked after by the IMS. A host of assistant surgeons, vaccinators, apothecaries, and so forth were needed The motive was both utilitarian and hegemonic. Dokter Djawa started in 1851, but its purpose remained unclear for a long time. Was it only to train vaccinators with some knowledge of medicine, or was it to be a place for training medical practitioners? The curriculum was primitive, the duration was short, and the medium of instruction was Malay. As a recent critique argues, it was linked with the larger imperative of how to control the intellectual developmental of the colonized while keeping the colonizers medically fit (Verma 1995: 130–41). The very first director of the Djawa School was honest enough to admit: "it did not lie in the government doctrine of that time to allow children of the autochthons, even if they were from indigenous chiefs or local nobility, to enjoy the same education as was available to the children of the ruling nation" (Lauw 1987: 4).[4]

In contrast, the British in India had developed fine distinctions in terms of what to teach, how to teach, and whom to teach. By 1856 the Calcutta Medical College, for example, had chairs in anatomy, physiology, zoology, chemistry, botany, materia medica, medical jurisprudence, midwifery, surgery, medicine, and ophthalmic surgery. In 1860, the students were divided into four classes: Primary, Apprentice class, Hindustani, and Bengal. The Primary students had the full course of five years in English and were eligible to sit for the Licence in Medicine and Surgery (LMS), the Bachelor of Medicine (MB), and the Doctor of Medicine (MD) examinations of Calcutta University. The course was on a par with the best in Europe. The Apprentice class, for the Eurasians, was like the other two classes of three years duration. In 1864 the Bengali class was subdivided into two: the Native Apothecary class, which trained students for hospital assistantship, and the Vernacular Licentiate class, which gave more extended clinical training in order to fit the students for independent practice among poor people (Director of Public Instruction Report, Bengal 1864–65: 19). This sort of divided system of education effectively met the most pressing local needs, particularly that of the army.

As for the question whom to teach, the British were very clear from the beginning. They needed a class of collaborators. The Brahmins and those in *Brahmannis-proximi* suited admirably. The British wooed the Brahmins desperately for the legitimation and consolidation of their rule. Caste wards/hospitals were created and in vaccination purity/pollution syndrome was carefully maintained. To quote an inimitable critique, the British, in a way, behaved like a lowborn indigenous ruler, desperately in need of a royal genealogy (A. Kumar 1998: 220–22)!

In striking parallel with British India, the Dutch also excelled in utilizing the divisions in the colonized society to their benefit. The Chinese were considered indispensable but were looked at with disdain. Even the Javanese nobility valued, not in a positive sense on their own merit, but mainly because of their useful intermediary function. Johannes van den Bosch unabashedly stated in his *Memorie* of 1834 that, because the Javanese could only be ruled through the medium of their own leaders, "it is in the well-understood interest of the government to ally itself with the higher classes" (quoted in van Doorn 1983: 3–6). How did the indigenous feel? To quote Raden Kartini, daughter of a Javanese regent who pioneered women's emancipation and education, "The Hollanders laugh and make fun of our stupidity, but if we strive for enlightenment, then they assume a defiant attitude toward us" (Palmier 1962: 6–7).

Medical Research

Medical education worked under constraints but did serve a purpose, however limited. Medical research remained sporadic and largely neglected. India and Indonesia were large natural disease repositories but their medical services were not geared to meet the task. There were no doubt scientifically trained persons, and most of the early investigations in natural history were made by them, but the medical service on the whole had a poor record of achievement in medical research per se. The development of the public health system and of medical science in Britain and Holland had been organic. In India and the Indies, this was not to be so. Curiously enough, the indigenous medical traditions were completely ignored and the study of Indian drugs found no place in the medical curriculum of the Indian universities. Some individuals talked about it, but nothing happened at the official level until 1896, when a Committee on Indigenous Drugs was appointed in response to growing nationalist demands (Dey 1894).[5]

By 1860, bacteriological advances had set bells ringing and given a new dimension to colonial health policy. If cholera was to be prevented, it had to be sought out, not waited for. A Cholera Commission was set up and sanitary commissions were established in the three presidencies in 1864. In 1883, Robert Koch discovered the cholera "Comma" bacillus in Egypt and visited Calcutta the same year to confirm the discovery. This was an important contribution and helped establish the theory of disease causation over the earlier miasmatic theories. This shift in focus had significant implications for the colonies. In 1890 a Leprosy Commission was set up and a bacteriological unit was opened in Poona. In 1896, a Plague Research Laboratory was established under W. M. Haffkine in Bombay.[6] But all these institutions worked under severe limitations. The research structure that eventually evolved was the result of a piecemeal and ad hoc response to sudden epidemic emergencies.

There was at least one original discovery of everlasting value—by Ronald Ross on the relationship between malaria and the mosquito. Gradually Ross developed interest in the practical implications of his work, seeing malarial control as a matter of reducing the population of mosquitos by destroying or treating their breeding areas. This was a practical and preventive approach but it involved considerable expenditure and large-scale sanitary measures. No wonder the governments in India and in England preferred to ignore Ross. And he mulled, "The government of India is a *mule* regards science . . . it *won't* do anything unless driven" (D. Kumar 1995: 151). The scientists at home and the colonial administrator both consistently held that scientists in India should leave pure science to Britain and apply themselves to the application of science. Russell wrote, "General fundamental problems are best worked out here (England) or in Europe or America where the number of workers is greater and where it is easy to get into touch with those able to render useful assistance" (Russell 1908: 236).

The Dutch Indies had a similar situation. The discoveries of the causes of traumatic infection, malaria, typhus abdominalis, cholera, pulmonary tuberculosis, amoebic dysentery, diphtheria, and tetanus, all made between the years 1880–1900, created great sensation in the Indies too, and aroused hopes of the possibility of efficient combat (Schoute 1937: 182). There was, however, one disease which refused to yield to the attacks of bacteriology—beriberi. C. Eijkman (1858–1930) had worked on it since 1883. He was given a bacteriological laboratory in 1886. By 1890, he had established a relation between disease occurring in chickens if fed a certain sort of rice and human beriberi. Gradually he noticed that a great difference appeared depending on whether the rice was polished or unpolished. This opened the way for the prevention and rational treatment of beriberi.

The turn of the century thus saw both a deep knowledge of tropical diseases and a viable institutional structure. In Britain, Neville Chamberlain could show these as proof of "constructive imperialism." The Dutch inaugurated what they called an Ethical Policy. Under this, the government allowed its public health officials great leeway in conducting investigations and setting up propaganda agencies. Vaccination was encouraged on a mass scale and several sanitary measures were enforced. But the health program sponsored by the government in both colonies, however excellent and progressive in certain aspects, would have required far greater outlays of funds, intensification of hygienic measures, and a greater number of hospitals to have the desired effect. The funds simply did not match the policy claims.

Foreign Philanthropy

To ease its burden, the colonial government looked for private support. Within the Indian municipal system, it was not easy to raise funds for public health through higher taxation. In some places, like Madras, the taxes were already high. In a study of the Calcutta Municipal Corporation, it has been found that the *rentier* class was extremely reluctant to pay higher taxes for public health purposes (Harrison 1994: 166–226). In some places, there was little or no surplus revenue. Under such circumstances the health programs of the Rockefeller Foundation (RF) came as divine intervention. Their focus was on the plantations in different parts of Asia and Latin America, which needed to be made lucrative through greater scientific input and the control of diseases that impaired labor productivity. In India, the RF's involvement began with the visit of Dr. V. G. Heiser to Madras in 1915. He looked into the prevalence of hookworm disease and felt that an enormous amount of work could be done at a comparatively small cost.[7]

During 1916, Dr. S. T. Darlin arrived in Java to study malaria work. The Dutch doctors and administrators were apprehensive and did not like the intrusion. Unlike the Dutch, the American and British doctors were cooperating closely in an international health network. The Americans on their part described the Dutch as "extremely rude" and "fat" (Mesters 1996: 51–62). J. L. Hydrick arrived as RF representative in Java in 1924, and he also first picked hookworm. A Hygiene Mantri School was started, where the public health specialists educated local midwives and traditional healers (*dukun*) in the principles of hygiene.[8] Hydrick enunciated the principle of "intensive rural hygiene work," which was never implemented. Hydrick's works were viewed with suspicion. In fact, preventive medicine was seldom appreciated by the Dutch doctors. As Hydrick reported:

The medical curriculum originates in Holland without the slightest flexibility toward local conditions. Holland's attitude toward modern public health instruction is proverbial. The consequence is that a health administration with a reoriented and modern viewpoint has so far been unable to obtain changes in medical education. (quoted in Mesters 1996)

The largest single investment of the RF in India lay in the establishment of the All India Institute of Hygiene and Public Health. It was expected to undertake applied research and instruction in public health, epidemiology, sanitary engineering, biochemistry and nutritional diseases, rural hygiene, and maternal and child welfare. Here the canvas was larger than that of the Mantri School in Java. And here again there was suspicion. The opening of the institute in 1932 was preceded by a great deal of bargaining between the Government of India and the RF. In a confidential minute, an official wrote:

I am strongly against the Government of India demeaning itself by going on its knees and holding out its hands for alms in America. It has to be borne in mind that the Rockefeller Fund in China has been lavishly dispensed in the founding of an immense university. What is this University? It is simply a trade development for the propagation of American commerce throughout China. (Charles 1923)

What did India gain from the RF? Going through the RAC records one does not get a picture that commercial interests dominated its Indian activities. No commercial evidence could be found. A functionary rather claimed that RF's object and success was that it aroused in both China and India "a medical-technical consciousness" that they had lacked. Was this true for Indonesia as well?

Health as a Nationalist Issue

Even at the height of colonial power, voices against the dominant medical discourse were heard. The indigenous practitioners vehemently denied that their system was unscientific or irrational, yet they did not see anything wrong in learning and benefiting from the new knowledge. Their emphasis was on reforming the system by adopting "scientific" method, not on changing the fundamentals of the system. Unani's encounter with modern medicine was located within a critical anticolonial public sphere.[9] The efforts of P. S. Varier (1869–1958) and Hakim Ajmal Khan (1868–1927) clearly show that the question of indigenous medicine was not one of medicine or medical science per se; it had become part of the upsurge of interest in India's cultural heritage, with all the accompanying political implications (D. Kumar 2001). Within the Western medical system, Indians demanded a better deal. In 1896, Indian doctors asked for a complete separation of the civil and military medical service and greater opportunity for indigenous talent.[10] This demand was repeated several times at the Indian National Congress and other forums. But the government would not budge. Only in the 1930s was Indianization of the medical services considered seriously and finally implemented, much to the chagrin of senior IMS officials.

In Indonesia, the Volksraad or People's Council (opened by the Dutch government in 1918) was the forum where the Indonesian nationalists discussed Dutch health policies (Abeyasekere 1986: 1–13). By this time, the motivations and opportunities for an effective health policy were far greater. Unlike the legislative assembly in India, the Volksraad members seemed to consider health to be a specialized matter, which was best restricted to budget discussions. They were not sure whether to ask for curative or preventive measures. They could not provide a comprehensive alternative of their own. Their Indian counterparts talked a great deal about indigenous systems and pledged support but did very little. Colonial medical hegemony still survives. Still medicine did figure in anticolonial discourse. When the Dutch government rejected a suggestion to train local midwives, Mohammad Ali (Volksraad member from Kalimantan, 1927–1931) protested: "A bird in hand is worth two in the bush, or rather one *dukun* with some medical knowledge is better than two certified midwives who are not there and infinitely better than *dukun* without that knowledge" (quoted in Abeyasekere 1986). This would be equally true for any village even in contemporary India!

No reference to the health debates in Indonesia would be complete without a reference to Dr. Raden Soetomo (1888–1938), a social reformer, political activist, and medical doctor.[11] In his writings and speeches he never referred to western ideologies; rather he would quote from Gandhi, Tagore, and Vivekanand. However, unlike Gandhi, he considered the difference between cooperation and noncooperation irrelevant. Interestingly enough, he opposed both Communist extremism and Muslim religious intolerance. He visited India in 1936 and was greatly disappointed "because conditions in North India with its poverty and slovenliness" depressed him. He also failed to meet his idol, Mahatma Gandhi, and was upset by a "somewhat rude reception and the neglected and dirty condition of Gandhi's quarters."[12]

Dr. Soetomo and his counterparts in India had to deal with a double text, one internal, the other alien, and had to carry on a two-pronged fight against the traditional and colonial hegemony. The pedagogic weapon they wielded had no primordial affinity with Western learning nor was it rooted in indigenous traditions. This resulted in an uneasy mix, an unequal war, and probably a split soul.

Nationalism, Transnationalism, and the Politics of "Traditional" Indian Medicine for HIV/AIDS

Cecilia Van Hollen

Traditional medicine. Complementary medicine. Alternative medicine. Herbal medicine. Complementary alternative medicine. These phrases have been flashing on radar screens of international public health organizations, pharmaceutical companies, and market investors since the late twentieth century and are gaining even more attention in the early twenty-first century. In May 2002 the World Health Organization (WHO) launched its first strategic program to monitor the use of traditional medicine worldwide and to make national policy recommendations for the regulation of traditional medicine. The guidelines for this strategy have been published in a WHO report, entitled *WHO Traditional Medicine Strategy 2002–2005* (2002.) The impetus for this strategy came from the acknowledgment that the majority of people in the "developing world" use some form of traditional medicine, as well as from the fact that there has been a rapid increase in the use of nonbiomedical types of medical treatment in richer countries.

The increasing global interest in traditional medicine has occurred simultaneously with the emergence and spread of the global pandemic of HIV/AIDS. Patients, medical practitioners, pharmaceutical companies, and individual producers of traditional medical remedies worldwide have been mining storehouses of traditional medical knowledge in search of treatments to cure HIV/AIDS, or at least reduce the symptoms associated with this disease. One recent study reports that 78 percent of people living with HIV/AIDS (PLWHA) in the United States use some form of "complementary alternative medicine" (CAM) (as opposed to 40 percent of the general population in the U.S. doing so) (WHO 2002a: 14). In India, too, traditional medicine is being given to PLWHA patients with varying claims attached. Treatments derived from

Āyurveda, Siddha, Unani, and homeopathic systems are being administered to HIV/AIDS patients throughout the Indian subcontinent, sometimes raising waves of controversy.[1]

India's systems of traditional medicine, particularly Āyurveda, have
been powerful symbols of nationalist identity and of resistance to Westernization ever since the late colonial period, when the British began
to push for the development and expansion of biomedical educational
institutions, hospitals, and clinics, claiming that biomedicine was scientifically superior to Indian systems of medicine. The colonial expansion
of biomedicine lent moral legitimacy to the colonizing process in India
and elsewhere, but the assumptions of the superiority of biomedicine
were questioned by Indian nationalists.

In contemporary debates about the use of traditional Indian medicine, nationalist arguments are still audible. This is evident in statements
by government officials and representatives of traditional medicine
pharmaceutical companies who want India to get its fair share of the
global market. It is also evident in statements made in defense of the
use of traditional Indian medicine to treat HIV/AIDS patients in India.
However, as traditional Indian medicine is increasingly marketed globally and becomes a transnational phenomenon, nationalist claims to
defend traditional medicine based on moral, anti-imperialist, and antic-
apitalist grounds that are reminiscent of some nationalist discourses in
the colonial era, are now ironically joined with claims to legitimacy
based on the degree of penetration into the global market and the
resulting high profits. This chapter examines the complex and uneven
role that nationalist discourse now plays in the context of the transnational flow of traditional Indian medicine, demonstrating that the social
character of "traditional medicine" in India (and elsewhere) is being
redefined in the twenty-first century.[2]

This chapter is based on ethnographic research conducted in India
with my research assistant, Sharon Watson, in December 2002 and January 2003.[3] It also draws extensively from newspaper, magazine, and
Internet articles; press releases; policy reports; a pilot documentary film;
and journalistic and academic books and articles pertaining to the subject of the global trends in traditional medicine use, particularly for
HIV/AIDS, and particularly in India.

"Traditional Medicine" and "Complementary Alternative Medicine"

The *WHO Traditional Medicine Strategy, 2002–2005* employs two primary
terms: "Traditional Medicine" (TM) and "Complementary Alternative
Medicine" (CAM). TM refers to a broad range of nonbiomedical sys-

tems of medicine and medical therapies as they are used in countries where those practices originated and where biomedicine (allopathy) is one among several types of medical practice incorporated into the national health care system.[4] CAM refers to nonbiomedical treatments used "in countries where the dominant health care system is based on allopathic medicine, or where TM has not been incorporated into the national health care system" (WHO 2002a: 1). In these situations TM is usually used to supplement biomedical treatment.

The report acknowledges the problematic nature of lumping all non-biomedical medical practices together in one category and then distinguishing them simply on the basis of whether they are part of a country's cultural heritage or recognized by a particular nation-state. As Pietroni's quote in the report states, "To speak of 'alternative' medicine is . . . like talking about foreigners—both terms are vaguely pejorative and refer to large, heterogeneous categories defined by what they are not rather than by what they are" (1992: 564–66, in WHO 2002: 8)

In this scheme, biomedicine is the normative category and everything else is "other." This othering of medical practice tends to reflect nineteenth-century racialized categories in which an emerging "Western" white societies' system of medicine was viewed as the "norm" and non-Western, nonwhite peoples' systems of medicine were "other." This typology also reproduces longstanding perceptions that "traditional medicine" is static and has remained unchanged since ancient times, whereas biomedicine is progressive and modern. Although the *WHO Traditional Medicine Strategy* is trying to move beyond these stereotypes to recognize the values of contemporary TM, the language and typologies used makes it extremely difficult to overcome these assumptions. Despite this critique, I use these terms here because the chapter analyzes the discourse on TM as it relates to the discourse of nationalism.

Nationalist Discourses on Medicine in Colonial India

The role of biomedicine in the colonizing project in India is a vast topic that has recently received extensive attention by historians.[5] Several of these studies have explored whether or not biomedicine was a "tool of empire,"[6] and have examined the ways in which colonial relations of power structured the practice and distribution of biomedicine in colonial India. Some of these studies also examine the ever-changing relationship between traditional systems of Indian medicine and biomedicine at various junctures in the colonial enterprise. Historians and anthropologists have looked, on the one hand, at the ways in which the organization and epistemological frameworks of biomedicine transformed indigenous systems of medicine. On the other hand, they have explored how indigenous systems of medicine and the sociocultural milieu within which they operated also shaped the practice of biomedicine in colonial and postcolonial South Asia.[7] Some have also explored how traditional medicines are being transformed into modern health products for middle class Indians and how transnational reworkings of traditional Indian medicine in the West have transformed the practice of Indian medicine within India (see, for example, Bode 2002; Zimmermann 1992). In short, this relationship has been dynamic and is not unidirectional.

The notion that biomedicine was a "tool of empire" employed by the British in colonial India, became an important trope in some anticolonial, nationalist discourses and a key factor motivating the revival and professionalization of traditional Indian medicine. Indian nationalist discourses, and specifically nationalist perspectives on biomedicine were not, however, uniform, and changed over the course of the colonial era. The medical historian David Arnold has presented us with contrasting ways in which Indian nationalists engaged science in general, and biomedicine in particular (2000: 176–85). For example, some argued that individual drugs or therapies from traditional Indian systems of medicine should be recognized and incorporated into biomedical practice without officially recognizing the indigenous systems per se. Others were adamant that the entire epistemology of traditional Indian medical systems had to be accepted.[8] Neither side of this debate, however, considered that the revival of traditional medicine would supplant biomedical practice or that biomedicine did not have benefits to offer society alongside traditional medical treatments.

Mohandas K. Gandhi, however, provided another view in his manifesto, *Hind Swaraj* (Indian Home Rule), originally written in Gujarati in 1908, in which he challenges the value of biomedical practice head on. Although his anti-"civilization" statements in *Hind Swaraj* may be regarded as highly polemical, and although he later detracted from the ferocity with which he condemned biomedical practice,[9] his statements in *Hind Swaraj* are emblematic of one brand of nationalist critique of biomedicine used by advocates of Indian medicine.

It is important to note that comments in *Hind Swaraj* do not represent the sum total of Gandhi's views on the relationships among the body, medicine, and nation. Joseph Alter's book *Gandhi's Body* provides a picture of the complexity of Gandhi's views on these themes. Alter argues that to understand Gandhi's politics overall we must appreciate Gandhi's "rational science of moral health," which is "at once, national— and, indeed, transnational—and also strictly self-oriented" (Alter 2000: 19). In *Key to Health* (first published in 1948), far less politically charged than *Hind Swaraj*, we see Gandhi constructing a template for the requirements of good health that critiques both Āyurvedic doctors (*vaids*) and biomedical doctors. Gandhi attempts to synthesize the then-popular European-inspired "nature cures" with Hindu notions of *bramacharya* (self-control) to develop a biomoral self-help guide to healthy living. The underlying theme in Gandhi's *Key to Health* is that it is every individual's duty to constantly strive to promote and preserve his/her own health in order to be able to serve god (Gandhi 1992: 3, 13).

Despite Alter's more nuanced representation of Gandhi's views of medicine and the body, it is Gandhi's critique of biomedicine in *Hind Swaraj* that is most evident in the nationalist tenor of contemporary advocates of the use of traditional Indian medicine to respond to HIV/AIDS. Three important themes are evoked in Gandhi's discussion of biomedical doctors in *Hind Swaraj* that have salience to my analysis of the nationalistic nature of the discourse surrounding the use of traditional medicine in the treatment of HIV/AIDS today. First, Gandhi clearly represents biomedicine as a tool of imperialism when he states, "The English have certainly effectively used the medical profession for holding us. English physicians are known to have used their profession with several Asiatic potentates for political gain (Gandhi 1938: 52–53). And, he adds, "To study European medicine is to deepen our slavery" (54).

Second, he constructs an opposition between biomedicine as a quick fix to alleviate symptoms but with only temporary effects versus indigenous Indian medicine's more holistic and spiritual approach that views illness and health as caused by a mind-body connection and that requires much greater effort and self control on the part of the patient to heal but that ultimately gets to the root cause of the problem and heals the patient. As he writes,

Let us consider: the business of a doctor is to take care of the body, or, properly speaking, not even that. Their business is really to rid the body of diseases that may afflict it. How do these diseases arise? Surely by our negligence or indulgence. I overeat, I have indigestion, I go to a doctor, he gives me medicine, I am cured. I overeat again, I take his pills again. Had I not taken the pills in the first instance, I would have suffered the punishment deserved by me and I would not have overeaten again. The doctor intervened and helped me to indulge myself. My body thereby certainly felt more at ease; but my mind became more weakened. A continuance of a course of medicine must, therefore, result in loss of control over the mind. (1938: 58)

The third of Gandhi's critiques of biomedicine that I want to mention is his contention that the bottom line is that biomedical doctors are avaricious:

We become doctors so that we may obtain honours and riches. I have endeavoured to show that there is no real service of humanity in the profession, and that it is injurious to mankind. Doctors make a show of their knowledge, and charge exorbitant fees. Their preparations, which are intrinsically worth a few pence, cost shillings. (1938: 54)

Other writers comparing Indian traditional medicine to biomedicine often reiterate this theme, arguing that biomedicine is unnecessarily more expensive than indigenous medicines. Some point out, that according to classical textual accounts of Āyurveda, the *vaids* were depicted as knowledgeable doctors and spiritual gurus, who would only accept payment from their clientele if the patient was successfully healed.[10] Throughout Gandhi's account of biomedical doctors, we hear echoes of the well-analyzed discursive opposition between a materialist West and a spiritual India that reverberated throughout colonial-nationalist debates.[11] Later I will show how these themes prevail today as well but are tempered by the fact that traditional medicine is fast becoming big business and therefore has great potential for material gain.

Traditional Medicine as Big Business in the Twenty-First Century

According to a 2002 WHO policy report entitled, "Traditional Medicine—Growing Needs and Potential," many "developing" countries' populations use traditional medicine for their primary health care needs. This report states that in Ethiopia 90 percent of the population use TM for primary health care, while in Rwanda, Benin, and India, 70 percent do so (WHO 2002b: 1). This report shows that in Canada 70 percent of the population used CAM at least once within a given year, with figures for France, 49 percent, Australia 48 percent, and the United States 42 percent used CAM. One thing these figures suggest is that today there is a high global demand and booming market for nonbiomedical traditional therapies. According to the WHO, "The world market for herbal medicines based on traditional knowledge is now estimated at US$60 thousand million. In the U.S. herbal sales increased by 101 percent in mainstream markets between May 1996 and May 1998" (12). Expenditures on traditional medicine in many parts of the world are significant and growing rapidly. Despite the fact that the U.S. has a lower percentage of its population using CAM than the other Western countries listed, it has the highest CAM annual expenditure, estimated at $2,700 million for 1997 (12).[12] Total annual CAM expenditures for Canada, the UK, and Australia were US$2400 million, US$2300 million, and US$80 million respectively (2).

Given this boom in global consumption of and expenditure on TM, India finds itself in competition with other nations to cash in on profits from the trade. In July 2001 India's health minister, Dr. C. P. Thakur,

revived a debate dating back to the colonial era concerning the integration of traditional systems of medicine and biomedicine in medical
education. He argued that Āyurveda, Unani, homeopathy, Siddha,
naturopathy, and yoga should all be integrated into the medical school
curriculum. His statement came in response to actions taken to inte-
grate information about traditional medicine into the curricula of some
medical schools in Western nations. As he said,

In the U.S., the National Institute for Health (NIH) is dedicating huge infra-
structure and financial resources not just on research but also on training pro-
fessionals. Out of 300-odd medical colleges and institutes in the U.S., over 125
are integrating courses. Alternative medicine is taught there in one form or the
other. In the UK too, the teaching institutes have started combining these practices with modern medicine. Why should we lag behind? (Joshi 2001)

But his concern clearly extends beyond the comprehensive training of
physicians, to ensuring that India gets a fair share of the financial profits
associated with the spread of traditional medicine. This is clear, when
he goes on to state,

Regardless of what people say, I want to put traditional medicine back on the
national agenda. China is exporting Rs. 40,000 crore worth of Āyurvedic and
other forms of traditional medicine. India's exports barely touch Rs. 400 crore.
Isn't it shameful that even countries like Thailand do much more business in
traditional medicine than we do? (Joshi 2001)[13]

These comparisons between India's exports of TM and the exports of
other countries, most notably China, appear frequently in speeches
made by government officials working in the area of health, as well as by
representatives of India's pharmaceutical companies dealing in the sale
of traditional medicine.

    These statements often include critiques against laws that are felt to
prohibit the free trade of India's traditional medicines to other countries. For example, members of India's traditional medicine industry
protested the government's 1996 laws against exporting endangered
plants (including medicines made with endangered plants), arguing
that such laws make it impossible for India's traditional medicine companies to compete with exporters of traditional Chinese medicine on
the global market.[14] More recently, exporters of Āyurvedic medicines
have voiced concern over a new law in the UK that designates Āyurvedic
medicines as "ethnic" and requires all "ethnic" drugs to pass much
stricter tests than other drugs before being imported into the UK. Critics
of this new law fear that under these new guidelines, approximately 95
percent of Āyurvedic medicines would not pass the stringent import

tests. This is viewed as a major threat to the industry since the majority of Āyurvedic exports from India are to European Union nations.[15]

The Potential for Traditional Systems of Indian Medicine in the AIDS Pandemic

With respect to HIV/AIDS, people working for the Indian government and for nongovernmental public health organizations, as well as some involved in medical education, have been calling for greater research into the possible beneficial uses of traditional Indian medicine to treat HIV/AIDS. Organizations such as WHO, the Indian Council of Medical Research (ICMR), UNAIDS, and the Population Foundation of India have actively organized meetings to address this issue, spurred on, in part, by the fact that traditional medicines found in east and southern Africa are said to yield positive results.[16]

In January 2000 a three-day international conference was held in Gujarat, attended by six hundred delegates who convened at the Gujarat Ayurved University to think collectively about the role Āyurveda could play in the fight against AIDS. At this convention Governor Sundar Singh Bhandari told delegates that the "Modern medical system had lost its hold on [the] holistic approach. With adverse drug reactions, people were looking for safe, alternative approaches . . . Āyurveda with its rich drugs obtained from nature and its philosophy of holistic approach could be a suitable alternative." He said that new research into the efficacy of Āyurveda in combating the AIDS epidemic "could be beneficial for [the] globalization of Āyurveda."[17] Addressing the same conference, the Gujarat state health minister also promoted the use of Āyurveda to combat AIDS, stating that "with the advent of the twenty-first century it was imperative that people have the inner strength to fight cultural invasion." It is not clear whether he was suggesting that AIDS itself has spread to India due to "cultural invasion,"[18] or whether "cultural invasion" refers to biomedicine. Regardless, he clearly views Āyurveda as an *Indian* weapon against this invasion.

Also speaking in 2000, the head of the department of internal medicine in Lokmanya Tilak Hospital in Mumbai echoed the widespread assumption that AIDS is caused by cultural "lifestyle" changes associated with modernity and views as a solution traditional Indian medical practices that engage holistic mind-body regimens: "High blood pressure, coronary artery diseases, diabetes, or even AIDS are caused by drastic lifestyle changes. The quality, quantity, composition and timing of our meals are incorrect. We should reduce the intake of the three 's'—saturated fat, salt and sugar and increase the other 's'—sports, salads, and spirituality."[19]

The Use of "Traditional" Systems of Indian Medicine for HIV/AIDS Patients in India

There are numerous examples of medical practitioners in India who are using traditional medicine to treat HIV/AIDS patients. Some claim to successfully alleviate symptoms; others claim to have found cures. One example is the Government Hospital for Thoracic Medicine in Tambaram, just outside Chennai.[20] PLWHA coming to this hospital are treated with a combination of at least three Siddha drugs that reportedly have immuno-restorative properties.[21] In 2002 there were over 300 patients daily taking this treatment in the eight wards designated exclusively for inpatient HIV care.[22] This endeavor is fully endorsed and supported by the government.[23] Critics, however, argue that this is simply a poor man's substitute for antiretroviral drugs and worry about the potential long-term side effects of the Siddha medicines, especially for immuno-compromised people (Jain 2002: 190–96). The superintendent of this hospital explained to me that, although many of the patients receive the Siddha treatments, the government only provides funding for antiretroviral treatments for those patients who have severe life-threatening conditions and are on the verge of dying.[24] Other critics voice a concern that governmental support of Siddha medicines at Tambaram will serve to legitimize the claims of other practitioners of traditional medicine who say they have found cures for HIV/AIDS.[25]

Dr. Nehru,[26] who has a Siddha clinic in Chennai, provides still another critique of the use of Siddha medicines at the Tambaram hospital. His complaint is that the doctors involved in the Siddha medicine program at Tambaram may have had some training in Siddha medicine through government Siddha medical colleges, but that that kind of training is not authentic, and therefore cannot be viewed as "traditional" medicine at all. According to him, real Siddha practitioners learn medicine as disciples, sitting at the feet of a guru for at least twelve years. And instead of using machines to process their medicines, "real" Siddha practitioners grind their medicines by hand with grinding stones. Furthermore, he argued that simply consuming Siddha medicines could not be considered true Siddha treatment, since authentic "traditional" treatments must include a spiritual, or psychological component. He explained it to me this way:

The spiritual thing is a must. As soon as a person has found out that he or she has a contagious, dreadful, life-threatening disease, immediately before medication he should be isolated, he should be first given a lesson to control himself in order to psychologically battle the disease he has. At the same time he should be taught yoga, spiritual divine classes, and meditation so he or she can develop his or her will power. Psychology is also part and parcel of the medication. Medication doesn't work unless the person cooperates with the full heart.[27]

When I met Dr. Nehru in Chennai in January 2003, he was trying to gain recognition for his Siddha treatments for HIV/AIDS patients. He was frustrated by what he viewed as the lack of government and industry interest in conducting clinical trials on traditional medical treatments for HIV/AIDS, and said that this lack of interest was due to the monopolistic nature of the biomedical establishment and governmental support thereof. Dr. Nehru also told me that the HIV virus was not at all new. He claimed it had been around in ancient times and that it had then gone dormant before resurfacing again in recent times. Therefore, he felt that there must have been ancient Siddha treatments to cure HIV, and he was working to recover this lost knowledge. Because of this, he was critical of anyone who claimed to have "discovered" a Siddha or Āyurveda cure for HIV/AIDS, since in fact such a cure had been discovered by the ancient Siddhars.[28]

There are several other examples of practitioners of Indian medicine who say the government and medical industry turned a blind eye to their attempts to get their treatments for HIV/AIDS tested. For example, Dr. Natwar Manilal Doshi claims that he has developed a cure for AIDS using traditional medicine. In 2001 he petitioned the Mumbai High Court to direct the Union government to get his drugs scientifically tested and to allow him to treat AIDS patients. Legal permission had to be sought in this case, since in 2000 the High Court restrained individuals and organizations from proclaiming that they had an AIDS cure.[29] In Delhi, in January 2001, Mr. Bhoop Narain Mandal succeeded in obtaining a Delhi High Court order for the central government to provide him with accommodations on the premises of a government hospital for one year to "prove his credentials" and pursue his Āyurvedic treatments for HIV/AIDS patients. Despite the court order, however, a month later Mandal complained that the government authorities continued to be "reluctant" to provide him accommodation. Before receiving the court order, Mandal claimed to have cured twelve AIDS patients over a two-year period, using the Dhanvantri branch of Āyurveda. He relies on what he refers to as "an old and sacred book" written in Maithili and Sanskrit, which he says has been with the Mandal family for generations.

Mandal views his work as a "one-man mission" to give "life" to AIDS patients. He took on this mission while living in Bihar when he read in the newspapers that AIDS is considered to be incurable by biomedical practitioners. Taking this as a challenge, he asks, "Who are these allopathic doctors to claim there is no cure for AIDS? After all it is a disease, and no disease is incurable." And holding the "sacred book" in his hand, he says, "Read the book and you will yourself find that our ancestors have developed [a] cure for all diseases." Finally, he confidently states, "One year is more than enough to prove that the Indian method has a cure for every disease."[30]

T. A. Majeed and ImmunoQR

Arguably the most widely known and controversial figure claiming to have found a cure for AIDS using traditional Indian medicine is T. A. Majeed, in Kochi, Kerala. As was the case with Mandal, Majeed seems to have eagerly stepped up to the challenge posed by biomedicine's failure to find a cure for AIDS. Majeed was working as an engineer in the Kolar gold mines and always had an interest in Āyurveda. But he left his engineering career to devote himself to an intensive search for Āyurvedic treatments for HIV/AIDS, though he never received formal training as an Āyurvedic doctor. Eventually Majeed developed a treatment combining over twenty different herbs and called his formula "ImmunoQR" (IQR).[31] He moved to Kochi (Ernakulam) to open a clinic called Fair Pharma and began administering his treatments there.

It was the story of Chitra Soman, an HIV+ woman, that catapulted Majeed into the public limelight. Chitra was a college student when she married her husband in Mumbai, where he worked for a tire company. When they married, she was unaware of the fact that he was an AIDS patient. Her husband died due to AIDS a year after their wedding, and three days after his death, in March 1992, Chitra gave birth to a baby girl. Chitra and her daughter were both found to be HIV+. Due to the intense stigma associated with AIDS in India, Chitra's house was stoned and she was shunned by her relatives.[32] Media reports of her difficulties generated sympathy and national and international financial support that enabled her to build her own house in her native place, Kerala. After much hesitation and skepticism, Chitra was convinced to try Majeed's IQR. This treatment consists of pills, syrups, and powders taken daily for 100 days. Majeed was charging Rs. 8,000 for a full course of treatment. This is certainly a hefty fee to pay for the average Indian citizen, though substantially less that the cost of antiretroviral drugs. According to Majeed, a patient who begins IQR treatment within three months of becoming infected with HIV can be cured in 30 days for the cost of Rs. 2,005. A patient is in the early stages of AIDS will be required to take the IQR treatment for 100 days at the cost of Rs. 8,400 (including taxes and courier charges). Majeed points out that his treatment is economical when compared with antiretroviral "cocktails," which he says cost Rs. 3,500,000 for three years (Majeed 2002: 2).

According to Majeed, after completing the IQR treatment Chitra returned for another HIV Elisa test. The clinic refused to test her since she had previously tested HIV+. Majeed's wife then convinced Chitra to disguise herself as a Muslim woman and go to another clinic for the test. That test, Majeed claims, showed Chitra to be HIV-.[33] This, he claims, was proof that IQR can destroy the HIV virus and cure AIDS patients. Majeed's popularity mushroomed and by December 2001 he had treated over 140,000 HIV+ patients.[34]

Majeed concedes that only a small percentage of patients who take IQR will convert from HIV+ to HIV- in an antibody test.[35] He argues that antibody tests are not the most useful to determine the impact of his treatments, since they only indicate the presence of antibodies to the virus, not the presence of the virus itself. For more conclusive proof of the effectiveness of IQR, Majeed recommends the HIV culture test and the CD4 count. These tests are, however, too expensive for many of his patients and are often not available except in major metropolitan centers of India.

Critics of Majeed and his IQR abound, and they challenge him to prove his cure through scientific trials. This is where the Majeed story becomes bizarre. According to Majeed, the ICMR already did a trial. He says that they began trials in June 1993 and that after one month they asked him to come to Delhi immediately. He then claims that the ICMR tried to cut a deal with him, saying that unless he promised to give them 25 percent of his business, they would not give him the results. Furthermore, he adds, when he refused to comply, the ICMR threatened to make a public statement that two patients had died due to IQR. He says that he still refused, despite these threats, and that the ICMR falsely claimed that the trial never took place.[36]

Furthermore, Majeed is critical of the fact that in order to obtain legitimacy, Āyurvedic treatments must be subjected to scientific tests based on biomedical epistemological grounds that demand proof through repeatable experiments in laboratories. He thinks that Āyurvedic epistemology is broader, and more accepting of the limits of our ability to explain natural processes in their entirety and it relies on experiential evidence as proof of efficacy. As he writes:

I have narrated the hurdles I had to face and am still battling. I must tell you that it is almost impossible to pierce the allopathic barrier. They stop all the other branches of sciences in the name of science! Now what is science? The best definition I have heard about science is that "science is polished common sense." How many scientists do have that? An American scientist recently remarked, "common sense is now very rare among scientists." We have to understand that science knows only 3–5 percent of the going-ons in this universe. The ayurvedic people are in no way bound to explain how the herbal medicines work—because the discoveries of elements and compounds are not complete and are never going to be complete for centuries. The recent science, that is allopathy, blocks an ancient science like ayurveda by asking us to explain its working in terms of a few compounds they know. If so it is their duty to prove how it works and not ours. The fact is it works—and that too without any side effects. Ayurveda is the real, time tested, ancient well established science on a firm footing. How can that be called an alternate science? It is the Modern science that should be called the alternate science. (Majeed 2002: 12–13)

Critics of Majeed portray him as the quintessential "quack" who takes advantage of gullible people in their time of great desperation. He is often accused of using steroids in his IQR formula in order to give AIDS patients an initial feeling of improved health (particularly increased appetite and energy), but ultimately further depleting the patients' immune systems, leading to a degeneration of health. Majeed retorts by saying that in his own laboratory tests, he has not found any evidence of steroids in IQR and that even in those reports that show the presence of steroids it is in such small traces as to be negligible (0.45 nanograms) and not a threat to the health of patients (Majeed 2002: 8–9).

One of Majeed's most outspoken critics has been Dr. I. S. Gilada, secretary general of the nongovernmental organization, Indian Health Organization (IHO). The IHO has been actively engaged in AIDS prevention, treatment, and awareness initiatives and Gilada views this organization as being "responsible for creating major awareness against quacks and fake claimants of 'AIDS Cures.'" In 1997 Gilada stated, "In the last decade India has witnessed everything from Human Faeces, to Snake venom as AIDS Cures, propagated by quacks,"[37] and placed Majeed squarely in the camp of "quacks." In another article, Gilada conjures up Orientalist phobias of an exotic, superstitious traditional India when he writes,

While I have no disrespect on authenticity of the alternative therapies, some of which have been known for marked achievements, I have strong skepticism on tall claims on AIDS-cures. Fraudulent claims are targeted to exploiting gullible people with HIV/AIDS. The remedies offered are, to name a few: Herbal concoctions, Sugar Coated pills, Hair therapy—by treating an infected hair of the infected person, Pendulum therapy, Heavy metals, Magnatotherapy, Snake venom in extract of Catachew etc. Each region of India, has several such claimants—prominent among them are T. A. Majeed from Kochin.[38]

Majeed and his supporters view such criticisms as a form of Western cultural imperialism that attempts to establish biomedicine as hegemonic and undermine the efforts of non-biomedical practitioners worldwide. They depict Majeed as a nationalist hero, a rugged individual, defending the beleaguered traditional practitioners of Indian medicine in the face of the onslaught of globalization. As one supporter, M. K. Harikumar, writes,

The man who found out medicine for AIDS, still stands as an amazement. The contemporary world order, which is ruled by Britishers is not conducive to accept the claim that a traditional doctor from Kerala, has found out the medicine for AIDS, "the global terror disease."

Allopathy, which is transforming into a global business will not cooperate with anything, which may affect its monopoly. As long as Diseases and Medicine are the biggest business of the developed world, indigenous practitioners like T. A. Majeed will have to fight alone.

Taking the role of doctor, manufacturer, distributor and promoter at the same time, the journey of Majeed is more difficult, adventurous, and challenging. (Harikumar 2001)

This rhetoric resonates directly with the anti-imperialist nationalist rhetoric that constructed biomedicine as driven by capitalist profit motives, as was voiced by Gandhi. And Harikumar even depicts the "Britishers" as the adversary in this nationalist struggle (while many other critics have come to view the Unites States as the imperialist power to be reckoned with in the postcolonial era). Majeed also argues that biomedical treatments for HIV/AIDS patients are overly aggressive, and that although a patient's life span may be extended through biomedical treatment, she/he will be "almost dead due to the destruction of cells in the body." In fact, he goes so far as to say, that there is an enormous conspiracy to cover up the damaging effects of antiretrovirals when he writes,

Scientists are hiding evidence that AZT accelerates death. In an effort to hide the emerging tragedy, the medical establishment either trivializes or disclaims the evidence that AZT causes diseases and accelerates death. Children [born of mother's who receive AZT to prevent MTCT] are born with serious birth defects, including holes in the chest, abnormal indentation at the base of the spine, misplaced ears, triangular faces, heart defects, etc. This speaks volumes about how far the MNCs can go on cheating the public for the sake of money. They are the only people capable of fooling all the people all the time. In the last budget Indian Govt revoked excise duty for "cocktail"! (Majeed 2002: 7)

Majeed's Āyurvedic treatment, on the other hand, is constructed as being a kinder, gentler, more holistic approach, which, it is claimed, will cure the patient rather than simply suppress the symptoms. Such statements resonate again with Gandhi's dichotomous depiction of biomedicine and Indian systems of medicine. Margaret Trawick (1992) has suggested that this opposition is a metaphor for the perceived cultural and material violence of globalization on the one hand, and an imagined alternative future on the other hand.

Like Mandal in Delhi, Majeed argues that IQR can cure any patient of a wide range of diseases, including AIDS, Alzheimer's, mad cow disease, and "mental retardation," among others. He claims that these diseases all have a common mechanism and that all can be successfully treated and cured with IQR.[39] Furthermore, in the midst of the post-September 11 anthrax episode in the U.S., Majeed said,

IQR is enough for the American scare Anthrax. I believe that Anthrax will not be cured by the medicine Cipra, which is largely spreading in America. There is something suspicious about [the] FDA's decision to entrust the right to one company for the distribution of this medicine. (quoted in Harikumar 2001)

In this last statement we note again reference to the monopolistic tendencies of biomedicine, echoing the earlier comment that "allopathy, which is transforming into a global business, will not cooperate with anything, which may affect its monopoly." This harks back to the familiar nationalist theme, expressed by Gandhi, that depicts biomedical practitioners, and here biomedical pharmaceutical companies, as being driven by capitalistic profit motives and devoid of humanitarian intentions.

At other times, however, Majeed's comments take on a distinctly different register, as he brags about his own great financial success with the Fair Pharma clinic. Although he takes pains to point out that the cost of IQR is a fraction of the cost of the antiretroviral cocktails, he also says that he himself earns Rs. 10,000 daily.[40] And he proudly proclaims that he is the highest tax payer in Kerala:

Inflow of AIDS patients to Cochin in search of my medicine for AIDS gained momentum day by day. The price of my medicine is 6000/- + taxes per patient[41] and to say that I paid an income tax of 1.43 crores of rupees by 2000–01 reveals that I have treated around 20,000 patients that year alone! (Majeed 2002: 8)

He makes such pronouncements about his tax bracket status in order to demonstrate that, despite his critics' representation of him as a "quack," his treatments are extremely popular. He goes on to stress that it is not only local patients in India, but also doctors in India and doctors and patients internationally who are buying IQR. Indeed the interest in his medicine globally, particularly in the West, is seen as legitimizing its use in India.

Some doctors working in South Africa, a country devastated by the AIDS epidemic, have responded positively to Majeed's IQR and have complained of the legal obstacles they face trying to import and prescribe the medicine (Sarguro 2001). Dr. Sudhir Borgonha from the Massachusetts Institute for Technology visited Majeed's Fair Pharma in 1995 and says that he underwent a transformation from being a skeptic to considering the possibility that there may be some clinical value to IQR for HIV+ patients. And in California, Dr. George Eassey, O.M.D. (Doctor of Oriental Medicine), heard about Majeed and became intrigued. He made a visit to Fair Pharma and, based on his assessment of the lab results there, decided to bring IQR back with him to treat his patients in California. Based on his own study of patients, Dr. Eassey claims that the IQR, in combination with a fitness and nutritional regime, can not only reduce symptoms related to HIV/AIDS but also reverse a patient's status from HIV+ to HIV- (Miners 1996).

Majeed speculates that Magic Johnson must have been treated with IQR by Dr. Eassey. Referring to a 1996 *Time* cover story about Johnson's recovery without AZT, in which Johnson and reporters suggest that Johnson's T-cell count increased due to positive thinking, Majeed says, "Magic Johnson should be asked to tell the truth. At least let him say if 'positive thinking' for him came in syrup form, tablet form, or powder form and from which part of the world?" (1996). Majeed informed me that the FDA has since prevented Eassey from treating patients with IQR in the U.S. and that Eassey fled California for London and later moved to the Czech Republic.

Majeed claims that Indian governmental organizations (especially ICMR and the National AIDS Control Organization), WHO, and the FDA in the U.S. are all conspiring to stop his practice because they have economic and political stakes in the multinational biomedical pharmaceutical companies. Many steps have been taken to legally block IQR in India and abroad (as will be discussed below). Majeed argues that if he were free to prescribe IQR in India and to export it, and if people in other countries were free to treat patients with IQR, it would transform the entire Indian economy. He writes in a brochure entitled "The Plight of Medicine for AIDS," "The Central Government should take note of the fact that this medicine is capable of solving India's balance of payment problem" (Majeed 2002: 14). And he concludes with the famous Indian nationalist slogan "Jai Hind" ("Praise India!"). In short, he portrays the potential global spread of IQR as a service to the nation.

Critics respond to the financial success and the international spread of Majeed's medicine, not by discrediting them, but by asserting that they are a sign of the problem. They point to Majeed's financial success as indicative of his ability to exploit "gullible" people at home and abroad. Gilada writes,

Through fraudulent misrepresentations and advertising widely in India and abroad, Majeed, who is not even registered with any statutory bodies of Medicine or Alternative Systems in India, has been minting money to the tune of Rs. 10 crore a year, prescribing spurious "herbal" medicines. (1997)[42]

Gilada also voices strong condemnation of the global spread of Majeed's medicines and the ways that is used to advertise his wares back home: "[The] internet has helped them further in global marketing of their fake remedies and then using that plank at home that their medicines are in demand all over the world" (1997). This is reflective of a broader concern over the possibility of medical malpractice over the Internet that has given rise to biomedically based organizations that seek to develop standards of reliability for medical information on the Internet (Hardey 2002: 207).

Opponents of Majeed are outraged by his advertising tactics and have made concerted efforts to ban his advertisements in the media. His advertisements claim that IQR is a cure for AIDS. In one ad the words "AIDS IS CURABLE" are typed repeatedly around the border. A number of NGOs working in the field of HIV/AIDS, including IHO, the Indian Network of Positive People (INP+), the Maharastra Network of Positive People (MNP+), and the Council for People Living with HIV/AIDS in Kerala (CPK+), among others, have successfully sought legal action to prevent Majeed from advertising IQR as a drug that "cures" HIV/AIDS.[43] Along with the concern that this advertising may take advantage of people, there is a broader public health concern that if people are led to believe that there is a cure for AIDS, they will be less inclined to take preventative measures to avoid contracting the HIV virus. These organizations thus feel that Majeed's advertising, presents an obstacle in their efforts to curb the spread of the disease.

The advertisements are of course not the only things to be alarmed about when it comes to prevention. Majeed's instructions to patients must also be taken into consideration. In addition to the possibility that people may take fewer precautions to prevent becoming infected with HIV, those who are HIV+ and take IQR may believe that they can no longer transmit HIV to others and therefore not take precautions. In December 2002, I spent a day observing doctor-patient interactions at the Fair Pharma clinic. On this day, Majeed's daughter was seeing the patients and prescribing medications. All the patients who came to the clinic on this day were men. In each case, there was discussion about how HIV would affect family life. Unmarried men were told that if they took the medication they could get married after six months without worrying about spreading the virus to their wives. Several of the men were married and their wives were pregnant. Indeed, it was often the HIV+ test of the wife during prenatal care that was the first indication that the men themselves might be HIV+. In these cases, the biomedical doctors overseeing the wife's prenatal care were typically advising an abortion and then antiretroviral treatment for the woman (if the family could afford it), or advising the pregnant mother to get a nevaripine injection during pregnancy and to administer nevaripine to the newborn in order to reduce the chance of parent-to-child transmission (PTMC) of HIV. The Indian government is now providing nevaripine treatments free of cost in some government hospitals. Majeed's daughter, on the other hand, told these patients that their pregnant wives should *not* take nevaripine to prevent PTCT because that would be dangerous to the health of the baby, and that they should *not* take antiretrovirals for their own treatment. Instead, she instructed the pregnant mother to take Majeed's medicine for 100 days during the pregnancy and then to give a quarter-tablet of the medicine to the newborn baby three times daily. She assured them that mother and child would be free of the HIV virus following these treatments.

The ban on Majeed's advertisements was of course a major setback to his practice. This was followed by the highly publicized death of Chitra, his most famed patient, in July 2001. Chitra's tragic death provided more ammunition for Majeed's opponents, despite the fact that Majeed argued that the cause of her death was unrelated to HIV/AIDS.[44] The most devastating blow, however, came on December 21, 2001, when the High Court of Kerala canceled Majeed's license for the production, manufacturing, and distribution of IQR and sixteen other medicines. On March 11, 2002, the Supreme Court gave back the license for all other medicines except IQR and directed the Kerala High Court to reexamine its verdict on IQR.[45] To date, Majeed remains suspended from treating PLWHA with IQR.[46]

Conclusion

In his often cited article, "The Nationalist Resolution to the Women's Question," Partha Chatterjee demonstrates how nationalist discourse in nineteenth-century colonial Bengal constructed a dichotomy between the home (India) and the world (especially British imperialism) that mapped onto a dichotomy between spirituality and materialism (Chatterjee 1990). The nationalist defense of traditional Indian medicine and critique of biomedicine in the colonial era, such as that of Gandhi, can generally be seen to reflect these overlapping discursive dichotomies.

My study of the contemporary debates surrounding the use of traditional Indian medicine to treat HIV/AIDS patients reflects a much messier discursive field. On the one hand, we can see the same kind of nationalist discourse that was evident in the colonial era, as individuals such as Majeed, Nehru, and Mandal rail against the imperialist, materialist interests of the biomedical industry and criticize national governmental organizations and international public health institutions for supporting the biomedical industry at the expense of traditional medicine. They represent themselves as the downtrodden underdogs of a Western-dominated global order, in which biomedicine is hegemonic, and present their medicine as having a more holistic, even spiritual dimension with a promise to rejuvenate and heal whereas biomedicine is depicted as a violent, temporary fix that depletes the body and soul.

However, Majeed and his supporters also loudly proclaim his material success and take pride in the extent to which his medicines have permeated the world. And, in light of the burgeoning markets for traditional medicine and CAM, they view the potential economic profits of exporting traditional medicine as the cure to the economic ills of the Indian nation. Former health minister Thakur also sought to promote traditional Indian medicine in order to cash in on potential global profits in light of the competition from China and "even countries like Thailand." Thus, as traditional medicine becomes a lucrative transnational phenomenon, its exclusive association with the home and the spiritual domain begins to break down. Ironically, it is in fact some of the critics of Majeed who view themselves as defending India's national interests in opposition to economic forces of globalization and criticize Majeed for exploiting the global market in traditional alternative medicine.

In essence, Gandhi's critique of biomedicine in *Hind Swaraj* and his broader critique of "civilization" can be boiled down to a condemnation of bourgeois capitalism's endless creation of insatiable desires in order to open up new markets. What seems to be at work in the discourse of Majeed and others, is an attempt to make use of a Gandhian style nationalist critique of imperial capitalism, while simultaneously celebrating the creation of new desires for the purchase of their own goods.[47] In his *Nationalist Thought and the Colonial World: A Derivative Discourse*, Partha Chatterjee wrote that nationalism "produced a discourse in which even as it challenged the colonial claim to political domination, it also accepted the very intellectual premises of 'modernity' on which colonial domination was based" (Chatterjee 1986: 33). The same could be said of the way in which Majeed and some other advocates of traditional medical treatment for HIV/AIDS condemn the global capitalist intentions of biomedical multinational corporations and global and national public health institutions, while simultaneously needing to demonstrate the merits of their own medicine based on their financial capital success and global penetration.

Chapter 7

Mapping Science and Nation in China

NANCY N. CHEN

The mandate of heaven (*tianming*) is a Confucian notion that anyone who is successful in seizing the reins of power retains the rightful authority to rule over China. Across the centuries, many imperial rulers and their contestants invoke *tianming* to declare each other as morally bankrupt while legitimizing their own form of hierarchy as better. In this chapter, I argue that the mandate of science operates as a particular formation in late socialism to anchor and legitimize state authority. Such a strategy offered bureaucrats the opportunity to define themselves as modern protectors of ordinary people from the influences of evil (*xie*) cults or superstition. The alliance of officials with scientists also facilitated the embrace of expert knowledge as the basis of governmentality.

On December 9, 1999, television broadcasts on China Central Television (CCTV) showed President Jiang Zemin visiting the bedside of Qian Xuesen, renowned scientist and father of China's missile system, who was ailing and needed to be hospitalized. The following day *Health News Daily* and *China Daily* devoted front pages to this visit in the manner of official receptions. The veneration given to "Uncle" Qian reflected the status accorded to Chinese scientists and how their projects are linked to the progress of the nation. How did scientists become such eminent state figures? Like medicine, science became integral to state formation and nation building especially during the socialist era. In the recent moment of market reforms under socialism, however, science has increasingly been utilized in the regulation of Chinese medicine. This chapter shows how science has been used to articulate national agendas and define the boundaries of contemporary Chinese medicine. Over the past decade, *qigong* circulated in transnational contexts as a form of "traditional' Chinese healing. However, within China, certain forms of *qigong* were deemed "superstitious" or pathological, while scientific forms were considered to be more acceptable. The state regulation of *qigong* with science generated an obsession with pseudoscience which continues into the twenty-first century. The goals of Chinese socialist modernization relied heavily upon discourses of scientific rationality and civilization. Science was embraced by both bureaucrats and *qigong* masters as a legitimating strategy for their own purposes. An engagement with scientific discourses is crucial to understanding the mobilization of allegiances between bureaucrats, scientists, physicians, and *qigong* masters in the formation of "scientific" or medical *qigong* that would be politically correct and sanctioned over more charismatic forms of healing.

Following Laura Nader's (1996) insight that an anthropology of science can reveal the boundary-making tendencies and ideological constraints of technoscience, my discussion will differentiate among the positions of masters, scientists, and officials. The roles of officials were ambiguous, as they not only represented the state but also avidly participated in the practice for their own health-seeking purposes. Chinese scientists were far more outspoken about the need to define clear boundaries between authentic *qigong* versus the more contaminated category of pseudoscientific *qigong* promoted by masters. Policing the newly constructed categories would eventually co-evolve with a state campaign for social order. Bureaucrats faced with forging socialist order in the post-Tiananmen period, framed by rapid transformations, were also aware that the fragmentation of social life and the appeal of multiple nonstate alternatives were spawned by state-sponsored economic reforms. The emergence of unofficial players and of cultural icons of power made the issue of defining political order, relying on scientific rationality rather than subjective knowledge, all the more important. Through science, bureaucrats reordered the classifications of *qigong* with scientists at the helm rather than *qigong* masters without scientific credentials. The first half of this paper documents the renewal of scientism and the widespread application of scientific discourse in this process.

In the 1990s, a loosely organized web of government representatives became galvanized in a campaign for the regulation of *qigong*. Official state discourses about *qigong* began to be situated apart from popular *qigong* debates. While testimonial accounts of *qigong* healing continued to abound informally and in popular press, there were calls to differentiate between "real" (*zheng*) and "false" (*jia*) *qigong* by state bureaucrats through internal memos and state media. This was an attempt to separate out those individuals who claimed to be masters and healed for lucrative purposes versus those with "true" abilities. The state appointed bureau to regulate *qigong* invoked the new category of scientific *qigong* (*kexue de qigong*) as a means to cleanse and discipline the ranks of "false" masters. Such categories were quite porous and difficult to maintain as the criteria for "true" abilities differed greatly among laypersons and officials. For ordinary Chinese the subjective experience of being healed was enough evidence of a master's abilities. However, for scientists and bureaucrats, double blind tests, lab studies, and board examinations were deemed crucial to determining "true" abilities. The state and its representatives thus became crucial gatekeepers to counter runaway popular imaginations of *qigong* masters. Science and visions of the modern life were an integral part of this construction. It became clear that the oppositional boundaries created between true science and false practices or "real" *qigong* versus "unscientific" *qigong* were defined by bureaucrats rather than practitioners in order to regulate *qigong* as a state enterprise. While charismatic masters and mystics were threatening to state order and not to be tolerated, *qigong* overall was nonetheless tolerated because the healing practice worked. Ordinary citizens and high level cadres alike still sought masters for chronic ailments and still practiced themselves in spite of the new regulations.

Early anthropological analyses have viewed science and magic in several ways—as dual opposites, as a linear progression of social progress, or as complex categories of indigenous knowledge (Tambiah 1990). In spite of the state's attempts to separate the two, there was also an ironic intertwining between science and popular forms of healing. Qian Xueshen (aka Tsien Hsueh-sen), one of China's most prominent scientists, was frequently cited as one of the most staunch public supporters of *qigong*. Qian studied physics in the U.S. and taught at MIT and Cal Tech before he returned to China in 1955.[1] His knowledge of rocketry and aerospace science placed him in a leadership role in touch with leaders such as Zhou Enlai and Mao Zedong. Over the past decades he received numerous accolades including "State Scientist of Outstanding Contribution," the highest honor a scientist can receive in China. Many scientists and masters alike that I interviewed mentioned in reverent tones how his support influenced the initial spread of *qigong* research. An article, "Dr. Yan Xin on Scientific *Qigong* Research," prominently invokes Qian:

Professor Qian Xuesen has unequivocally advocated the creation of human body science. *At the same time, he predicted that the integration of Traditional Chinese Medicine, qigong, special human body functions, and a unified theoretical and scientific work will result in a great leap forward in medicine.* Furthermore he suggested that this event will revolutionize modern science as a whole, and that a second cultural renaissance will arise and come to fruition in China.[2]

The patronage of China's premier scientist and the invocation of science by masters led to the privileging of science to measure the authenticity or power of *qigong*. In what follows I explore some of the concerns and debates that led to science as a form of "national consciousness" about modern life (Tang 2000 :23). Especially during the twentieth century, science represented a potent field of meanings in both the production of knowledge and subjects.

The Scientific Spirit in Twentieth-Century China

Intertwined notions about science and progress form a continuous strand between imperial China and the contemporary socialist state. Joseph Needham's (1954–2000) multivolume history of Chinese science and civilization has left a tremendous legacy in the study of science, medicine, and technology. His evolutionary approach to science and technology proclaimed the importance of ancient Chinese discoveries such as gunpowder, printing, and astronomy to world history. Yet, such a master narrative also held that science and technology were static after the Sung dynasty and any innovations emanated from the West due to industrial capitalism.[3] Debates about science and technology were central concerns in imperial China, particularly in the encounter with Western missionaries and diplomats. For instance, above the Jianguomenwai subway stop in Beijing lies the former observatory and seventeenth-century astronomy instruments of Father Matteo Ricci, the Jesuit priest who translated Western scientific texts into Chinese and became an imperial advisor to the emperor. Now a tourist attraction, the site is a silent reminder of how such instruments of scientific inquiry offered entry to imperial courts.[4] Such a binary opposition between traditional sciences of China and modern sciences of the West has been the subject of much consideration by scholars.

Instead of taking up the Needham question of why modern science did not emerge in China as it did in the West, my discussion examines how science became foundational in twentieth-century Chinese cultural politics. One reading suggested by Laura Nader is that "the politicization of science is unavoidable, not only because politicians, corporations, and governments try to use what scientists know, but because virtually all science has social and political implications" (1996: 9). How then can we begin to document the ways scientific inquiry becomes political? As Donna Haraway (1997) and Geoffrey Bowker and Susan Leigh Star (1999) have indicated, dual attention is necessary not only for the knowledge that is being produced but also on the invisible standards and categories that created such subjects.

Lydia Liu's (1995) project of translingual practice or the "examination of language, discourse, and text" in the making of historical events is particularly useful in understanding the formation of science in China. The term for science and its usage evolved in relation to debates about the philosophical aims of science. Prior to the contemporary usage of *kexue* as the nomenclature for science, *gezhi* and *gewu zhizhi* were more frequently used to connote scientific exploration. *Kexue* was a neologism from the Japanese term *gaku* and referred to the study of a specialized subject (Wang 1995). Wang Hui's study of early twentieth-century scientists and scholars indicates that these terms reflected an underlying tension between the embrace or rejection of either Western or traditional Chinese science. Scientism and assumptions of social and national progress were promoted by intellectuals and new elites at the turn of the century. In contrast to C. P. Snow's assertion that science and the arts or humanities were two separate cultures, scientism and humanism have been deeply intertwined in the formation of modern Chinese culture (Hua 1995). D. Y. Kwok offers a useful understanding of this framework: "Scientism, in general, assumes that all aspects of the universe are knowable through the methods of science. Scientism can thus be considered as the tendency to use the respectability of science in areas having little bearing on science itself" (1965: 3).

Science has always been embraced by Chinese state leaders as a national platform essential for modernization. During the Republican era of the 1920s, attaining modern science, medicine, and technology was viewed to be crucial for the development of the modern state.[5] Usually the interlocutors of such notions of modernity were Chinese scholars who had been trained abroad either in Japan or in Western countries and foreign missionaries. In the first quarter of the twentieth century, May Fourth intellectuals interrogated the relevance of traditional values in light of China's place in the world. Chen Duxiu, a prominent intellectual, held that science could be a "replacement for Confucian values" (Wang 1995: 38). Even as the May Fourth movement could be characterized as "anti-Confucian" or "antitradition," according to Wang Hui, remained, such as the importance of science in the ation.

construction of a modern nation occupied intellectu- ntury. Under Mao the problem of unifying the nation es rather than Confucian ethics continued. With the RC, the socialist state continued to forge ahead with as a national goal; the primary advisors were either e scientists who had trained in the Soviet Union. 950s and 1960s, national progress was charted in terms of scientific progress guided by Marxist principles. Adhering to this generativity of science, Mao believed in the transformative properties of science in building the socialist nation. Scientists were regarded as an intellectual elite that needed guidance. However, his vision of science was far more "utilitarian" and localized than early modernizers

(Feurtado 1986: 4). The motto "Serve the People" quickly incorporated science to advocate the mass participation of non-experts. Science for science's sake was meaningless if no immediate social function or progress was evident.

Mao's policies also differed somewhat from earlier intellectuals in the specific linkage of science with technology as a precondition to socialist modernization. During the early years of the PRC, many scientists were sent to the Soviet Union while Russian experts were brought to China to promote scientific and technological innovations. Mao's science policy in the 1950s emphasized science as an "independent 'force of production'" which nonetheless required political consciousness and proper values by its practitioners (Feurtado 1986: 99). "Red and Expert" and "Walking on Two Legs" were common slogans during the Great Leap Forward. Such statements indicate the ideological role of science and technology which was crucial to progress. The Maoist era solidified the relation between science and the development of the nation.

The post-Mao period opened with the 1978 National Science Conference, in which high priority for science and technology (*keji*) would become the cornerstones of modernization. Dengist reforms revised earlier interpretations of Marxist practice such that scientific research could be disentangled from political debates to focus on applied industrial and agricultural development to "serve the economy and society" (Saich 1989: 17). During this redirection of science policy, concurrent debates about scientism and humanism were being waged among intellectuals. According to Shiping Hua, three versions of scientism circulated during the post-Mao era: "The Marxist scientism of historical materialism, a Chinese style scientism of technological determinism, [and] the empirical scientism of systems theory" (1995: 6). Hua contends that three corresponding schools of humanism also emerged, "Marxist, Confucian, and critical humanism." The schools differently engaged with questions of human nature and how Marxism could be used in policies of liberalism.

Scientists were among the first citizens to travel abroad in scholarly exchanges. They have continued to occupy prominent and visible positions, as they are often viewed as earnest spokespersons for the well-being of the nation. For instance, during the student demonstrations of the mid-1980s, a middle-aged physicist named Fang Lizhi became a visible figure who spoke out about concerns with corruption. While the international press focused on his alliance with student demonstrations and calls for democracy, Fang maintained a wide audience in China primarily due to his status as a scientist. After Fang's departure to the United States, many other scientists within China continued to speak on national issues such as environmental concerns, population policy, and more recently market planning. During the 1990s science and technology policy was readjusted from an emphasis on production to a focus on economic growth. Such developments would require emphasizing basic research to enable new innovations (Yu 1999). Li Zhengdao, Nobel Prize winner in physics, gave the following metaphor about research and development in marketization:

Fish cannot survive without water and there won't be any fish market without fish. So when people try to develop a fish market they should, of course, prepare for more fish and, at the same time, a sufficient amount of water should never be neglected. (quoted in Yu 1999: 166)

Such a metaphor sought to rationalize the further deepening of limited goods which would be necessary in shifting to market reforms. The notion of science as critical to nation building is a particular ethos that has pervaded most of twentieth-century China. Ann Anagnost notes that during the early twentieth century, intellectuals distinguished between material and spiritual development in the notion of Chinese civilization. Reformers in the 1980s maintained such a "split" but privileged material civilization over spiritual development (Anagnost 1997: 84). Science has been a critical part of this process. Scientific and medical *qigong*, for instance, emphasized the material elements of *qi* as a source of energy rather than the spiritual qualities of healing, which can be far too subjective. The use of scientific discourse to create new categories of "real, scientific" and "false, unscientific" *qigong* evolved after specific interest groups came together. Continued emphasis on scientism in the twenty-first century reveals how integral science and technology are to socialist modernization.

Pseudoscience and "False" *Qigong*

Qigong presented a critical tension between *mixin* (superstition) and science on rightful authority. In order to combat superstition or pseudoscience, scientists vehemently opposed popular claims about the practice. If *qigong* was to promote a better life, then modern science was necessary to prove its reality and efficacy. However, many masters invoked science to claim that their forms were sound. How would it be possible to combat pseudoscience when scientific discourse had been already appropriated in the popular context?

During the 1990s there were two movements that were foundational to the state's containment policy toward "false" *qigong*: secularization and medicalization. The move to demystify and secularize *qigong* was taken up by scientists. Scientists, especially physicists, were involved in empirical research to test the phenomena of *qi*. Publications in Chinese journals such as *Ziran* (Nature) tried to establish *qi* as a physical element similar to wave particles. Another project based at Qinghua University involved experiments with masters such as Yan Xin, who was also trained as a Chinese medical practitioner. This process of secularization to take control of *qigong* discourse was closely related to the medicalization of *qigong* deviation.[6]

The overlap between traditional Chinese medicine and *qigong* healing was further institutionalized when several traditional Chinese medicine clinics offered *qigong* as a new addition (Hsu 1999). Yet the classification of *qigong* as a part of traditional Chinese medicine was not satisfactory to the medical scientists who were also bureaucrats of the post-Mao state. Masters with no formal training, who claimed to be able to cure anything, were still legion. Such healers were viewed as counter to the medical system that was founded as a state institution on scientific principles. The medical bureaucrats wished to create order (*zhengli*) and distinguish between those healers who cured without formal training versus those healers who were officially recognized by the state. Popular practices, such as mass healing lectures or practices in the parks, began to be cast as *mixin*). Secular and medicalized versions of *qigong*, referred to as medical *qigong*, which reduced hallucinatory effects and removed the need for charismatic masters, were introduced. The move to medicalize *qigong* deviation and promote medical *qigong* was a key strategy to promote surveillance by doctors and licensed practitioners. Medicalization, according to Allan Young (1997), has always been about the assignment of symptoms and somatized disorders into routinized medical categories. Categorization has often been deeply politicized, such as the recently medicalized disorders of posttraumatic stress disorder (PTSD), chronic fatigue syndrome (CFS), and attention deficit disorder (ADD), among others.

Individual practices and magical claims about *qigong* in contemporary China existed within the same spaces that were created for post-Mao economic reforms and Chinese modernization. Just as nostalgic Mao figures emerged as popular cultural icons and as commodities, the term *mixin* also began to reappear. *Mixin* was a neologism, borrowed from Meiji modernizers, which referred to superstition or feudal thoughts during the early socialist era. The term was also used extensively during the Cultural Revolution (1966–76) to purge heterodoxy. In the resurgence of state policy to contain *qigong* with superstitious overtones, there was an attempt to insert early Maoist socialist values to assert state order. In the ensuing battle to define clear lines between legal forms of *qigong* research and practice from more charismatic forms, *mixin* emerged as an effective rhetorical device with chilling resonances to earlier campaigns during the 1950s.

During the 1990s a renewed form of scientism emerged. Discourses about pseudoscience would be used to distinguish between practices that undermined the credibility of scientific knowledge and national progress versus state-sanctioned forms of enterprises which embraced the scientific spirit that cultivated the nation-state. The state sports federation figured prominently in the growing surveillance of healers. The charge of this agency was to prevent illegitimate healing practices of "corrupt" masters who only sought monetary gain. Internal articles documenting the fate of individuals who sought help with healing only to end bankrupt or with cases of *qigong* deviation were circulated between state agencies such as the Ministry of Health, Public Security Bureau, and the State Medical Bureau. A formal public health campaign was initiated after more informal networking between such agencies took place.

The increased popularity of *qigong* and, by extension, masters of this art presented several concerns to the state. First, the proliferation of informal social networks based on breathing exercises harked back to the days of the Boxers and other millenarian cults who in times of rebellion oppressed the state. These groups often incorporated spiritualistic practices which involved immediate allegiance to a leader or master rather than any formal units of the party or state (P. Cohen 1997; Esherick 1987; Naquin 1976; Spence 1996). In following with the long history of rebellion and movements to challenge the mandate of heaven, there were powerful continuities such as charismatic leaders, breathing exercises, and utopian views of a better future after the apocalyptic end of the regime. However, there were also some fundamental differences. Specific new technologies and changes in the transmission of such practices in the post-Mao era have meant that such practices tended to be urban based rather than originating from peasant groups in marginal regions. More women and literate individuals became practitioners and, most significantly, the cosmopolitan travel of masters transformed such practices from village based organizations to global empires.

Second, these informal social networks helped to support the power of masters with little or no formal medical training to the extent that these individuals accumulated exalted powers of health and wealth in a socialist market economy. Like rock stars in the West, these individuals had much charisma and garnered great attention and respect wherever they went. Rather than facing official audiences of stiff clapping hands, these individuals could move thousands to tears as they rocked to and fro in their chairs convulsing with the power of *qi*. The masters fit into this desire for charismatic leadership after Deng's succession in the late 1980s. Their emergence depended upon the renewal of the social sphere referred to as *minjian* (folk) that was nongovernmental and increasingly influential.

Third, a major consequence of these mass audiences was that individuals left the lectures feeling infused with the power of *qi* and ready to heal themselves or others. The sensations of *teyi gongneng* (paranormal abilities) led many to perceive supernatural even alien entities that would not be possible to control without extensive practice. When such individuals were unable to control these sensations and were instead brought into clinics of state medical institutions, the masters were accused of dabbling in superstition. From the perspective of the state bureau it became necessary to call for regulation in a practice where *luan* (chaos) had taken over. Accusations of corruption and *mixin* were directed at specific masters who had amassed tremendous capital during mass healing sessions or in private.

The main concern of the state regulatory bureau was social order and morality. This required maintaining a fragile balance between modernization and meeting the material and social needs of the world's largest population. The unrest of the Tiananmen demonstrations described earlier only furthered the resolve of the government to direct its efforts at economic revitalization, to quell popular protest over issues of material disparity and corruption.

A series of internal documents calling for the regulation of *qigong* began to be circulated among several state bureaus and ministries. Beginning in 1990, a few articles about deviation were published in major newspapers. The state regulation of *qigong* became even more aggressive in 1991. Private entrepreneurial book carts were raided by public security officers for any book titles that promoted "unscientific" (*wu kexue*) or "false" (*jia*) *qigong*. As one state official told me, it was necessary to reduce the feverish interest in *qigong* (*jiangwen yidian*). Masters who wished to practice officially were required to register with the state *qigong* association. One could become licensed in several ways: by already having a medical degree and taking additional courses at a traditional medical school; by training with an officially recognized master; or by performing before a select board of officials and bringing in former patients to certify one's healing powers. State authority was also inserted into the parks in two ways. Practitioners had to be formally registered members of an official school. Red and yellow banners appeared in parks stating what form was being practiced by a nearby group and the date of certification. For individuals who practiced without such markers, regular raids by public security were conducted. Practitioners of banned forms were taken in by local police to be questioned.

Though it would appear that the state had initiated and implemented a hard strike against pseudoscience and false *qigong*, such a campaign would not be entirely possible without the involvement of masters. Such a task could have been difficult due to the eclectic nature of this group. Masters came from diverse backgrounds—not only were there multiple forms or styles, masters came from all ages, occupations, and regions. The move to regulate *qigong* nonetheless mirrored the views of many masters who felt that the entrepreneurial promotion of miracles by some colleagues was going too far.

Master Liu, a woman master in her mid-fifties, was outspoken about the need for scientific *qigong*. Though she had been trained in the "traditional" way through the direct passage of knowledge from her father who was a healer, she was concerned about contemporary forms of transmission. In her eyes,

Qigong needs to be controlled because it will go downhill from here. There are fewer and fewer people who understand it; we are all so busy. There are too many newcomers with very little *gong* (skill) who practice at a popular level and do a lot of damage. If patients try to give me money, I return it.

Her views were amplified by Master Dong, who was slightly older, in his sixties, and had overcome cancerous tumors. He believed that *qigong* needed to be moral and develop a whole ethical system without money or hierarchy. Many other masters had differing views about three masters who became infamous. Most of the masters I interviewed concurred that Dr. Yan, the TCM doctor and master, was indeed skillful and capable of healing. However, their views about a popular female master were quite disparaging. With a disdainful sneer, Master Song tersely stated, "She deals with *mixin* and *yuzhouyu*; [her form] is pure trickery."

The debate as to whether or not *qigong* healing should have been regulated by traditional masters or by medical doctors became a much contested issue. Initially most healing in the popular realm was undertaken by specialized masters, while traditional medical doctors utilized *qi* healing in combination with massage, herbal medicine, and sometimes acupuncture. With the increased popularity of *qigong* practice, individuals were encouraged to cure themselves or, if capable, to cure others rather than relying on traditional Chinese medicine. Concern for this widespread development led to the mobilization of the state apparatus by scientists, especially medical doctors, to secularize *qigong* as a solely medical practice rather than a spiritual one. Science came to be used as a metaphor of what was upright (*zheng*) and progressive for the development of the nation. On the other hand, pseudoscience needed to be purged in order to restore *qigong* to its rightful place as an official healing system.

The containment of *qigong* via science revealed state projects of civilization such as the transformation of bodies into appropriate subjects.

Steps to establish order (*zhengli*) in the social realm of *qigong* through science set the foundation for a renewed scientism which was much more public and widespread than earlier debates in the 1920s. New participants besides intellectual elites such as *qigong* masters, ordinary practitioners, and their families became involved. Sima Nan, a former master turned investigative reporter and pseudoscience buster, devoted himself to public challenges of masters and healers who claimed to have extraordinary abilities. In addition to producing CCTV programs that debunked "false" *qigong*, he invited James Randi, an American magician and debunker of psuedoscience, to discuss tricks of the trade such as sleight of hand. Members of the Committee for the Scientific Investigation of Claims of the Paranormal (CSICOP), based in the U.S., sent a delegation to China with the challenge that it would pay one million U.S. dollars to anyone who could prove their special abilities. The scientized version of medical *qigong* continued to be promoted and in 1994 the State Council of China announced moves to strengthen the education of science.

The contemporary situation of *qigong* within the PRC remains distinct—defined by an ever watchful yet ambivalent state policy eager to harness the popularity and power of *qigong* to the mandate of science and socialist modernization. While it appeared that the social world of *qigong* had receded and given way to consumer life and the discipline of markets endorsed by the party, most charismatic leaders did not quietly retreat or become relics of the past. Though there was an immediate departure from Beijing, the center of the secularization campaign, most masters were quite resourceful and relocated their quasi-empires to more favorable climes elsewhere in the provinces, and more notably abroad, where extensive networks of overseas Chinese and foreigners greeted the charismatic leaders with bated breath. Such a move was predicted by all the masters I interviewed. Even with the regulation of *qigong* through science, most masters believed that the events in China were just the beginning and that "*qigong* will continue to grow." Tales of miraculous healing paved the way for entrepreneurial masters to go transnational. Despite the reinforcements of scientization and medicalization to further the ideals of a socialist civilization, the flexibility and appeal of masters abroad led to the continued growth of *qigong* and charismatic forms of healing outside China.

Summary

My examination of *qigong* in China traces a divergent trajectory from its transnational circulation. Within the PRC, the cultural politics of popular healing have been subjected to intense management and regulation through scientific modernization. Elsewhere, *qigong* continues to be promoted as a traditional healing art. The social worlds of *qigong* reflect a vast network that facilitate transnational translations of the practice. The tensions concerning superstition and pseudoscience are largely unseen and unknown by most practitioners. Chinese scientists and physicians, however, have focused in recent years on transmitting medical *qigong* as the appropriate form to teach abroad.[7] The move to contain heterodox forms of healing can be found in other medical systems, especially biomedicine. For instance, in the early twentieth century, medical institutions in the United States that did not adhere to scientific standards outlined in the Flexner report were shut down (Ludmerer 1999; Reed 1932). The majority of institutions closed in the name of combating medical "sectarianism," quackery, and unscientific practices included schools of midwifery, naturapathy, chiropractic, and medical programs for predominantly African Americans. Despite such regulation, many of these modalities returned in the form of alternative medicine in the late twentieth century. By mapping the ways science is invoked, we can trace how scientific discourses not only maintain classifications of authentic knowledge or pseudoscience, and also apprehend how these are foundational to the formation of modern subject-citizens. In both contexts, the cultural logic of science enables particular forms of modernity and nationalism to operate.

Chapter 8
Sanskrit Gynecologies in Postmodernity: The Commoditization of Indian Medicine in Alternative Medical and New Age Discourses on Women's Health

MARTHA ANN SELBY

> What is significant about the adoption of alien objects—as of alien ideas—is not the fact that they are adopted, but the way they are culturally redefined and put to use.
>
> —*Kopytoff (1986: 67)*

The two earliest extant medical compendia in Sanskrit, the *Caraka Saṃhitā* (circa second century C.E.) and the *Suśruta Saṃhitā* (circa mid-third century C.E.)[1] contain detailed information about women's bodies throughout their pages in various taxonomic and narrative forms, but this information primarily emerges in the *śarīra-sthānas* (or "chapters on physiology") in both texts, embedded in prescriptive writings on conception, pregnancy, and postnatal care. In this chapter, I will examine how proponents of Euro-American New Age and alternative medicines have transformed early Āyurvedic ideas about women's health into an essential and influential segment of the postmodern wellness industry. I will analyze different modes by which we might chart the ebbs and flows of medical knowledge from India through Europe and America, paying particular attention to the ways Āyurvedic gynecology has been "presented" to the West in various packages. This is by no means an easy task, but what I would like to accomplish in these pages is to focus on three different ways in which this knowledge has been transmitted. First, I look carefully at translations of these early texts that were made in India during the last century and how the "Sanskrit to English" shift has resulted in serious misunderstandings of Āyurvedic formulations in regard to their constructions of gynecological and obstetrical ideas. Second, I examine books by Euro-American authors that claim to represent Āyurvedic gynecological notions and look at how the general collapsing of Āyurveda into yoga has affected the structuring of ideas about women's bodies in general—this conflation has been documented by many observers, Joseph Alter being chief among them (1999, 2004). Third, I look at the ways Āyurveda and notions pertaining to women's health in general have been transmuted into a huge and booming cosmetics industry in Europe and the United States, in which health has been largely replaced by beauty, resulting in a popularized, exoticized, and watered-down version of Āyurveda for the Western (or "Westernized") female consumer. But before I move on to these three strategies, I would like to comment briefly on Āyurvedic education in the United States and its two main models of operation, the "formal" and the "casual." I will close with a meditation on just how we might view "practices" such as Āyurveda and yoga as "commodities."

Āyurveda, Spa Culture, and American Medical Bricolage

There are several institutes in the United States that offer formal training and issue certificates in Āyurvedic medicine. These include places such as Vasant Lad's Ayurvedic Institute in Albuquerque, New Mexico,[2] and others like it in San Francisco, New York, and so on. Lad's institute, founded in 1984, provides a very interesting mélange of representations of Indian medicine. Not only are there formal courses offered in Āyurvedic "healing"—I have noted that the word "medicine" shows up in written materials fairly infrequently—but there are also offerings in "Vedic" astrology. The word "Vedic" is used in this context, as in many others, as a kind of brand name—an index, if you will—that simultaneously conjures up notions of antiquity and authority, no matter how false or misleading. The yoga department at Lad's institute also offers instruction in something termed Ayuryoga, an excellent neologistic example of the conflation of practices that I noted above, described on the institute's Web page as a "blending of Ayurveda Medicine and Yoga poses and pranayama." The institute has also chalked out for itself a niche in American spa culture by offering a package of *panchakarma* treatments that include "oil massage, herbal steam treatments, shirodhara, cleansing diet, herbal therapy, lifestyle education, and other therapies."

I was told by an informant, a participant in the Fifth International Congress on Traditional Asian Medicine in Halle, Germany, in August 2002, that Vasant Lad returned to India recently, reportedly in disgust, because of his frustrations with the United States Food and Drug Administration. In fact, the FDA is probably more complicit in the Āyurvedic cosmetics phenomenon than good old American or Indian entrepreneurial spirit. During a recent visit to the FDA Web page,[3] I found warning letters, consumer advisories, and refusal reports issued for many Āyurvedic products manufactured in India proper, including pills and needles but mainly herbs and other medicinal foodstuffs. It is likely that this sort of constant watchdogging by the U.S. government has led to the import and/or the stateside manufacture of noninvasive, nonconsumable "for external use only" items that would fall under the cosmetic category—soaps, shampoos, make-up, lotions, skin-care items, and so on.

The second model of instruction is much less formal. For instance, in the *Informal Classes* catalog issued in the summer of 2002 by the Texas Union at the University of Texas at Austin, sandwiched between "Couple Massage I" and "Essence of Essential Oils" is a class titled "Ayurveda—Intro." Again, the Ayuryoga conflation appears in an excerpt from the course description, which reads, "Ayurveda, or the Indian Science of Life, is a whole health approach popularized by Dr. Deepak Chopra [yet another brand name] that works to correct systemic imbalances through nutrition and yogic practices. . . . In class, we will determine our own prakriti . . . and learn how to use food seasonally to balance our beings. You will receive guidelines for diet and exercise geared to your own body type, designed to help you achieve systemic balance and a greater sense of physical and emotional well-being."[4] I signed up for this class in the summer of 2002 for fieldwork purposes, but it was canceled due to low enrollment. In both models—the formal institute setting as well as the more casual settings of extension courses—medicine meets and is transformed into wellness, in the brave new world of option and alternative.

Textual Misrepresentations

But what about classical textual bases for contemporary practices? This is where I want to position my first strategy in terms of flows and circuits of transmission. I would like to say at the outset that I do not view medical texts in Sanskrit—or any knowledge system from India or anywhere else, for that matter—as static, originary, or even, I might add, "indigenous." I hold to the firm belief that there is no thing in the world that we can call "indigenous," though we might call many things "indigenized." The classical texts of Sanskrit Āyurveda are no exception to the rule, but have most definitely undergone a process of indigenization that have led them to their current forms as "foundational" texts, and that have also led them to be used to further all kinds of political and nationalist agendas. There are two main ways in which Indian translators of the early medical *saṃhitās* have presented these texts to the English-speaking world. The main strategy is that of skewing the texts in such a way that they align more comfortably with Western notions of "the scientific."[5] This appears most radically in terms of the measurement of substances. In most translations of the *Caraka Saṃhitā*, for instance, amounts of herbs, oils, milk, meats, and other substances used in treatment are relayed to English readers in terms of grams, liters, and the like, while in the Sanskrit of the original text, one sees terms that have rough equivalents in meaning to "handfuls," "gobs," "pinches," and even "die-shaped plugs" of the substances used in formulating treatment, leading to a view of a system that is intuitive, infinitely adjustable according to conditions of patient and substance alike, and by no means "fixed" in terms of exact quantity, but descriptive in its own terms, and very useful as well, when it comes to issues such as judging proportions, or so one would imagine.

In the realms of female anatomy and treatments for gynecological and obstetrical difficulties, there are a number of strategies used by these first translators to knock these texts into alignment with Western knowledge and expectations. One is that of total elision; the other is a strategy similar to the one I just described regarding systems of measurement. When it comes to certain items that are simply left out of English versions, an early translator of the *Suśruta Saṃhitā*, is the guiltiest party. Kaviraj Kunjalal Bhishagratna published a quite readable version of the text in the early 1900s. He had a tendency to leave out long passages of text that have to do with what might seem more "imaginary" or "fanciful" to Western eyes than other items of information. For example, in discussing the issue of breast milk, the authors of the text describe milk production in a woman's body as being analogous to that of semen in a man's. This analogy is drawn out at quite some length. According to the *Suśruta Saṃhitā*, both substances have their own occult circulatory systems in the body, and both respond to the same sorts of stimuli in terms of concentration and emission—a man ejaculates from the stimulus provided by a beautiful woman; a woman emits milk when she sees a beautiful child.

The passage in question occurs in an early section of the *Suśruta Saṃ hitā*, the *nidāna-sthānam*, or "section on pathology," where the author(s) are discussing *stana-roga*, or "diseases of the breast." The following is my own translation of the section, found at 10.19–21:

Just as semen is not seen even in limbs that have been cut up, and due to the fact that it permeates the entire body, it (breast milk) is said to be analogous to semen. And, just as semen is emitted at the sight of a desirable young girl, or at the memory of her, or from listening to her words, or at her touch, or because of sexual excitement, and, since the cause of sexual excitement is said to be a pellucid heart, so do women thus emit milk, because it has its origin in the essence of food.

Perhaps out of a sense of what Bhishagratna may have had of Western propriety or prudery, he collapses this very interesting and elaborate passage in its entirety into one romanticized English paragraph on milk production and mother love (Bhishagratna 1963: 70–71), leaving the clearly drawn erotic analogies largely up to his readers.

Then there is the question of the egg. When I first began casually looking at Āyurvedic texts, I noticed immediately that all available English translations of both *saṃhitā*s at the time were using this word "egg," or "ovum," "ova," or "ovae," the latter Latinized usage appearing in Bhishagratna's translation of the *Suśruta Saṃhitā*. "How can this be?" I asked myself, since I knew that eggs in female humans were not discovered until quite late in the history of medicine, in the mid-1800s. And sure enough, the words that were being translated as "egg" were all terms for menstrual blood: *śonita*, *ārtava*, and the like. What is more, one cannot comprehend classical understandings of embryology, sex determination, or even bigger issues of selfhood and sexual orientation that these texts provide for us with such elegance and fluidity unless one understands that, medically speaking, all these elemental concepts are driven by notions of how the substances of blood and semen mix and mingle in a woman's womb. Substituting an "egg" for a measure of "blood" does not unlock the imagination that it takes to comprehend the dynamics of sex and conception, no matter how "unscientific" or "backward" that blood might seem.

There are other misconstruances as well. Consider stretch marks, for instance. In its passages that describe the female form during late gestation, the *Caraka Saṃhitā* describes striations on the skin of a woman's belly that in some instances cause itching. The texts employ a word that, when you run to any standard Sanskrit dictionary to look it up, is defined as some sort of subcutaneous worm, and "worm" is how these "striations" are translated. A quick trip to the enlightened Sanskrit commentator Cakrapāṇidatta tells us that "worm" is a metaphorical usage employed to describe the fissures that appear on a woman's skin as her belly stretches and grows during pregnancy.

What is perhaps the most disturbing, though, is the way Europeans and Americans have adapted the basics of Āyurveda to formulate "wellness" regimes for women that totally elide patriarchal and hierarchical—even misogynist—elements that are shot throughout these texts. I now turn to my second strategy, that of the representation of Āyurvedic notions by contemporary Euro-American authors and gurus who write for a female audience and offer treatments to their female patients.

The first text that I would like to offer up for analysis is *Āyurvedic Healing for Women: Herbal Gynecology*, written by one "Atreya" (also the name of the putative "author" of the second-century *Caraka Saṃhitā* and first published in the United States in 1999 by Samuel Weiser ("Atreya" 1999). According to the biographical information printed on the book's back cover, Atreya hails from Southern California. He studied "meditation, pranic healing, Ayurveda, and yogic psychology" in India for six years, and now resides in France, where he "practices Ayurveda and pranic healing . . . he is also the author of *Prana: The Secrets of Yogic Healing* (Weiser 1996) and *Practical Ayurveda: Secrets for Physical, Sexual and Spiritual Health* (Weiser 1998)." The cover of the book visually reflects many of the paradoxes and conflicts that much of the remainder of this paper will explore. An emaciated woman, sporting a jog bra and a pair of Lycra shorts, is seated in a meditative posture next to a voluptuous *yakṣī*, encapsulating a stunning contrast in cultural attitudes toward feminine physical "perfection."

The contents of the book itself fit into the "self-help" genre that has become a major component of the contemporary trade publishing industry, and rather than address issues of "gynecology" and "obstetrics" head-on, Atreya takes us through rhapsodic romantic visions of what the world would be like if women never had menstrual cramps. The inside front cover of the book promises us instructions on "how to use dietary changes and herbal supplements to treat PMS, mitigate premenopausal symptoms, prevent osteoporosis, and reverse many other ailments." Of particular interest to me are chapter 2, "You as an Individual Woman," and appendix 2, "Pregnancy and Childbirth According to Ayurveda." Atreya takes us through the humoral system upon which classical Āyurveda is based, explaining the three humors, or *doṣa*s, in relation to a woman's body type and, interestingly, her menstrual flow.

There are indeed chapters in the classical texts which provide us with such descriptions, and Atreya is not terribly far off the mark here, but what is fascinating about these descriptions is that they focus on complexion, hair quality, how well the skin tans, and relative fatness or thinness, followed by descriptions of menstrual difficulties for women of each type. The types are *vāta* (the "windy" woman), *pitta* (the "bilious" woman), and *kapha* (the "phlegmatic" woman). The *vāta* category is the least healthy in this taxonomical system; the *kapha* person is constitutionally the strongest. And what is fascinating to me is that the voluptuous *yakṣī* on the book's cover is of the *kapha* body type, round and glossy, while the Lycra-bedecked *yoginī* seated by her side is of the *vāta* body type, painfully thin, slight of frame, and extremely bony. In his appendix on childbirth, Atreya authoritatively states, "This subject is worth a book in itself." Why was I under the impression that this was somehow what the book was mainly going to be about when I bought it? He continues, "In fact, the main text of ancient Ayurveda, the *Caraka Samhita*, spends about one-fourth of its many hundreds of pages just on women's health pertaining to childbirth." A factual error, to be sure, in that the text covers this information in very dense narrative form that ranges over only a few chapters among hundreds on unrelated topics. But what probably bothers me the most about this particular section is that he represents hatha yoga as being a practice essential to a healthy pregnancy, when the Sanskrit texts themselves are quite divorced from such practices—in the classical world, these two lines of thought about the care of the body were quite separate and rarely, if ever, interacted.

Throughout his text, Atreya claims that ancient Āyurveda was a system that affirmed women and held the female body in rather high esteem, when the Sanskrit texts themselves hold that very body in such esteem only as a vessel for the production of sons, or as a useful aphrodisiac, and little else. There is no hint in our modern-day Atreya's book of how this medicine might have been actually practiced "on the ground" in the classical period, when, for instance, a caesarian section would only be performed, except in rare circumstances, after the woman had died in the throes of a difficult delivery but still had a viable fetus inside her. What is more, where questions of difficult menstruation, miscarriage, and difficult but not life-threatening labor are concerned, the "clinical voice" of the physician defers as a last resort to the "experiential voice" of a class of women labeled in the texts as the *āptā-striyah*, or "accomplished women," as I've come to think of them: elderly, multiparous women who have not outlived their husbands, and whose voices are largely elided in Atreya's representation of Āyurveda.

On Yoga, Beauty, and Wellness

In regard to yoga, there are two texts that I would like to examine briefly. The first is a yoga classic—I have had it on my shelf since my high school days—*Richard Hittleman's Yoga: 28 Day Exercise Plan* (Hittleman 1988). It was first published in 1969, and, riding the wave of the 1960s mystical craze that swept the United States, had undergone 23 printings through 1988. Though Hittleman's book does not mention Āyurveda per se, it does herald the fitness movement in the U.S. by promising "astonishing results—loss of weight, greater firmness, more energy, relief from pain, freedom from stress and an overall feeling of youthfulness and well-being," all in just 28 days! My favorite chapters include "Beauty Through Poise and Balance," "The Beautiful Woman" (this chapter concludes, by the way, with this promise: "Because she has found herself, she is able to give of her beauty—to her friends, family and husband and it is in this giving that true fulfillment is realized"; 210) and, best of all, "Yoga and the Housewife." In this section, Hittleman writes, "Work, according to the Bhagavad-Gita, is a great privilege and through it inner growth and development are achieved. If the housewife does not experience such satisfaction from her work, if housework is continual drudgery and without meaning, she becomes irritable, frustrated and depressed and these feelings are passed on to other members of the family. This morbid situation prevails in many homes and makes for very unhappy living" (153–54). Hittleman recommends "making a ballet" out of sweeping and cleaning, adding that "you will be surprised at how quickly your body assumes added grace and beauty and at how quickly this is noticed by your family and friends" (154).

This appropriation of yoga by American fitness gurus has led to some interesting conversations with many of my Indian friends in Austin. My friend "Pārvatī," a recent immigrant from Tamilnadu, told me one day over lunch that she was very bored. I asked her if there was anything that she'd like to try, and she said, "Well, I'd like to take a yoga class, but I've noticed that in America (lapsing into Tamil), *yoga uṭampukku tāṉ irrukkum. Uṭampum manasum tani-taniyāka ille*" ("In America, yoga is only for the body, but the body and the mind are not separate things").

A latter-day version of Hittleman is a beautifully produced German guidebook, *Im Einklang mit dem inneren Mond: 28-Tage-Yoga für Frauen* ("In Harmony with the Inner Moon: 28-Day Yoga for Women"), by Reinhard Bögle (2000). Obviously based on Hittleman's scheme, Bögle promises "beauty and health," but also something a bit more "feminist" in its orientation: "A power program for women—simple, but intense." His poetic title also suggests attunement with a woman's inner biological cycles that wax and wane with lunar phases, implicit in Hittleman's earlier title, but here made explicit by Bögle.

Āyurveda as Brand

Returning to the issue of the "branding" of Āyurveda as a lucrative marketing strategy for American women consumers, I would now like to explore a world in which classical Āyurvedic ideals are entirely inverted. Do keep in mind my description of the paradoxical cover of Atreya's book, as it will serve as an excellent illustration. We are about to go where academic angels fear to tread, the world of the American supermodel, Christy Turlington's world, specifically. Her cosmetics line, "Sundāri" (never mind the misspelling), is based on the tri-humoral system of Āyurveda. On her beautifully designed Web site,[6] Turlington explains to us that

In Sanskrit, Sundāri translates as "beautiful woman." Today, it also represents a system of natural Ayurvedic skin care suited to meet the needs contemporary women face in developing their individual inner and outer expressions of beauty. . . . Ayurveda teaches that the balancing of mind, body and spirit will ultimately lead to peace, harmony and lasting beauty. Together these women [Turlington and her partners] have reinterpreted this exotic yet practical Indian philosophy and developed the foundation for the ever-evolving Sundāri brand. At Sundāri beauty is being well, a natural vitality inspired by balance, a radiance that shines from the inside out. Fused from Eastern and Western beauty practices, our philosophy empowers women to embody beauty and discover their own inherent balance. To embody beauty is a creative process, an active quest towards a deeper understanding of ourselves and the world we live in. Sundāri invites you to join us in this universal quest.

Here is Turlington's own representation of Āyurveda from her Web site's FAQ page:

Historical evidence has traced the origin of Ayurveda back to ancient times pre-dating religion when only the wisest of men would congregate on the slopes of the Himalayas in hopes of gaining knowledge of the science of Ayurveda from Indra, Lord of the Immortals who is said to have learned the invaluable science from the physicians of the gods. Thousands of years later the Western world is just beginning to embrace the truth and effectiveness of holistic Eastern philosophies and as ambassadors of this movement, Ayla, Cavan [her two partners] and Christy created Sundāri to share these beauty secrets with the rest of the world. Ayurveda enforces the conviction that every living organism has a natural and unique proportion of universal elements: Air, Space, Water, Fire and Earth. Ayurveda proposes that there are three governing forces called *Doshas*, made up of these elements, at work in each of us at all times to create our constitutions. Regardless of skin type, balanced Doshas are exemplified through smooth, clear, beautiful and radiant skin. Sundāri products were founded on this principle and reveal that one's skin is a direct reflection of their inner state of being. The emphasis for a Sundāri is on inner beauty first and foremost.

On the Web site itself, one can determine one's own skin type by navigating through a series of questions to figure out which products to buy—figuring out whether you have *vāta*, *pitta*, or *kapha* skin determines which range of products is right for you. Anita Roddick of Body Shop fame also sells the Ayurvedic brand name with a line of body-oil mists that are geared toward one's own humoral tendencies, available only in her UK and European stores, interestingly enough.[7]

But the specter that keeps looming over all this material is, as I've mentioned, the total inversion of the Āyurvedic ideal of the *kapha* body type, the well-padded, sturdy woman with glossy skin and excellent constitution. What is held up for us instead, in the postmodern world of the supermodel where the long, thin, emaciated, bony frame is the aesthetic ideal, is, as one Web site I visited puts it, "the *vāta* babe." The *vāta* babe extraordinaire? Cameron Diaz, just in case you were wondering, according to one of the many sites I surfed. Oprah Winfrey is our *kapha* heroine and Fergie our *pitta* beauty. One Web site prescribes different brands of nail polish with lists of colors according to the consumer's humoral tendencies.

There are many more questions to ask (and many more product lines to explore), but what I hope I have demonstrated above is a fascinating phenomenon of the Euro-American marketplace, the endpoint, at least for now, in the mutating *paramparas* of the transmission of several Sanskrit knowledge systems, in a glittering world of celebrity appropriations, erasures, and elisions of old hierarchies replaced by new and perhaps more sinister paradigms of postmodern body images, where looks trump wellness and medicine, and where beauty, now more than ever before, seems to know no pain.

Conclusion: "Eastern" Practices as "Western" Commodities

Can we really think of bodily practices such as Āyurveda and yoga as commodities, as "goods"—"circulating things"? The current demand for these practices in Euro-American contexts seems driven by a New Age Orientalist desire for esoteric Eastern knowledge.[8] Items "for sale" are purity, wellness, and enlightenment. These are abstract concepts, to be sure, but the very vagueness of these principles is what has, in fact, led to the development of very diversified and lucrative market strategies. In Arjun Appadurai's incisive and very influential introduction to his edited volume, *The Social Life of Things: Commodities in Cultural Perspective*, he describes "regimes of value" in which "specific things (or groups of things) . . . circulate in specific cultural and historical milieus" (Appadurai 1986: 4). There are ways in which the practices in question fit in, at least partially, with standard definitions of what commodities are. These practices are, in Appadurai's own words, certainly "thoroughly socialized things" (1986: 6), and if we can for a moment imagine these practices as objects, they partially fit the classical Marxian definition of commodity as well. These practices are "outside us;" they are things that by their properties satisfy "human wants of some sort or other" (quoted in 1986: 7).

But there are other useful and perhaps more fruitful modes by which we can visualize and understand Āyurveda and yoga as commodities. The easy way out is to label these practices as "services" and call it a day; the New Age consumer plunks down her money and purchases an hour's worth of carefully constructed and packaged tranquility; or, outraged or made suspicious by western biomedicine, she exercises her rights as a free-market medical consumer and chooses a round of *panchakarma* treatments; or, if well-heeled, she hops on a plane to India and indulges herself in what Jean Langford has so aptly labeled "medical tourism."[9] I use the feminine pronoun here with great purpose: the New Age consumer is by and large female, to such a degree that a cartoon in the *New Yorker* depicts a man surrounded by women in a yoga class. All the participants have assumed the *adhomukhaśvanāsana* or "downward-facing dog" posture, in which the body is bent over in a wedge with palms flat on the floor, forming a triangle with the buttocks at the highest point. A woman next to the male participant turns to him and comments, "You do yoga like a guy."[10]

Too, if we think of these practices in terms of their social contexts, then viewing practice as commodity becomes a bit easier. I have already referred to Āyurvedic spa culture, which is more marginalized and not as accessible in the United States as is the now ubiquitous culture of the yoga studio. In thinking about the mainstreaming of yoga in this country in the past few years, it is quite easy to see just how yoga has become a viable, buyable product, and how malleable it is in terms of location and consumer trends. To give a sample of yoga alternatives available in Austin, Texas, the local center where one can enroll in classes in Bikram Yoga (the now copyrighted and controversial "hot box" practice) is named Yoga Vida, mixing "East" with the American "Southwest" in a rather curious way. In an attempt to appeal to the funkier customer in Austin alternative society, there is another studio in town called Yogagroove. But the most prominent space to purchase this practice in Austin is the strip mall. In Austin, I have yet to see a yoga studio in a mainstream megamall, but these studios are quietly proliferating in spaces constructed by the tastemakers of alternative America. Its ubiquity emphasized in its name, the Yoga Yoga chain of studios in Austin (there are now three altogether) seems to have developed its marketing strategies along the same lines as Whole Foods Market, Whole Earth Provisions Company, and other trendy "alternative but not quite" businesses, some of which sell lines of Āyurvedic cosmetics in their aisles along with organic foods, thereby maintaining a hazy consumer ambience of progressive, alternative "choice."

The Yoga Yoga studios provide their "products" to their customers much in the same way as might a school of dance. The client can purchase an individual class for $15 or buy different configurations of tickets that offer "packages" at a slight discount. And, just as at a dance school where one might choose a class in ballet, jazz, or tap, at Yoga Yoga one can choose classes in any of yoga's several varieties: *hatha, aṣṭāṅga, kuṇḍalinī,* and so on. Most instructors are female, and tend to follow two models of instruction: the first mimics the quasi-mysticism of the traditional Indian guru/student relationship; the second seems more like a standard course in physical education, wherein various postures and stretches are carefully explained to students in kinesthetic terms.

As seems to be the case in other realms of exercise-conscious America, clients at Yoga Yoga are also encouraged to purchase all sorts of gear. There are CDs, cassettes, and all sorts of books (cookbooks and books on Āyurveda and on yoga) available for purchase, and yoga "sticky mats" available for rent and purchase in trendy colors (my own teal-blue sticky mat is the Tapas Ultra model). Consumers can also buy silk bags made out of Indian saris that perfectly fit their mats. It seems, in fact, that these "ideas" and "practices" from the East have been spun in a centrifuge, and yoga and Āyurveda precipitate into tangible products. In Igor Kopytoff's words, this is a part of the process of material production that moves a concept or a practice into the realm of a distinct, culturally-marked "thing" (Kopytoff 1986: 64). The practices themselves are "commoditized," but the byproducts of these practices are what circulate most noticeably in alternative consumer spaces.

We can also note the proliferation of yoga gear in any number of catalogs, and in those that specialize in feminine attire, especially. In the summer 2002 Gaiam Living Arts catalog, for instance, one could purchase CDs and videotapes with titles such as "Yoga for Abs" and "The Secrets of Sacred Sex," and. in a featured advertisement on the catalog's back cover, a "free cotton golf towel, biodegradable eco golf tees, golf balls, and organic cotton golf cap" were all available with the purchase of a "Yoga for Longevity Kit" priced at $73.00.[11] Perhaps this can serve to emphasize just how mainstream yoga has become, since we now seem to be inhabiting a world in which Ben Crenshaw and Tiger Woods can comfortably rub shoulders with Bikram Choudhury or T. K. V. Desikacar. In the land of merchandising, everything gains an equivalence, and all combinations seem infinitely possible.

Chapter 9
China Reconstructs: Cosmetic Surgery and Nationalism in the Reform Era

SUSAN BROWNELL

Biomedicine as a Transnational "Empty Frame"

Most of the contributions to this volume trace the paths followed by local medical practices as they travel across national, regional, and other boundaries. This chapter, however, traces a reverse direction of travel: it describes the transnational development of the field of cosmetic surgery and how it was appropriated into local, everyday practices in China. In this chapter, I take some of the conventional thinking about transnationalism and add to it a distinctly anthropological twist—in the form of insights from anthropologists Victor Turner and John MacAloon—which, I believe, creates a better framework for inquiry into the meaning-making processes that go along with transnational practice. I illustrate the advantages of this conceptual framework by describing how, from the 1980s onward, the transnational practices of cosmetic surgery were adopted in China both by cosmetic surgeons, who linked their skills with assertions of patriotic nationalism, and by patients, whose desires created a market for cosmetic procedures—most notably eyelid surgery—linked to meanings of (racialized) national identity.

Transnationalism is understood to refer to "processes which transcend the state-society unit and can therefore be held to occur on a trans-national or trans-societal level" (Featherstone 1990: 1). Ulf Hannerz observes that transnational cultures today tend to be more or less clear-cut occupational cultures tied to transnational job markets. He states that a particularly important occupational class is that of intellectuals, whose profession has a built-in affinity with transnationalism because they trade in a decontextualized knowledge that can be shifted to different local settings (1990: 27). The general label for this kind of decontexualized knowledge is "science," and biomedicine is one of its subfields. Of course, scientific knowledge is often stamped with the character of Western culture, but it is at least decontexualized enough to operate in non-Western settings. Biomedical practitioners constitute a rather clear-cut transnational occupational class that is knit together by relationships formed through international medical associations, international conferences, medical and educational institutions, international journals, international exchanges, personal friendships, and a host of other practices.

Because of their "trans-societal" nature, transnational communities of medical specialists are in a position to act as mediating "bridgeheads" (Hannerz 1990: 245) to influence directions of social change within the local, territorialized cultures between which they travel. Victor Turner considered "pure scientific research" to possess "liminal" qualities, along with sports, fine arts, literature, and many other activities (1974: 16; 1982: 86). Turner hints that, like the other "liminoid genres," modern scientific research is a "liminal," in-between activity set apart from the normative social structure and mundane everyday practice.[1] As such, it has the potential to bring new social forms into existence because it provides participating members opportunities to experience moments of detachment from everyday life when they can reflect upon their own norms and customs:

> those genres which have flourished since the Industrial Revolution (the modern arts and sciences), though less serious in the eyes of the commonality (pure research, entertainment, interests of the elite), have had greater potential [than preindustrial genres] for changing the ways men relate to one another and the content of their relationships. Their influence has been more insidious. Because they are outside the arenas of direct industrial production, because they constitute the "liminoid" analogues of liminal processes and phenomena in tribal and early agrarian societies, their very outsiderhood disengages them from direct functional action on the minds and behavior of a society's members. (Turner 1974: 16)

Turner's processual perspective emphasized that human social life ebbs and flows between hierarchical processes that distinguish human beings and set them apart from each other (*societas*) and liminal processes that create a sense of bond and union between them (*communitas*). This social ebb and flow can also be seen in the relationship between nationalism and transnationalism: John MacAloon, a student of Turner, has observed that since the eighteenth century, the nation-state has emerged as the most important segmentary unit of modern political organization, but "simultaneously with these modern principles of segmentation, institutions appeared which seek to constitute an international and even transnational identity of humankind" (1992: 12). Science is one of these institutions of transnational identity-making because it "carries a weight of authority recognizable, if not always recognized, by all persons in some places and some persons in all places throughout the world. . . . It is unquestionable that modern science is ideologically and practically engaged in the production of trans-personal, trans-national, and pan-human identities " (1992: 12).

MacAloon has developed the notion of the "empty form" to conceptualize the relationship between nationalist and transnationalist processes in international sports. It hardly requires mention that the world of international sports is characterized by intense national rivalries; we expect it, and we believe that such rivalries compel the world's athletes to achieve greater and greater performances. At first glance, it might seem unusual to assert that the world of international medicine is similar in its rivalries and in the fact that competition drives elite surgeons to achieve increasingly amazing results. Nonetheless, in plastic and cosmetic surgery there is a great deal of competition to establish "firsts" and claim superiority, and the most salient political units in this competition are nations. Thus, the transnational and national structures of international sports can shed some light on the transnational and national structures of international medicine. What sports and Western biomedicine have in common is that they are both forms of social and bodily practice that came into existence in the modern era, largely tracing their roots to the West, with major administrative centers that are still largely headquartered in the West; but in the last century and a half they have spread with remarkable rapidity around the globe, penetrating grassroots social life almost everywhere to some degree. This makes them both exemplary models of *transnational* body practices.

One reason that they have spread so wide and far is that they are very malleable in the meanings that can be attached to them and the uses to which they can be put. "As pure, that is purely empty forms for the constitution of intercultural spaces, they present themselves to the human groups interconnected by them for refilling with diverse cultural meanings" (1995a: 234). While at one level the repertoire of body techniques they involve would seem rather fixed and limiting, at another level the international communities and bureaucracies that form around them offer countless opportunities for multicultural interactions and the heated exchange of different viewpoints (for example, at the level of the World Health Organization or the International Olympic Committee). The forms of the practices may be dictated by transnational organizations, and may be transmitted across national boundaries by communities of transnational elites (often trained in the West), but the *meanings* assigned to them are often very nationalistic (MacAloon 1995b: 33–34). The usefulness of the notion of the "empty form" is that it helps explain how these phenomena can be both *transnational* and *national* at the same time.

While it calls up a useful mental image, the concept of the "empty form" is unsatisfactory because it creates an artificial distinction between form and content, making it seem theoretically possible that sport and scientific practices can be *completely* emptied of their original local (in this case Western) cultural content in a mechanistic process not unlike turning a bottle upside down to spill out its contents before refilling it.[2] This image does not do justice to the intense conflicts, cross-cultural negotiations, and even personal suffering that have historically accompanied the spread of transnational cultural forms. As will be discussed, when transnational cosmetic surgery arrived in China, it was never a completely "empty" form awaiting refilling with local meanings. Because of its identification with "bourgeois" vanity, its practitioners were attacked and denounced in socialist China from the 1950s until the 1980s. It was only the half-century-long period of accommodation to the West that allowed cosmetic surgery to finally flourish from the 1990s onward.

Adopting a slight shift in terminology, then, I will prefer the phrase "empty frame." This borrows Erving Goffman's notion of the "frame," which refers to the basic elements people use to organize experience by creating definitions of social events and their subjective involvement in them. A frame is the answer to the question, "What is it that's going on here?" (Goffman 1974: 10–11, 8) "Science"—scientific inquiry, research, and the worldview that is disseminated as the result of them—is one of the primary frameworks that people around the world now use, to greater or lesser degree, to organize large chunks of experience. Goffman's concept of the frame is useful because it emphasizes the situatedness of the meanings that are assigned to a given "strip" of experience: they are contingent, can be contested, change over time, are often defined by processes of social negotiation, can even, in retrospect, be "wrong." When applied to transnational biomedicine, the conception is useful because it reminds us that what Hannerz called "decontexualized knowledge" does not just suddenly emerge emptied of its local context, but rather is socially produced by communities of deterritorialized intellectuals seeking a common language with which to speak to one another. Entering into this community involves stripping oneself of one's local beliefs, or at least excluding such beliefs from the frame of scientific inquiry and discussion.

In the discussion that follows, I will begin by discussing the transnational origins of cosmetic surgery and the ideological struggles in China over its meaning. I will then discuss how three processes—the reinvention of history, insertion of new meaning, and mixing of forms—have contributed to the naturalization of cosmetic surgery as a Chinese practice. I will conclude with a discussion of how all of these issues have played out in a particular surgical technique, the double eyelid operation, illustrating that transnational cultural flows and geopolitics have repercussions at the level of minute, mundane body practices.

The Transnational History of Cosmetic Surgery

In 1942, during the Anti-Japanese War, several soldiers with lower jaw injuries were sent to the Dental Institute at the Western Chinese Medical University in Chengdu; as described by one of the students there, Song Ruyao, "everyone just stared blankly at these anti-Japanese soldiers with malformed faces, unable to speak, unable to eat, suffering psychological and biological agony."[3] At the same time, a pilot with burns on his face and both hands was sent to an associated hospital, and the doctors—who were among the best in China—were unable to treat him. He was sent to the United States, where he underwent over a year of treatment at a cost of over U.S.$100,000. When he returned, skin grafts had been done on his hands, but the scars on his face had not yet been dealt with. Realizing that it could not afford to send every untreatable wounded soldier to the U.S., the Nationalist government decided to send someone there to study plastic and reconstructive surgery, so that he could return to China and establish the discipline. Song Ruyao was selected (1987: 241). In 1943 he was sent to the University of Pennsylvania Medical School to study under famed plastic surgeon Robert H. Ivy. Like most classic plastic surgeons, Ivy did not perform cosmetic surgery and held it in contempt. However, other surgeons did perform it (the most common operation was the "nose job," or rhinoplasty) and Song learned the techniques. In 1948 he received his Doctor of Science there, and returned to Chengdu, where he got his Doctor of Dentistry (D.D.S.), and Doctor of Medicine (M.D.) degrees in 1951. He became China's first professor of plastic surgery, and China became the first Asian nation to have a full professor and offer a course in plastic and reconstructive surgery (Song 1987: 241). However, he had returned after the defeat of Japan in the war, just as the Nationalists were preparing to retreat to Taiwan and leave the mainland to the Communists. The Nationalist government gave no support to his work, and he seldom had patients.

In 1948, three other Chinese students also studied plastic and reconstructive surgery for a month in Shanghai under another well-known U.S. surgeon.

Song Ruyao's idle period did not last long. In 1949, the People's Republic of China was established, and in 1950 the Korean War broke out. Song observed that, "Except for not using the atomic bomb, the U.S. military used every kind of modernized weapon" (Song 1987: 242). He spent 1951–56 treating Chinese soldiers wounded on the frontline.

"I, this doctor who had studied plastic surgery in America, was from 1951 to 1956 treating nonstop the injuries produced by the American army. You ask, is this a bit of *Mockery*?" (Song 2001) ("mockery" was written in English while the rest was translated from the Chinese by me).

Historically, the techniques of cosmetic surgery have arisen out of plastic and reconstructive surgery, which mainly developed in response to the terrible wounds of modern warfare, beginning with World War I. There is a bit of gendered irony here, in that techniques invented to repair the bodies of men wounded in war were modified in peacetime to serve the pursuit of beauty by women. In the West, cosmetic surgery has been regarded as the bastard child of plastic and reconstructive surgery, held in contempt by "real" surgeons who believe they are fixing "real" problems, not psychological ones. The relationship between plastic and cosmetic surgery has always been conflicted, even though the basic principles (tissue grafting and implants) are the same, and the line between them is often not clear: is reconstructive mammoplasty after mastectomy for breast cancer merely a "vanity"? Does it substantively differ from skin grafting to repair scar tissue from a napalm burn?.

The great impetus for the development of plastic surgery was the need to repair the damage done to the body by the techniques of modern warfare. Nothing else mutilates human bodies to a degree and scale similar to that of war. But the impetus for cosmetic surgery did not come just from the plastic surgery techniques developed in wartime; it also required the production of a desire for those techniques. And it appears that war also created this desire, both in the West and in Asia. After World War II, Asians began asking for eyelid surgery and nose implants in large numbers, first in Asia, then in the U.S. (Haiken 1997: 200). Postwar Japan seems to have been the originating point for the popularization of cosmetic surgery in East Asia. In 1957, the one-day record of Jujin Hospital of Cosmetic Surgery in Japan was 1,380 double eyelid operations. In the 1960s, Tokyo clinics gave double eyelids to 200,000 women each year (Haiken 1997: 203). Liquid silicone was probably first used in breasts in Japan around the time of the war. A commonly used formula was developed in Japan in 1954, but did not become common in the U.S. until the mid-1960s (Haiken 1997: 243). The Korean War stimulated the growth of cosmetic surgery in Korea and among Korean Americans. One U.S. surgeon recalled his first Asian patient as a Korean war bride who, in the early 1950s, asked to have her eyelids and nose done because her husband was ashamed of her. Another was barraged by requests while stationed in Korea in early 1954. Finding that little had been published, he designed his own techniques and reported them in a journal in 1955 (Haiken 1997: 201). During the Vietnam War, more Vietnamese women sought cosmetic surgery. Surgeons noted that many

were bar girls who wanted to attract American GIs. The GIs had introduced *Playboy* pin-up girls into Vietnam, which influenced the bar girls'
ideals. Other women wanted to attract American husbands or jobs
(Haiken 1997: 204).

After his return to China in 1948, Song performed a few cosmetic eyelid operations for people who had heard of wonderful American cosmetic surgery techniques, but requests were rare. While he did not
perform cosmetic surgery during the Korean War, Song writes that "the
spirit of beauty (*meirong*) was present in my medicine and teaching from
start to finish" (Song 2001). He realized that the line between plastic
and cosmetic surgery was not so clear while treating the soldiers
wounded in the Korean War: "Through my actual work, I came to
understand: the vast majority of soldiers fighting wars on behalf of a just
cause do not fear death, but they fear being wounded, having a malformed face, terrifying and sickening people wherever they go, living a
life in which they are alive but not completely alive, dead but not truly
dead! The pain and suffering in their innermost hearts moved me
deeply. I didn't perform cosmetic operations, but I tried my best to
restore their normal form" (Song 2001).

Function over Form: Cosmetic Surgery as a Contested Frame in China

When transnational cosmetic surgery arrived in China, its link with stereotypical bourgeois vanity was maintained. As political turmoil heated
up, plastic and cosmetic surgery were also politicized. The battle over
political ideology revolved around the notions of "form" (*xing*) versus
"function" (*gongneng*). As Song described it,

During the period of 1950–1953, when I was performing plastic surgery treatments on those wounded in the Korean war, the Chinese government repeatedly
instructed us: "Right now our nation is not yet wealthy; in treating the wounded,
emphasize the recovery of function [*gongnengde huifu*], and do not do cosmetic
surgery operations." Later, a few experts applied the concept of class struggle
even more, and said, "Emphasizing form is a capitalist style of treatment; a proletarian ought to emphasize the recovery of function." Thus the phrase "plastic
and reconstructive surgery" [*zhengfu waike*] appeared.

He explained further,

"*Plastic Surgery's "Plastic"* comes from the Greek *Plastikos,* meaning *Mold,* meaning it can be molded. The Chinese "plastic" [*zhengxing*] is not a translation of
the word but of the meaning: it means the repair [*xiuzheng*] of malformations
[*jixing*] due to combat injury, traumatic wound, burn, congenital developmental
abnormalities and surgical removal of tumors. The character for "form" [*xing*]
in plastic [*zhengxing*] surgery in the past has provoked some serious problems.

Traditionally medicine emphasized function [*gongneng*]. Plastic surgery pays attention to form [*xingtai*], which clearly departs from medical tradition. (Song 2001).[4]

In 1956 Song was sent to the USSR for half a year to visit hospitals in Moscow and Leningrad. There he learned from the Soviets how to perform limb reattachments on dogs; in 1963 his hospital performed the first human hand reattachment in China. In 1957 the government asked him to establish China's first plastic surgery hospital, and in its first two years he trained fifty students, many of whom later became professors themselves. However, in 1957 a political campaign was carried out in the world of medicine, preceding the better-known Anti-Rightist Campaign. This campaign, known as the "attack the seven white banners" campaign (*da qi baiqi*—so called because white is an inauspicious color in China)—targeted the seven most prominent medical doctors in China, one of whom was Song. Because of his youth, he endured the attacks better than many of the other targets, some of whom committed suicide.

Song and his wife, who was also a medical doctor, both endured repeated attacks during the Cultural Revolution (1966–76). In 1969, at the height of the Cultural Revolution, the Plastic Surgery Hospital personnel were sent to Jiangxi for labor reform. Plastic and cosmetic surgery were at a virtual standstill for the decade. Song's wife never recovered from the trauma of the Cultural Revolution period. Her back had been broken and she walked with a stoop. After ten years of enduring attack, she felt old and useless and had lost her desire to live. She died not long after the Cultural Revolution ended.

During the Cultural Revolution and into the late 1970s, Song's "aesthetic viewpoints" and style of work in plastic surgery were denounced as "bourgeois," and he was accused of emphasizing form over function. In the 1950s, he had always used the word for "plastic" (*zhengxing*) that contained the character for "form" (*xing*): he had used it in the name for his training hospital, and when he presided over the establishment of a scholarly association and a journal, he called the association the Chinese Plastic Surgery Association, and called the journal the *Chinese Plastic and Burn Surgery Journal*. As a result, he became militantly attached to the notion of "form," and after he was rehabilitated he stubbornly continued to use the Chinese phrase *zhengxing*, using it in the name of the Beijing Badachu Plastic Surgery Hospital that he was asked to establish in the 1990s.

The opposing attitude is evident in a textbook written in 1976 and published in 1979, in which the battle for the soul of plastic surgery is evident in the title: *Reconstructive Surgery* (*Zhengfu waike*) uses a different label from that chosen by Song, in this case consisting of the characters for "completion" (*zheng*) and "recovery" (*fu*). In this book the author notes,

Before Liberation, our nation's reconstructive surgery was a gap in learning. Although there were a few people doing a little work in plastic surgery, essentially they were only doing some cosmetic operations on a few people. After Liberation, under the guidance of the proletarian revolutionary line of Chairman Mao, a team of specialist corrective surgery was gradually established, and the work of corrective surgery began to develop. Now the main object of service of this specialty are the injured workers, soldiers, and peasants who were honorably wounded during the socialist revolution and the socialist reconstruction. (Wang 1979: 1)

He further comments,

In capitalist nations, they use "cosmetic surgery" to serve the capitalist class as the main content of the specialty, and pile up huge collections of essays in their magazines, books, and newspapers recording how to correct a nose, reshape a breast, remove wrinkles of the face, and other cosmetic procedures. However, in our socialist nation, we place our top priority on restoring the function of the disfigured or malformed tissues and organs of the injured workers, peasants and soldiers who were wounded in the line of duty in national defense, industry, and agriculture. Therefore, our corrective surgery is at the opposite end of the spectrum from that of capitalist nations, not only in the object of its service, but also in the content of its work.

In chapter 2, the author begins by arguing that corrective surgery must consider both function and form in combination, with function considered more important than form. "In this, we oppose carrying out cosmetic operations simply for the pursuit of external appearance, and we must criticize and resist the corrosive effects on our socialist endeavor of the capitalist class's 'cosmetic surgery'" (Zhang 1979: 4).

However, the attitude expressed in this book would soon be swept away by the changes initiated in the era of reform and opening-up (ca. 1978). The Plastic Surgery Hospital reopened in 1979, and Song immediately reestablished his international contacts. He met William Shaw, the Taiwanese-born chief of plastic surgery at UCLA Medical School, and they became good friends and visited frequently. Song and his second wife spent two years in the United States in the 1990s. Beginning in 1981, Song organized numerous Sino-U.S. plastic and cosmetic surgery exchanges and meetings. Experts from Japan, England, Australia, Canada, Poland, and other nations were invited to China to lecture and give training in procedures. At that time, medical textbooks in foreign languages, whether new or old, were very hard to acquire because they were too expensive. Also due to economic limitations, very few cosmetic surgeons were able to go abroad to study. In this time period, Song felt that the U.S. influence on the development of the field was the greatest, mainly through the channels of American medical journals and Sino-U.S. scholarly exchange conferences (Song 2001).

Coincidentally, China's reopening occurred at the same time that cosmetic surgery as a discipline began to officially recognize that the techniques that had been developed by largely white surgeons on largely white patients could not be applied wholesale to people of color. In July 1981, an international seminar on Cosmetic Plastic Surgery for the Nonwhite Patient was held in conjunction with the 87th annual convention of the National Medical Association (an association formed to serve African American physicians) in Atlanta, Georgia. It was the first of its kind in the world and was linked with the formal recognition by the NMA of the new Section on Cosmetic Plastic and Reconstructive Surgery (Pierce 1981: frontispiece). The proceedings, published as *Cosmetic Plastic Surgery in Nonwhite Patients*, were edited by Harold Pierce of Howard University Medical School. (The influence of an outdated anthropology of race can be seen in Pierce's chapter on "Ethnic Considerations," which begins with an overview of the concept of race that cites a 1950 publication, Coon, Garn, and Birdsell, *Races: A Study of the Problems of Race Formation in Man*).

More than many other medical subfields, cosmetic surgery presents a challenge to the universalist assumptions of biomedicine. On the one hand, concepts of beauty vary across cultures, and the kinds of surgeries that are sought vary by national and ethnic background. One clear example is eyelid surgery, which is commonly requested by East Asians and rarely sought by Europeans. Research on the anatomy of East Asian eyes revealed a different anatomical structure, which accounted for the different eye shape. Surgeons had to derive new techniques from existing techniques used on European eyelids to correct other problems (such as entropion, or inward-turning eyelashes). Bodies respond differently to surgery: for example, Asian noses can tolerate larger implants than European noses because of thicker skin on the nose, but excessive scarring is a greater problem for Asian skin. Human biology is universally similar enough to form the basis of transnational biomedical knowledge, but it is not universally the same.

In China in the 1980s, the "pursuit of beauty" was extolled as a backlash against the repression of the Cultural Revolution, and cosmetic surgery began to gain rapidly in popularity. By far the most popular operation was—and still is—the "double eyelid" operation (*chongjian chengxing shu*, or colloquial *shuangyanpi shoushu*), a relatively simple procedure in which a fold is added to the eyelid, transforming it from a stereotypical "single eyelid" Asian eye into a "double eyelid" eye, which is considered stereotypically European. I will return to this below.

This brief summary of the establishment of cosmetic surgery in China and the career of its founder, Song Ruyao, illustrates the importance of the transnational flow of medical techniques through study abroad, conferences, visiting experts, medical journals and textbooks, and personal friendships. These techniques developed and moved around the globe in response to movements of people and culture that preceded them: to use Arjun Appadurai's labels, cosmetic surgery moved along the terrain of the ethnoscape and technoscape (and was also conditioned by the finanscape and mediascape) of global culture (Appadurai 1990: 295–310).

In short, cosmetic surgery did not arrive in China completely "emptied" of its Western meanings. On the contrary, those particular meanings took on new significance in the global and domestic political context of the 1960s and 1970s. Cosmetic surgery was associated with the bourgeois pursuit of beauty then, and it still is. The difference is that within China the pursuit of beauty was formerly attacked and denounced, but after the end of Maoism it was glorified as a natural expression of human nature, of the personal freedom and individuality that had been suppressed under Mao. As of now, it does not yet appear that in China cosmetic surgery has become the symbol of artificial, decadent, and superficial beauty that one might think it is in the U.S., if one were to take the Hollywood comedians seriously. (However, its popularity in the U.S. puts the lie to that stereotype.)

This history illustrates the notion of the "empty frame." Cosmetic surgery was a kind of bodily practice constituted within definite social and political contexts, and these contexts shaped the meanings that were attached to the practices. When these practices were associated with nations perceived as enemies, they were denounced and viewed with exaggerated notions of threat, rather than being neutralized, naturalized, and accepted. Ultimately, the changing domestic and international political context led to their neutralization, naturalization, and acceptance in China from the 1980s onward. It is important to remember that this process occurred at the cost of great personal suffering by practitioners like Song Ruyao.

Nationalism in Chinese Cosmetic Surgery

Since 1978, cosmetic surgery has been reinvented and reinvested with new meanings in the Chinese context. As outlined by MacAloon, the three main channels through which previously Western forms come to be invested with diverse meanings are the appropriation of history, the naturalization of the practice, and the hybridization of forms (1995b: 3–4).

Appropriation of History

It is a stock feature of Chinese cosmetic surgery textbooks to include an introductory historical overview of the history of cosmetic surgery in China and the West, beginning with China. A typical entry begins, "Although Chinese traditional cosmetic medicine did not form into an autonomous disciplinary system, it still has a long history; it originated at almost the same time as Chinese medicine, developed in step with it, and established a good foundation for subsequent generations to develop cosmetic medicine, pharmaceutics, and procedures" (Liu 1997: 4). The history of cosmetic surgery in China is traced back as far as evidence for the use of rouge in the Shang dynasty.

Naturalization

The main way in which the Western origins of cosmetic surgery are neutralized, and its practices naturalized, is through claims that Chinese surgeons can best the West (and to a lesser degree, Japan and the other Asian Tigers) at its own game. Chinese cosmetic surgeons relate with a great deal of pride their stories about successfully correcting the mistakes made by other cosmetic surgeons. The pride is particularly great when the first surgeon was from one of the nations known for its advanced cosmetic surgery.

Despite the suffering that he endured at the hands of colleagues, former students, and Party officials for two decades, Song Ruyao still comes across as an ardent nationalist. When I asked in a questionnaire if he had learned his cosmetic surgery techniques in the U.S., he replied with sarcastic humor: "Naturally [after my return to China in 1948] I could teach students American rhinoplasty. But American rhinoplasty is used to reduce the height of the nose. Chinese people's noses are not very high, and if you were to carry out American rhinoplasty you would create a deformed saddle nose, so you couldn't call that a cosmetic procedure." He also related with some relish:

[One time a] famous foreign American plastic surgery professor demonstrated a blepharoplasty (eyelid surgery) procedure at my medical school (Beijing Badachu Plastic Surgery Medical School). Before the operation, many Chinese girls heard that this professor was charging 5,000–10,000 U.S. dollars to perform blepharoplasty in his own country, but now it was free, and they fought to be his patient. During the demonstration, the professor's operation was clean, dexterous, everything in the exemplary style of the great professor. The audience could not help but admire him! They didn't expect that after the swelling in the upper lids receded, the double eyelids slightly resembled deepset Western [*xiyang*] eyes, making her appear elderly! I gave her another operation and pulled down the subcutaneous tissue of her upper lids to pad underneath her double eyelids, but the sunken situation was not improved.

After establishing China's first plastic surgery hospital in 1957, Song Ruyao decided that "we should strive to create plastic surgery methods that suited the national conditions in China, or you might say, to create 'plastic surgery with Chinese characteristics'" (1987: 242–43). One of their main goals was to reduce the total number of surgeries necessary to carry out reconstructions. For example, at that time in England and the U.S., the reconstruction of a missing nose required three to four surgeries, and in the Soviet Union it required four or more. Reasoning that the Chinese population was much larger and the people missing noses more numerous, it was decided that the Chinese path should be to achieve reconstructions with fewer surgeries. In 1961, they successfully reconstructed a nose in a one-step procedure. Moreover, the reconstructed nose was comparable to the multiple-surgery nose in appearance and function, and was superior in the fact that it had sensation (Song 1987: 243).

Another cosmetic surgeon I interviewed, Zhang Shen, had been sought out by a Chinese singing star, Chen Lili, who had established a successful career in Tokyo, where she had also had botched eyelid surgery. After the surgery she wore dark glasses in public and was afraid to take the stage. When she went to the cosmetic surgery center at Xiehe Hospital, the older surgeons were afraid to take on her case for fear that failure would reflect badly on them. Zhang Shen was the youngest surgeon and had nothing to lose, so he studied her case for hours and decided on a procedure. He successfully corrected the scar tissue that made her hardly able to shut her eyes. Normally cosmetic surgery patients prefer to keep their operations secret, but Zhang Shen requested that she allow him to publish her story, and a photo of the two of them together, in a major newspaper, and out of gratitude she reluctantly agreed. The story appeared in Star News (Mingxing bao) (Jiang 1994).[5] Thus Zhang Shen was able to launch his career as a well-known cosmetic surgeon in Beijing whose skill was superior to Japanese surgeons; he became a frequent guest "expert" on radio talk shows.

MIXING OF TRADITIONAL CHINESE AND MODERN MEDICINE

Almost any Chinese medical textbook will contain the phrase "Our nation has both an ancient and time-honored ancestral medical tradition and a rich and varied modern medicine." The combination of Western and Chinese medicine has been a key principle of the Chinese medical system since the Communist takeover. In cosmetic surgery, the combination of Chinese and Western techniques is manifest in two different ways, which are nonetheless not clearly separated. The first is when traditional Chinese medical practices are used by cosmetic surgeons. For example, a traditional belief is that healing occurs more quickly when the weather is cool. In order to minimize scarring, many people prefer to have their surgeries done in the fall when the weather is cool, and to avoid surgery in the hot summer weather. The second way is when a surgeon who is a Chinese national comes up with an innovation that contributes to the development of the field, such as those described above. Although these might seem like different kinds of phenomena, they are both considered a blending of Chinese and Western medicine.

Another form of hybridization comes in the form of joint investments, which were one of the initial driving forces behind the development of cosmetic surgery centers in urban China in the 1990s. The Tongren Medical Cosmetic Center was opened in 1994 as a joint venture between the famous Tongren Hospital and a Singaporean food company. Next door to the cosmetic surgery center was a glasses/contact lens center that was a joint venture with a Japanese company. Government policy prevented foreign investments in hospitals, but it allowed these centers for two reasons: (1) cosmetic procedures existed in a gray realm between institutionalized medicine and commodified beauty salons, and (2) the state could not provide enough funds for modern facilities to meet the demand. In 1995, Zhang Shen complained that he felt the amount of work he had to put in was hardly worth it because he only had a monthly wage of 500 yuan and had to fulfill a quota of 30,000 yuan, after which he got 5 percent. He would frequently perform five operations in a day, but most of the profit went to the Singapore partner and the center. He wanted to open his own institute so he could make more money.

COSMETIC SURGERY AS A GLOBAL COMPETITION BETWEEN NATIONS

Finally, it is clear that this process of reinvestment of a transnational form with "authentic" Chinese meanings occurs in an atmosphere of international competition.

Song concluded his 1987 article on the history of plastic surgery in China by noting, "At this moment, as China's plastic surgery workers, our ancestral nation demands of us, the people demand of us, and the times also demand of us, that we cannot simply imitate English and American plastic surgery techniques without changing them; we must eliminate our weaknesses, work hard for national prosperity, develop research work that suits the national conditions, carry out reform, and create plastic surgery techniques with Chinese characteristics, in order to better serve the Chinese people" (Song 1987: 243).

Badachu Plastic Surgery Hospital occupies 20,000 square meters, with more than 300 beds and more than 100 doctors, and is currently the largest plastic surgery hospital in the world. Song concluded in his letter to me,

China's upsurge in cosmetic surgery was rather late. China has the world's largest population, and the numbers of people requesting beautification and the numbers of doctors performing cosmetic surgery occupy the top spot in the world. The accumulation of such huge amounts of experience could move Chinese cosmetic surgery into the ranks of the world's most advanced in the not too distant future, or even in some areas it could be that "the late starter takes the lead" [houlai jushang]. We will wait and see. (Song 2001).

The Double Eyelid Operation: From Transnationalism to Nationalism

Double eyelid surgery, the cosmetic surgical procedure that is currently most popular in China today, illustrates transnational processes at work. How popular is eyelid surgery? Surgeons have stated that it is the most common cosmetic surgery in the Far East, accounting for more than half of the total number of patients requesting cosmetic surgery (McCurdy 1990: 3; Harahap 1981). Zhang Shen, who had a lively practice in Beijing, estimated that it constituted 80 percent of the surgical procedures he performed. It is so common in China that if you ask any middle-class urban Chinese woman between the ages of about eighteen and forty-five about it, it is almost certain that she has had the procedure herself (though chances are good she will not confess), or that she knows someone who has had it.

As related to me by Song Ruyao (2001), the history of this procedure is that it originated in the late nineteenth century. An ophthalmologist named Hotz discovered an operation to make the eyelid turn outward as a cure for entropion (inward-turning eyelid). In the West, sufferers are not numerous and this operation is not common. But in pre-Revolutionary China, especially in the farm villages, shayan (lit. "sand eye," trachoma) was very common and frequently caused a loss of vision in people as young as the early thirties because inflammation caused the eyelid to turn inward and rub against the cornea. So the Hotz procedure was common in China. People discovered that it not only could cure entropion, but also could produce the "double eyelid" shape. Song notes, "However, in clinical practice this aesthetic shape sometimes appeared and sometimes did not appear, and then again when it appeared, sometimes it was excellent and sometimes poor." The classic ophthalmological surgeon emphasized curing disease and looked down on cosmetic treatments (*meirong*). Before the 1980s, it was rare for an ophthalmological surgeon to use the Hotz procedure to give the double eyelid operation to a healthy person who did not suffer from trachoma.

Meanwhile, as mentioned, cosmetic surgeons using a modified Hotz procedure found a rapidly growing desire for the operation, first in Japan and then in areas with many overseas Chinese, such as Hawaii, Singapore, the Philippines, and so on, as well as in Korea and Vietnam. As it has developed over time, the most common and long-lasting technique involves cutting away a crescent-shaped sliver of skin, fat, and muscle from the eyelid and suturing shut the incision. When healed, it produces the desired fold in a crescent shape above and parallel to the eye opening.

Song concludes that in China, "After the reforms and opening up, people's lives became wealthier, and they started to request cosmetic treatments. The double eyelid operation spread rapidly throughout all of China, and became daily work in cosmetic surgery" (2001).

Chinese people tend to divide the shapes of eyes with reference to an Occidental/Oriental dichotomy. "Westerners (Occidentals)" (*xifangren*), also called "Europeans" (*Ouzhou ren*), or sometimes "Europeans/Americans" (*Oumei ren*), have "big eyes" (*da yanjing*) with "double eyelids" (*shuangyanpi*). "Easterners (Orientals)" (*dongfang ren*), also called "Asians" (*Yazhou ren*), or "Chinese" (*Zhongguo ren*) have "little eyes" (*xiao yanjing*) with "single eyelids" (*danyanpi*). These categories differ from the typical American racial categories; rather, the labels applied to eyes give primacy to the presence or absence of a fold in the eyelid, and the labels applied to people give primacy to geographical or national categories. Double eyelid surgery might seem to be a result of an attempt to "erase" one's race, but it is important to keep in mind that the categories attached to eye shape are not racial categories. Therefore, it is more accurate to say that eye shape is associated with meanings of regional (Asian) or national (Chinese) identity. Surgeons vary in their assessment of whether Asians seeking double eyelid surgery desire a more Western appearance.

An Indonesian dermatologist, himself an "Oriental," stated outright in 1981 that double eyelid surgery is an imitation of the Western eye. "The Oriental, striving for a more Occidental appearance turns to surgery for the creation of the palpebral fold" (Harahap 1981: 78). He commented, "Just why many Orientals prefer to 'Westernize' their eyes is not known, although it is thought to stem from the influence of motion pictures and the increasing intermarriage of Asian women and Caucasian men, particularly since the second World War" (1981: 78).

Most surgeons deny that the majority of patients desire to look like

Westerners, noting that double eyelid surgery does not actually create a European-looking eye. Such surgery, while more radical, does exist, but is very rarely requested. Song recalled:

I remember that in 1948 when I was a professor at Chengdu Western Chinese University, there was a wealthy woman who asked me to give her the double eyelid operation. At that time I had just come back from America, my brain full of American thinking. When I solicited her opinion before the operation, she also said she wanted slightly wider double eyelids. And so during the operation I made her double eyelids as wide as Western double eyelids. After the operation, her husband called her "the big double-eye bourgeois" [*shuangyan dazi*]. I had no choice but to perform another operation to narrow her eyelids.

The two surgeons I interviewed, Song Ruyao and Zhang Shen, said that while it was true that their patients explicitly denied a desire to look Western, they still felt that the influence of Western culture accounted for the popularity of double eyelid surgery.

Surgeons from China, Korea, Japan, Los Angeles, and Hawaii insist that the operation is not caucasianization or Westernization of the Asian eye. The surgeons rationalize that such a request is not abnormal because double eyelid eyes exist in their own ethnic group (estimates vary from 30 to 50 percent) (Haiken 1997: 202, 208). John McCurdy, after practicing in Hawaii since 1976, wrote a book in 1990 entitled *Cosmetic Surgery of the Asian Face* (1990). "It is important that the facial plastic surgeon thoroughly understand that, at the present time, most Asian patients who request facial cosmetic surgery do not wish to have their features 'westernized' but desire rather conservative changes that improve facial balance and harmony while maintaining, and in some cases accentuating, desirable Asian characteristics" (1990: vii).

Despite the disclaimers by surgeons, however, it is clear that in cosmetic surgery the European face is the norm and the Asian face is typically defined in terms of deficiencies relative to it, and in general negatively.[6] McCurdy's 1990s text, which is so careful to say that Asians do not want to "Westernize" their eyes, repeatedly makes reference to "standard" eyelid surgery (blepharoplasty), which refers to surgery on Caucasians. He uses phrases to describe Asian eyes like: "sad, tired" eyes, "correction of this problem" (the epicanthial fold), "imparts an air of mystery and stoicism," "characteristic puffiness," "excess skin and fat." The Asian nose is "thick-skinned," has "deficient" tip projection, "characteristic bulbosity" of the lobule, with "attenuated lower lateral cartilages" (McCurdy 1990: 4, 5, 43, 61).

Zhang Shen, on the *Dream Garden* radio talk show, October 1995, also revealed his tendency to take European eyes as the standard of beauty:

if people consider that just because eyelids are double they're beautiful, this is an error. It's more correct to look at the beauty of your eyes as part of the beauty of the entire face. This face is a part of the entire body and manner [*qizhi*]. So let's say that it's only that the eyelids are a little bit double—how beautiful can that be? But if it's really the case that the eyes are excessively small—especially Orientals [*dongfang ren*], our eyes tend to be a little bit small—if the eyes are a little bit bigger, if the eyeball shows a bit more, certainly it will improve a person's impression of elegance, certainly it can strengthen a person's sense of attractiveness, increase a sense of beauty. And so this beauty is not to say that eyelids are only beautiful if you make them double, but how can you make the eyes bigger, increase the proportionality with the face—only this can be called beauty. But if, on the contrary, you very simply say, "I'm here, now you give me double eyelids," this can be a mistake.[7]

In interviews with women who had undergone cosmetic surgery, I also found that they did not state outright that they want to look European. They said that the eyes are the window to the soul, that large eyes are more expressive and make a person seem more intelligent, that they just wanted to improve their own individual appearance. However, it is also clear that the decision to seek out surgery is conditioned by medical and popular discourses that associate double eyelids with Europe and America and single eyelids with Asia, and value double eyelids over single eyelids.

Conclusions: The Double Meaning of "China Reconstructs"

If we take eyelid surgery as an example of a transnational form that has been reinvested with uniquely Chinese meanings, our analysis of the larger picture reveals the complexity of the overarching context. The larger picture is that this is a medical technique that originated in Western Europe and spread throughout the globe in the past 120 years. Its dissemination into China was part of a highly contested process in which transnational flows of culture produced national currents and countercurrents within China. In the process, the Western meanings of cosmetic surgery were reshaped, both at the official institutional level and at the popular level. And the final result was the production of a set of medical techniques and a pool of popular desires that merged to produce a tremendously widespread fad, which is now literally reshaping tens of thousands of Chinese bodies.

This history of cosmetic surgery illustrates how the total set of relations that structures today's geopolitics—in which the scientific worldview is the dominant worldview, and national and transnational communities are the dominant political units—affects everyday body images and practices at the most minute levels. Whether through war, military occupation, or simply the mingling of different peoples in enclaves such as Hawaii, these moments of transnational cultural flow have sparked the growth of cosmetic surgery. What is remarkable is that the body proves so malleable. Thanks to modern medicine, "race" is no longer any more fixed and immutable than "culture." It is easier to undergo an eyelid operation than to learn English. Thus, the link between the double meanings of the title of this paper—"China reconstructs"—is not arbitrary. There is a relationship between the political "face" of China and the "faces" of ordinary people, with implications for the meanings attached to each. This is why a focus on bodily practice can be a particularly important approach in understanding issues of national/racial identity and transnational flows of culture.

Notes

Chapter 2. Āyurvedic Acupuncture—Transnational Nationalism: Ambivalence About the Origin and Authenticity of Medical Knowledge

1. The response of King Udayana of the Upper Indus after questioning Hui-Seng and Sung Yun about "The Land of the Sunrise" and listening to them speak of the philosophy of Confucius and Lao Tzu as well as the medical science of Hua Tho and the magical power of Tso Tzhu. English translation of E. Chavannes's "Le Voyage de Song [Sung] Yun dans l'Udayana et le Gandhara" (1903). Quoted in Needham (1965: 209).

2. Tibetan Buddhism is by definition a Tantric tradition: this applies to the four major orders (the Nyingmapas, Kagyupas, Sakyapas, and Gelugpas), as well as to the Dzogchen and other syncretistic traditions. Much of the ritual of the medieval Chinese state was Tantric, and it was from China that nearly all the Buddhist Tantric traditions of Japan were transmitted. In China Tantra has survived since the twelfth century C.E. in Daoist ritual practice, and it has been said that Daoism is the most enduring monument to Tantric Buddhism (Strickman 1996: 49). Elsewhere the Chinese Chan (a Sinicization of Sanskrit *dhyāna*, "meditation") school lives on in Japan as Zen Buddhism. In Burma, the Zwagyis, Theravāda monk-alchemists, have for centuries combined elements of Theravāda Buddhism, Daoism, and Tantric alchemy in their practice. Cambodian inscriptions indicate the presence of Hindu tantrikas (practitioners of tantra) there in the medieval period (White 2000: 8).

3. Evidence of trade between polities in South Asia and Chinese dynastic entities dates to the late second century B.C.E. This trade seems to have been well established by the fourth century C.E. and flourished between the third and eighth centuries, a period characterized by intensive philosophical and religious ferment. It seems clear that ideas that eventually came to take shape as what is now known as Buddhism were in circulation in what is now China as early as 50 C.E. By 450, an early Tantric text, the *Ratna-Ketu-Dharani*, which had been earlier translated into Tibetan, was further translated into Chinese.

4. As Needham points out, although most scholarship on contact between India and China is concerned with the history of religion, it is clear that many Buddhist monks—perhaps most importantly I-Ching—were concerned with questions of protoscience manifest in alchemy as well as in mathematics, geometry, physics, and astronomy along with medicine (Needham 1965: 209–14, in particular 212–13).

5. In *Science and Civilization in Ancient China*, Joseph Needham points out—in a manner that underscores the problem of thinking about medicine in nationalistic terms—that the communication between "China" and "India" was not just bidirectional but circular (a pattern that probably also characterized the

exchange of ideas between the northern Mediterranean region and the area
from Baghdad south and west). Third-century ideas about embryonic breathing
found their way into Mahayana texts in South Asia and were "refined" into
"erotic-yogic" techniques by Natha yogis in the ninth and tenth centuries, but
were earlier—probably in the fourth or fifth century—reintegrated into Taoist
practices. As White points out, following Needham: "when Indian tantrism was
first introduced into China in the eighth century by the Buddhist monks Subha-
karasimha, Vajrabodhi, and Amoghavajra, a certain number of its techniques
were merely "returning" to their country of origin, from which they had been
exported but a few centuries earlier (1996: 63).

As Buddhism began to decline in southern Asia, it became formalized and
increasingly institutionalized in what is now Tibet. Many early Sanskrit texts—on
yoga and tantra—are known primarily through their translation into Tibetan by
Marpa in the eleventh century, his disciple Milarepa's translations and original
work in the eleventh and twelfth centuries, as well as through the Tibetan historian Buston's fourteenth-century scholarship.

6. *Doṣa*, which is translated into English as humor, defect, or fault—which
reflects a similar imprecision—was translated into Chinese as *tu*, meaning poi-
son in English (Unschuld 1985: 142).

7. The Sanskrit term of this era for the area of Tibet and China is, not surpris-
ingly, politically ambiguous. *Mahacina* means greater China, and one wonders
where exactly—if they were concerned with exactness at all—travelers to the
northwest of Kashmir and north of Assam drew the line.

8. It should be noted that the term "Islamic medicine" is an exception to the
rule. The term *Unani* medicine is used in India to designate Islamic medicine,
but etymologically it is an Urdu word that means the medicine of Greece. Why
not Persian medicine, since many of the ideas can be linked to Baghdad in the
tenth and eleventh centuries? Sometimes Tibetan medicine is also referred to as
Buddhist medicine, and here there is a similar ambivalence and ambiguity
between geopolitics, culture, and religion.

9. For a clear awareness of the interweaving of modernity, politics, and medicine by a scholar who has played a major role in defining the field, see Leslie
(1976; Leslie and Young 1992, 1992: 177–208). See also Brass (1972); Crozier
(1968); Unschuld (1992: 44–62).

10. Technically, of course, the capitalized acronym TCM is a modern designa-
tion for "traditional" practices that are now practiced under the political, cultural, and financial aegis of the PRC.

11. One of the earliest treatises on acupuncture is the *Huang ti chia I ching*,
which dates to 280 C.E. Archaeological evidence based on the excavation of
stone, bone, and metal needles provides interesting material for earlier system-
atic practice, but without significant contextualization it is difficult to know
whether a needle is a needle used for needling, a tool used for lancing boils, or
something else altogether. Figurines with marked circulation tracts are, of
course, much more compelling and provide the kind of cultural contextualization that is needed to make sense of other less "textual" kinds of *materia medica*
(see He and Lo 1996).

12. Since the argument here is about nationalism in the context of Āyurvedic
acupuncture, no attempt has been made to present Chinese acupuncture in anything more than the most rudimentary terms. However, it is worth quoting Sivin
(1987), who summarizes the work of Lu and Needham (1980) while providing
a translation of various Chinese accounts of theory and practice:

The term *ching* has been known in the West only as the name for the linear arrays of acupuncture loci on the surface of the human body that we call circulation tracts. But the word has a much deeper meaning than this, denoting a basic physiological conception in ancient Chinese medicine founded on the theory of the Two Forces (*yin* and *yang*) and the Five Elements (*wu hsing*), which recognized six patterns of physiological function and pathological dysfunction. This sense emerges in the ancient and mediaeval Chinese system of diagnosis now called *liu ching pien cheng* (differentiating the syndrome in accordance with he six *ching* patterns. (Needham, Lu, and Sivin 2000: 64)

13. Paul Unschuld's *Medicine in China: A History of Ideas* (1985) and the relevant volumes in Joseph Needham's *Science and Civilization in China* provide comprehensive overviews of medical history on this scale and scope.

14. In many ways the at times subtle and at other times rather abrupt shift in the discourse about needles or fingers in the comparison between Indian and Chinese acupuncture extends directly into the domain of other related modalities of treatment, in particular surgery and surgical technology, heat therapy and various heating technologies, and bloodletting and various bloodletting technologies (see, in particular, Devasena 1981).

15. *Nāḍī* is a very important term in the conceptualization of Āyurvedic acupuncture, although much of the meaning assigned to it seems to be drawn from a theory of yogic physiology (see Alter 2004). Most sources translate *nāḍī* as nerves and both the subtle and gross conduits for the flow of substances through the body. Since one of the subtle substances that flows through or along the *nāḍī* is conceptualized as vital energy, it is possible to think of *nāḍī* as providing a conceptual framework for the conflation of nerve impulses, sensory perception—including pain—and vital energy. Many modern texts on Āyurvedic acupuncture allow for this "easy" conflation across domains, whereas other sources are adamant that *nāḍī* are either one or the other.

16. See also Filliozat (1969).

17. Here Shigehisa Kuriyama's book *The Expressiveness of the Body and the Divergence of Greek and Chinese Medicine* (1999) is a perfect case in point. Whereas the subtle and extremely interesting comparison and contrast of Greek and Chinese views of the body provide for a much better understanding of the history of medicine in general, and a much greater appreciation for the "depth" at which cross-cultural variation in the construction of medical knowledge is relevant, to make this comparison and contrast it is necessary to reify medicine as Greek and Chinese. This reification rests uneasily on the foundation of historical analysis, all the more so as the degree of historical detail becomes important.

18. Within the field of religious studies things are somewhat different, given the transnational spread of Buddhism, Hinduism, Islam, and Christianity. Therefore, it is not surprising that those features of medicine that are most directly linked to religious ritual and doctrine tend to be dealt with with less direct concern for bounded boundaries as such. Of particular relevance in this context is the literature on Buddhism and Tantra (see, for example, White 2000).

19. In his comprehensive *Encyclopedia of Indian Medicine* S. K. Ramchandra Rao makes no reference to needling. Reference is made to the importance of *marma* for surgery—so as to avoid causing trauma to a patient—but there is no reference to *marma cikitsā*. There is also no reference to what Ros terms Bhedan Karma, or "Piercing-Through Therapy" (1987).

20. Devasena (1981) has provided a detailed overview, analysis, and ethnographically contextualized study of a Sinhala text called *Salla Vidya* (referred to as the Sugathadas Samararatne manuscript). Based on an analysis of grammar,

syntax, and spelling, the text probably dates to 1880 or 1890. There was also a text called *Salya Cikitsā Vidhi* in the library of the Purana Vihara temple in Gandara. Devasena quotes a lay student of the chief incumbent of the temple through 1950 as saying that this manuscript "contained instructions on puncturing and pressurizing of *nila* points (function centres), . . . together with illustrations of instruments and human figures depicting crucial loci" (1981: 15). Another text referred to as *Vidum Pilissum Potha* contains information on cauterization of loci on the body to treat ailments at points that are not coterminous with those loci (17). Devasena makes note of eight other manuscript of uncertain antiquity that clearly need to be further analyzed (41–46).

21. Lo (2002) provides an excellent account of the early stone technology associated with acupuncture.

22. In a condensed version of a longer but unpublished paper entitled "Acupuncture in Ancient India" (1991), C. B. Desai makes a number of interesting points but the bulk of his analysis revolves around the description and classification of needles. After pointing out that the term for needling used by Suśruta is *vedhana*, he goes on to explain that *vedhana* is included as one of eight surgical manipulations (1991: 62) Other terms used for needling are *vydhana* and *sūchithodana*.

23. In this regard Unschuld (1985: 144–48) documents the fascinating case of cataract surgery being incorporated into medical practice in China as a "mechanical" procedure. It is clear not only that the technique was developed in the "Western lands," but the procedure as described in Chinese texts involved needles, needling, and poking. Whether the Indian technique derived from an earlier Greek method is unclear—as is the question of whether the tool in question was called a needle in southern Asian practice. Wujastyk points out (1998: 124) that needles are classified by Suśruta as knives, of which there are twenty types. There are two types of needle, one for draining and one for suturing—but it is intriguing to consider that cataract surgery might be regarded as a kind of needling/surgery that drains off the "brain fat" that has accumulated in the eye, much as acupuncture in some interpretations is used to drain off excess *qi*.

24. In his discussion of bloodletting techniques in the context of "Asian acupuncture techniques," Thatte, quoting Suśruta, delineates twelve types of leeches, six poisonous and six nonpoisonous (1988: 105–7).

25. This point has been made brilliantly by Shigehisa Kuriyama with respect to the pulse, which was understood and felt as a radically different thing in early China and early Greece (1999).

26. But is puncturing with a "double bladed needle" really puncturing in the same sense as puncturing with a straight gold needle as thin as a hair?

27. This raises an important question concerning the relationship between acupuncture and martial arts in China, as well as questions about a transregional "antinationalist" history of martial arts that might parallel the history of medicine being discussed here.

28. Those familiar with the literature on body cultivation and power in China will note the close similarity between the 108 vital points that must be attacked and protected in the application of various Chinese martial arts, notably in the southern style involving *dianxue* (Cantonese *dim mak*) (Mooney 2001: 38), and the 107 *marma*. It could be argued that a more logical approach to the question of nationalism might develop around the transnational communication of these ideas (and we will see this is, in fact, relevant in terms of the South Indian mar-

tial art of Kalarippayattu and *varma cikitsā*), but the fact remains that in India the question of nationalism has much greater significance with regard to the domain of medicine, whereas in China the martial arts have enough "cultural currency" to stand on their own as indexically nationalistic (see Mooney 2001: 33, 41–43; Henning 2001).

29. Thatte, making a somewhat subnationalistic distinction between North and South Indian traditions of Āyurveda, points out that the North Indian tradition defines *marma* as constituted of *soma, maruta, tejas, sattva, rajas,* and *tama* (1988: 5). This is an interesting and somewhat curious concatenation of substances and qualities. However, in defining *marma* at another point in his text, Thatte references Suśruta and speaks of the "five anatomical structures" being "collectively present" in the *marma* (1988: 15).

30. Thatte argues that the skin is important not simply because it provides a clear perspective on the surface contours of the body, but because it is the "specialized seat of vyana vayu," which is important in terms of circulation of energy. Thus the skin is important functionally rather than as a kind of default place marker (1988: 5).

31. On the specific rationale for this cosmophysiology, see White (1996).

32. Here Thatte provides an interesting discussion of how herbal poultices having the character of a particular humor can be used to massage specific loci based, it seems, on the humoral character of the loci (1988: 32).

33. See Eliade (1997); Feuerstein (1990, 2001); White (1996). For an analysis of the ways *nāḍī* in particular and yoga in general are integrated into a modern scientific discourse of medicine in India, see Alter (2000: 55–82; 2004)

34. This would be analogous to what Kuriyama says about the importance of *mo* conduits independent of a theory of needling or of evidence for needling as such (1999: 44)

35. Thatte's scheme, derived from what he refers to as the Tamila Marmas Sastra, recognizes 108, although these are divided into the standard two subdivisions of *padu* (relatively more important) and *thodu* (relatively less so) (1988: 23). See also Dharmalingam, Radhika, and Balasubramanian (1991: 16–19), who lists 63, one—number 12—being listed twice. Although referred to as *varmam*, the points appear to be *adangal* loci.

36. Dharmalingam's usage is difficult to sort out, but although he seems to blur the distinction between *varma* and *adangal* at some points in his text, at one point he writes: "*adangals* can be used as key points to activate the actual *varmaas.* . . . We can use these *adangals* where the concerned *varma* points cannot be touched or stimulated" (1981: 49).

37. In fact, no counter-application seems to involve just "hitting" the opposite point. It usually requires other kinds of massage and medication.

38. One way to think through the confusion surrounding the relationship between *adangal* and *marma* is to recognize two forms of loci-oriented therapy, one centered around *adangal* as independent of *marma*—numbering 51—and one centered around a series of 108 points that correspond, in theory if not in fact, to the *marma* in a relationship of binary complementarily. Thus pain and suffering caused by damage to a marma can be counteracted by treating a point on the opposite side—or is it configured of an opposite ratio of substances?—of the body.

39. Charting points along the radial, median, and ulnar nerves of the arm's flexor surface, Thatte identifies 5 similar and 9 dissimilar points. On the extensor surface there are 2 similar, 8 dissimilar, and 5 approximately similar points.

On the extensor surface of the leg there are 2 similar points, 12 dissimilar, and 5 approximately similar points, and on the flexor surface there are 3 similar, 3 dissimilar, and 1 approximately similar (1988: 47–95). Of course, if the total number of points in TCM is counted, then the ratio of dissimilar to similar points increases significantly.

40. Devasena points out that "As we have seen it was because of the existence of libraries that many capable individuals were able to instruct themselves on cauterizing and puncture and on other aspects of traditional medicine. Research into these library centers of the seventeenth, eighteenth and nineteenth centuries will reveal interesting facts" (1981: 26).

41. It is interesting to note that skepticism about the idea that *nila* points at one place on the body could be stimulated to address some problem experienced at a significant remove from that point seems to have factored into the very etymology of the term used to designate these points. As Devasena points out, the term *nila* means confusion, confounding logic, obscurantism, and darkness as opposed to clear insight, and in many instances was used derisively (1981: 55–57). In a section entitled "points that can be needled," Desai indicates that the classical texts of Āyurveda say that any point on the body *other than* a *marma sthāna* can be needled, but then he goes on to say that since the *marma* are therapeutically relevant, they should be counted as acupuncture points (1991: 65).

42. It is interesting, in terms of the relationship between enumerating points on the body and devising technology to manipulate these points, that the author of an early twentieth-century Sinhalese work on cauterizing (Abeysinghe 1934), points out that there are 101 instruments for cauterizing cataloged in the *Suśruta Saṃhitā*, and that Vagbhata, in what seems to be the textual equivalent of "throwing up one's hands," points out that there can be as many different kinds of cauterizing tools as there are ailments that require cauterizing (in Devasena 1981: 52).

43. The term itself is of Portuguese derivation.

44. Kuriyama notes the probable historical link between bloodletting, cauterization, and acupuncture in China (1999: 204). Given the profound importance of bloodletting in Āyurveda, the logic of bloodletting, *prāṇic* flow, and *nāḍī* physiology and cauterization deserves to be studied much more carefully. In other words, there is no reason to fetishize needles as the definitive technology in the history of acupuncture, either national or transnational.

45. David Frawley has written a large number of popular books on Āyurveda and Yoga, among other topics. From the standpoint of established, academic scholarship his work is controversial. Although intent on promoting the transnational flow and global popularization of so-called Vedic ideas, what he has written about the history of Hinduism plays into the politics of nationalism.

46. Harjit Singh provides a similar synthesis (1998: 30–46)

47. Mehta (1999); see also Gala (n.d.) and Goel (2000); for Sri Lanka see Jayasosoriya and Fernando (1979) and Premaratne (1978).

48. There is convincing evidence that "pressure" points were important in the training and care of elephants and horses (Desai 1991).

49. Unfortunately a book entitled *Vedic Health Care System: Clinical Practice of Sushrutokta Marm Chikitsa and Siravedhan* (Sah, Joshi, and Joshi 2002) came to my attention after this chapter was written. However, it seems to confirm the central argument I have tried to make by pushing the synthesis of Āyurveda and TCM to an even higher level of detailed integration than achieved by Ros. Sah, Joshi, and Joshi claim that Suśruta articulated a theory of acupuncture based on the

delineation of *dhamanī* meridians, *sira* points, and *rasa* vital energy. While they are explicit about making a comparison of Suśruta's acupuncture with the Chinese variant, they clearly use the Chinese variant to reconstruct a classical Āyurvedic system.

50. Remembering, that is, what is easy to forget in the context of transnational health consciousness: Nature Cure originated as medicine that was distinctly associated with southern Germany, although, since it came into being at a time when European borders were shifting, and just as nations as such were being established, the strongly "nationalist" label "German" is more linguistic and cultural than anything else.

51. I-Ching's aversion was probably to cow dung and cow urine, but also to a whole panoply of animal excreta that factor into Āyurveda, and perhaps also human urine and excreta that are used in various aspects of Tantric practice and some features of esoteric yoga.

Chapter 3. Deviant Airs in "Traditional" Chinese Medicine

1. In addition to their academic professions, both authors originally trained and practiced in European centers of "traditional Chinese medicine" and bring to the study intimate professional knowledge of the complex layering of different acupuncture cultures in Britain. Many scholars and colleagues gave advice and help in the course of our research. In particular, we would like to thank Mark Kane, Michael Loewe, Volker Scheid, and Bob Withers.

2. D.C. Lau, (1996), 12; 34).

3. Sibu Beiyao Shanghai: Zonghua Shuu 4.13, 2.

4. Sibu Beiyao Shanghai: Zonghua Shuu 7.43, 3–4.

5. Sibu Beiyao Shanghai: Zonghua Shuu 10.71, 7–10.

6. Sibu Beiyao Shanghai: Zonghua Shuu 1.4, 10–14.

7. Sibu Beiyao Shanghai: Zonghua Shuu 5.20, 1.

8. Sibu Beiyao Shanghai: Zonghua Shuu 8.27, 8b–11b.

9. Sibu Beiyao Shanghai: Zonghua Shuu 8.27, 9.

Chapter 4. Reinventing Traditional Medicine: Method, Institutional Change, and the Manufacture of Drugs and Medication in Late Colonial India

1. There were several strains within the Swadeshi movement. The broad movement comprised those who felt that there was a need to check the drain of capital through goods that were imported. There were those like Coomaraswamy who professed a "higher Swadeshi," premised on a theory of traditional aesthetics anchored in the craft tradition (Visvanathan 1985: 40).

2. There is a general tendency among scholars of the nineteenth century to subscribe to the binary typology of westernization/revivalism. David Kopf (1970) recognized a third response, revitalization. The efforts of men like Varier and Ajmal Khan represent an effort to revitalize whatever was salvageable from the past. Both Āyurvedic and Unani movements were open to modern advances in medicine during the period under consideration.

Chapter 5. Health and Medicine in British India and Dutch Indies: A Comparative Study

I am grateful to a young Dutch scholar Han Mesters for both inspiration and discussion.

1. See also Home Department, Public Branch, no. 18, Keep With pt. A, July 18, 1838, preserved in National Archive of India, New Delhi (NAI).

2. For details see H. M. Griffin (1972).

3. Home, Public, no. 20, March 7, 1835, NAI.

4. quoted in Verma (1995).

5. Home, Medical, nos. 54–57, Aug. 1896, NAI.

6. Haffkine had a rather unusual career in India. For details see Deepak Kumar (1999: 239–71).

7. International Health Board, 5/2/sp. Report, Box 49, f. 304 a, Rockefeller Archive Center (RAC).

8. Mantri is a Javanese name for a certain lower rank in the government hierarchy.

9. To quote a verse from a hakeem in 1910, "Kuch-Ilaj Aya Na Kuch Charagiri Ayee:Tibb-E-Unan Ke Munh Doctory Ayee Band Sheeshe Mein Vilayat Se Pari Ayee: Lal-Peeli Hui, Gusse Mein Bhari Ayee Chaman-e-Tibb se Guldasta Uda Kar Layee: Nayee Tarkeeb Se Bandish Saja Kar Layee" [Knows no method of treatment, but Doctory dared to challenge Unani. In a closed bottle a fairy has come full of anger from foreign lands. The bouquet stolen from the garden of (Unani) Tibb has been rearranged in a new fashion]. Jogi Dakani, quoted in Qaiser (2000: 29–42).

10. *Selections from the Records of the Govt. of India,* no. 377, Calcutta, 1900, p. 28, NAT.

11. For interesting details, see van der Veur (1987).

12. Soetomo noted ruefully, "The high mountain is only beautiful and spotless when one observes it from a distance" (van der Veur 1987: 33).

Chapter 6. Nationalism, Transnationalism, and the Politics of "Traditional" Indian Medicine for HIV/AIDS

A version of this paper was presented at a conference on Asian Medicine: Nationalism, Transnationalism, and the Politics of Culture organized by the Asian Studies Program, University of Pittsburgh, November 13–16, 2002.

1. Āyurveda and Siddha are both indigenous to India. Whereas Siddha is largely confined to the regional area of South India, particularly to the state of Tamil Nadu, Āyurveda is used throughout the country. Unani is derived from a form of ancient Greek medicine originally introduced into India via the early Islamic migrations. Homeopathy originated in Germany but is widely practiced throughout India.

2. In this chapter, I will not address the question of the efficacy of traditional medicine to treat HIV/AIDS since such an analysis is beyond my expertise.

3. This research was funded by the Institute for Scholarship in the Liberal Arts (ISLA) at the University of Notre Dame and by the Department of Anthropology at the University of Notre Dame.

4. A definition of TM provided in the *WHO Traditional Medicine Strategy 2002–2005* (WHO 2002a: 1) is "'Traditional medicine' is a comprehensive term used to refer both to TM systems such as traditional Chinese medicine, Indian *ayurveda* and Arabic *unani* medicine, and to various forms of indigenous medicine. TM therapies include medication therapies—if they involve use of herbal medicines, animal parts and/or minerals—and non-medication therapies—if

they are carried out primarily without the use of medication, as in the case of acupuncture, manual therapies and spiritual therapies."

5. For example, see Arnold (1993, 2000); Bala (1991); Ernst (2002); Harrison (1994); D. Kumar (1995, 2001); Lal (1994); Mills and Sen (2003); Pati and Harrison (2001).

6. This is a term used by Daniel R. Headrik (1981), and discussed in Arnold (1993, chap. 1).

7. In addition to the authors mentioned in note 5, see also, Leslie (1976); Leslie and Young (1992); Obeyesekere (1992); Van Hollen (2003).

8. Compare for example, Arnold's discussion of Ram Nath Chopra and G. Srinivas Murti (Arnold 2000: 182–84).

9. See, for example, his letter published in *Young India*, January 1921, printed in the 1938 edition of *Hind Swaraj.*

10. For discussion of the role of the *vaid* in classical Āyurvedic texts, see Basham (1967).

11. For more discussion on this discursive opposition, see Chatterjee (1990); Nandy (1983).

12. This was comparable to the projected 1997 out of pocket expenditure for all physician services.

13. 1 crore is equal to 10 million.

14. From "Ayurveda—the Indian System," *Far East Focus* (Business and Industry section), February 1997.

15. Under this new law, Chinese medicine is also designated as "ethnic" medicine. However, according to the Ayurveda industry, the Chinese government has taken an active role to persuade the British authorities to place individual Chinese medicines on the more easily approved list; whereas the Indian government, these critics complain, has not taken an active role to assist the Ayurveda exporters in this matter. From K. Santosh Nair, "Ayurvedic Exports from India in Jeopardy, UK Plan to Classify it as Ethnic Remedies"; www.pharmabiz.com/newsfeat/alter233.asp, August 5, 2002).

16. For example, see "Doctors Look for Traditional Medicine for AIDS Cure" written by a staff reporter, *Times of India*, November 9, 2000.

17. From "Ayurveda Seminar Inaugurated," *Times of India*, January 6, 2000.

18. This is a fairly common argument; for discussion, see Dube (2000).

19. Chitra Siddharth, "From "Modern Medicine with an Open Mind," *Times of India*, January 31, 2000.

20. This hospital was originally established as a tuberculosis sanatorium but has increasingly become a hospital for HIV/AIDS patients, many of whom are suffering from TB as an opportunistic infection associated with AIDS.

21. The three Siddha drugs administered to PLWHA are Rasagandhi Mezhugu, Amukkara Chooranam, and Nellikai Leyham.

22. Personal communication with Dr. P. Paramesh, superintendent of Government Hospital of Thoracic Medicine, December 23, 2002, Tambaram.

23. See "Funds for AIDS Research at Siddha Institute," *Hindu*, November 22, 2001.

24. Personal communication with Dr. Paramesh.

25. Personal communication with Kausalya, founder of Positive Women's Network, December 21, 2002, Chennai.

26. At Dr. Nehru's request, I have retained his real name.

27. Interview with author, January 6, 2003, Chennai.

28. He viewed Siddha and Āyurveda medicine as essentially the same, and referred to them as "siblings."

29. "Health—Indian Doctor Claims AIDS Cure Through Traditional Medicine," *Pakistan Press International, The Pakistan Newswire,* August 20, 2001.

30. Yojna Gusai, "Ayurvedic Doctor Claims Cure for AIDS," *Statesman* (India), February 21, 2001.

31. For more information of Majeed's trajectory see Miners (1996). According to this article, ImmunoQR contains the following ingredients (according to Caraka's classification of drugs, with original spelling):

Embelica—Phyllantis	Curcuma Angustafolia
Glycyrrhiza Glabra	Indian Winter Cherry
Adhatoda Vasica	Periploca Indica
Tinospora Cardifolia	Tiarldaum Ind
Vitis Vinifera	Plumbago Zeylanica
Sugar Cane	Dasamoola
Cypern Rotundus	Syzygium Gambolanum
Santalum Album	Pinus Deodara
Zingiber Officnale	Terminalia Chebula
Aeglemarmelos	Avi
Piper Longam	Spaeranthus Indica
Asparagus Racemosus	

However, in an interview I conducted with Majeed on December 26, 2002, he stated that he does not disclose all the ingredients on the IQR label because, according to him, in Āyurvedic medicine most doctors never disclose all the ingredients as an informal way to protect their patents.

32. See "Nationwide International New Headlines," *Press Trust of India,* July 19, 2001. For more in-depth discussion on stigma and AIDS in India, see Jain (2002) and Dube (2000).

33. This account of the story is portrayed in the pilot film *Medicine in Cochin,* produced by Graham Day for GFilm Productions, 2000. For further information about the film, contact Graham Day at gd@gfilm.f2s.com.

34. This is according to "AIDS Cure Messiah Ready to Prove Claims," *Times of India,* December 4, 2001.

35. Such as the Elisa test or the Western Blot test.

36. This account of the story is portrayed in *Medicine in Cochin.*

37. From Dr. I. S. Gilada, "ASCI Bans Ads on 'AIDS Cure'; IHO Requests Media to Cooperate with ASCI," Indian Health Organization Press Release, October 8, 1997.

38. From Dr. I. S. Gilada, "Traditional HIV/AIDS Care," in Sea-AIDS (message 1984), www.hivnet.ch:8000/asia/sea-aids/viewR?1984.

39. Personal communication with T. M. Majeed, December 26, 2002, Ernakulam. For further discussion on this see Majeed (2002:10–12).

40. From *Medicine in Cochin.*

41. This is the cost of IQR minus the tax and courier charges.

42. In response to the criticism that he is not a licensed medical practitioners of any sort, Majeed writes, "This is just a very desperate statement to stop my medicine. They forget the fact that the greatest of scientists, Luis Pasteur, was not a doctor" (2001). He claims that since he was not trained in one form of medicine or another, he is not confined by his training and can think more freely and therefore is more likely to make important new discoveries (personal communication, December 26, 2002).

43. See "Supreme Court Dismisses Majeed's Petition," SEA-AIDS@healthdev.net, Thursday, April 4, 2002.

44. According to one report, Majeed claims that Chitra's death was caused by "consumption of fat and vomiting." See Akhel Mathew, "'Cured' AIDS patient Chitra is Dead," *Gulf News*, July 21, 2001. Another report indicates that Majeed stated that Chitra's death was caused by tuberculosis since she did not take her medicines regularly. For this account see "AIDS cure Messiah Ready to Prove Claims" (note 34). He gave me the latter explanation in my meeting with him on December 26, 2002.

45. This information was obtained through personal communication with Graham Day, producer *Medicine in Cochin*, October 22, 2002, and "Supreme Court Dismisses Majeed's Petition," SEA-AIDS@healthdev.net, Thursday, April 4, 2002.

46. Personal email communication with T. A. Majeed, May 26, 2003.

47. This is not to say that their motives are purely monetary, since they claim to want to alleviate people's suffering through their medicine.

Chapter 7. Mapping Science and Nation in China

1. The circumstances of his return are discussed extensively by Iris Chang (1995) as well as several Web sites, the most notable being the Federation of American Scientists.

2. International Yan Xin Qigong Association, 1999, http://www.twm.co.nz/-sai/DrYan_qi.htm, June 11, 2001. Original emphasis.

3. Francesca Bray's (1997) reading of Needham's work offers a compelling assessment about its consequences.

4. See J. Waley-Cohen (1999) for further discussion of this site in its historical context.

5. The May Fourth Movement, following protests of the Versailles Treaty of 1919, coalesced into fervent social, literary, and political activity which questioned Chinese culture and China's place in the modern world. The rejection of "traditional" principles of Confucianism and patriarchy, for instance, forged new intellectual directions that embraced science as well as Western art and culture.

6. I discuss *qigong* deviation in detail elsewhere (Chen 1999, 2003).

7. For instance, the 2002 Fourth World Congress on Qigong focuses on medical *qigong*, whereas previous congresses did not make such a distinction.

Chapter 8. Sanskrit Gynecologies in Postmodernity: The Commoditization of Indian Medicine in Alternative Medical and New Age Discourses on Women's Health

1. For the very interesting and complex question of dating early medical texts in Sanskrit, see Dominik Wujastyk, *The Roots of Āyurveda*, rev. ed. (2003: 2–5, 63–64). The dates I give are probable ones for the composition of the "cores" of these texts. As is the case for most works of this sort, these two medical *saṃhitā*s were composed in layers and revised over periods of several centuries.

2. The Ayurvedic Institute's Web address is http://www.ayurveda.com (last accessed September 10, 2003).

3. The U.S. Food and Drug Administration web address is http://www.fda.gov (last accessed October 10, 2003).

4. *Informal Classes*, June-August 2002, p. 10. Course catalog published by the University of Texas at Austin on behalf of Texas Union Informal Classes.

5. See Jean M. Langford, *Fluent Bodies: Ayurvedic Remedies for Postcolonial Imbalance* (2002: 116–22) for her lovely and quite sensitive exposition on aphoristic and expository "textures" in the *Caraka Saṃhitā* and other works on Indian medicine.

6. The Sundāri Web address is http://www.sundari.com (last accessed October 13, 2003).

7. The Body Shop's Web address is http://www.thebodyshop.com (last accessed October 13, 2003).

8. This phrase is New Age Orientalist Vijay Prashad's; see *The Karma of Brown Folk* (2000: 47–68).

9. This is a concept Langford discusses throughout her book.

10. The cartoon, penned by Eric Lewis, appeared in the August 12, 2002 issue.

11. *Gaiam Living Arts: The Catalog for Total Well-Being*, summer 2002. The company's Web address is http://www.gaiam.com (last accessed October 13, 2003).

Chapter 9. China Reconstructs: Cosmetic Surgery and Nationalism in the Reform Era

Thanks to William Kirby for suggesting this play on words. *China Reconstructs* is the title of an English-language propaganda magazine published by the Chinese government for foreign consumption. For many decades, when China was closed to the outside world, it was one of the few available current sources in English on the PRC, and so every Sinologist is aware of the phrase. The label "reconstruction" (*jianshe*) referred to the construction of a new socialist society under the guidance of the Communist Party. In English, the language that the Party-state applied to "building the new face of China" also applies to individuals who are building new faces for themselves through cosmetic surgery—which until recently was denounced as bourgeois and decadent by the Party. (This pun does not work in Mandarin Chinese.) The second insiders' joke is that *China Reconstructs* featured many an article on the achievements of Chinese doctors in limb reattachments (one of the main techniques of plastic and reconstructive surgery), often illustrated in gory detail, which were a key way of proving that China had become a modernized nation with modernized medicine.

1. I should emphasize that this is only a "hint"; this connection was only briefly mentioned in his published writing, although based on my participation in his seminar at the University of Virginia, I believe that I am accurately representing his way of thinking on these matters.

2. My reformulation of the notion of the "empty form" was aided by discussions with Pamela Stewart and Andrew Strathern at the conference on Asian Medicine: Nationalism, Transnationalism, and the Politics of Culture, University of Pittsburgh, November 14–16, 2002.

3. Song Ruyao, letter written in Chinese to the author in response to a list of questions, July 28, 2001. All translations are by the author.

4. English and Greek words in italics were written in English in the original.

5. Jiang Xin, " '94, Chen Lili jixing gaozhao" ('94, Chen Lili's lucky star shines high), *Mingxing bao* (*Star News*), 1994 (date and page unknown).

6. Compare Emily Martin's (1987) description of the tendency in Western medicine to take the male body as the norm and to consider the female body as a deviation.

7. Zhang Shen (1995).

References

Premodern Texts

Agniveśa. *Carakasaṃhitā*. Revised by Caraka and Dṛdhabala with the Āyurveda-dīpikā commentary of Cakrapāṇidatta. 4th ed. Jādavjī Trikamjī Ācārya. Varanasi: Chaukhambha Sanskrit Sansthan, 1994.

Bhishagratna, Kaviraj Kunjalal, trans. and ed. 1963. *An English Translation of the Sushruta Samhita Based on Original Sanskrit Text*. 2nd ed. 3 vols. Varanasi: Chowkhamba Sanskrit Series Office.

Chao Yuanfang. 601. *Chaoshi zhubing yuanhou lun* (Mr. Chao's Origins and Symptoms of Medical Disorders). Zhubing yuanhou lun jiaozhu edition. Beijing: Renmin weisheng, 1991.

Dash, Bhagwan and Ram Karan Sharma, trans. *Agniveśa's Caraka Saṃhitā*. 7 vols. Varanasi: Chowkhamba Sanskrit Series Office, 1976.

Gujin yitong daquan (Great Completion of Medical Tradition, Past and present). 1556.

Guoyu (Sayings of the States). Traditionally attributed to Zuo Qiuming (fifth century).

Houhanshu (History of Later Han. 445 C.E. Ed. Fan Ye (398–445). Beijing: Zhonghua, 1996.

Huangdi hama jing. Weishing huibian edition, 1823. Reprint Beijing: Zhongyi guji, 1984.

Huangdi neijing suwen. Sibu beiyao Shanghai: Zhonghua shuu, 1927–35.

Huangdi neijing lingshu. Sibu beiyao Shanghai: Zhonghua shuu, 1927–35.

Huangfu Mi. *Zhenjiu jiayi jing* (ABC of Acupuncture). Comp. 256–282 C.E.

Liji (Record of Rites). attr. Liu Xiang (78–8 B.C.E.). In Legge (1885).

Lushi chunqiu (The Annals of Lu Buwei). 239 C.E. In Reigel (2000).

Mengzi. In D. C. Lau, ed., *A Concordance to the Mengzi*. Hong Kong: Shangwu yinshu guan, 1995.

Shijing (The Book of Songs 1,000–600 B.C.E.). In Waley (1937).

Sun Simiao 581–682?. *Qianjin yaofang* (Essential Prescriptions Worth a Thousand). Renmin Weisheng edition. Beijing, 1955.

Suśruta. *Suśrutasaṃhitā*. Ed. Kavirāja Ambikādutta Shāstri. 9th ed. 2 vols. Varanasi: Chaukhambha Sanskrit Sansthan, 1995.

Wang Tao. 752 C.E. *Waitai biyao* (Arcane Essentials from the Imperial Library). Gao Wenzhu ed. Beijing: Huaxia chubanshe, 1993.

Xunzi. c. 298 C.E. In D. C. Lau, ed., *A Concordance to the Xunzi*. Hong Kong: Shangwu yinshu guan, 1996.

Yinshu. c. 186 B.C.E. See Zhangjiashan 247 hao Hanmu zhujian zhengli xiaozu. *Zhangjiashan Hanmu zhujian*. Beijing: Wenwu, 2001.

Modern Texts

Abeyasekere, Susan. 1986. "Health as a Nationalist Issue in Colonial Indonesia." In *Nineteenth and Twentieth Century Indonesia*, ed. D. P. Chandler and M. C. Ricklefs, 1–13. Monash: Monash University Press.

Abeysinghe, P. M. P. 1934. *Agni Karma Vidhi*. Columbo: W.E. Bastian.

Adams, W. 1868. *Report on Vernacular Education*. Calcutta, 1868.

Adas, Michael. 1990. Machines as the Measure of Men. New Delhi: Oxford University Press.

Alter, Joseph S. 1999. "Heaps of Health, Metaphysical Fitness: Āyurveda and the Ontology of Good Health in Medical Anthropology." *Current Anthropology* 40: S43-S66.

———. 2000. *Gandhi's Body: Sex, Diet, and the Politics of Nationalism*. Philadelphia: University of Pennsylvania Press.

———. 2004. *Yoga in Modern India: The Body Between Science and Philosophy*. Princeton, N.J.: Princeton University Press.

Anagnost, Ann. 1997. *National Past-Times: Narrative, Representation, and Power in Modern China*. Durham, N.C.: Duke University Press.

Appadurai, Arjun, 1986. *The Social Life of Things: Commodities in Cultural Perspective*. Cambridge: Cambridge University Press.

———. 1990. "Disjuncture and Difference in the Global Cultural Economy." In *Global Culture: Nationalism, Globalization and Modernity*, ed. Mike Featherstone. London: Sage.

Arnold, David. 1989. *Imperial Medicine and Indigenous Societies*. Delhi: Oxford University Press.

———. 1993. *Colonizing the Body: State Medicine and Epidemic Disease in Nineteenth-Century India*. Berkeley: University of California Press.

———. 2000. *The New Cambridge History of India: Science, Technology, and Medicine in Colonial India*. Cambridge: Cambridge University Press.

"Atreya." 2000. *Ayurvedic Healing for Women: Herbal Gynecology*. New Delhi: Motilal Banarsidass. Reprint of 1999 Weiser edition.

Bagchi, Asoke K. 1997. *Medicine in Medieval India: 11th to 18th Centuries*. Delhi: Konark.

Bala, Poonam. 1991. *Imperialism and Medicine in Bengal: A Socio-Historical Perspective*. New Delhi: Sage.

Banerjee, Madhulika. 2002. "Power, Culture, Medicine: Ayurvedic Pharmaceuticals in the Modern Market." Paper presented at the Fifth International Conference on Traditional Asian Medicine, Halle, Germany, August 19.

Basham, A. L. 1967. *The Wonder That Was India*. New Delhi: Rupa.

Beal, Samuel, 1869. *Travels of Fah-Hian and Sung-Yun, Buddhist Pilgrims from China to India (400 A.D. and 518 A.D.)*. London: Trübner.

Bernal, Martin. 1987. *Black Athena: The Afroasiatic Roots of Classical Civilization*. London: Free Association Press.

Birch, Steven J. and Robert L. Felt. 1999. *Understanding Acupuncture*. Edinburgh: Churchill Livingston.

Bivins, Roberta E.. 2000. *Acupuncture, Expertise and Cross-Cultural Medicine*. Manchester: Palgrave.

Bodde, Derk. 1975. *Festivals in Classical China: New Year and Other Annual Observances During the Han Dynasty, 206 BC-AD 220*. Princeton, N.J.: Princeton University Press.

Bode, Maarten. 2002. "Indian Indigenous Pharmaceuticals: Tradition, Modernity, and Nature." In *Plural Medicine, Tradition and Modernity, 1800–2000*, ed. Waltraud Ernst, 184–203. New York: Routledge.

Bögle, Reinhard. 2000. *Im Einklang mit dem inneren Mond: 28-Tage-Yoga für Frauen.* Munich: Knaur/MensSana.

Boomgaard, Peter 1996. "Dutch Medicine in Asia, 1600–1900." In *Warm Climates and Western Medicine: The Emergence of Tropical Medicine, 1500–1900*, ed. David Arnold, 42–64. Amsterdam: Vill.

Bowker, Geoffrey C. and Susan Leigh Star. 1999. *Sorting Things Out: Classification and Its Consequences.* Cambridge, Mass.: MIT Press.

Brass, Paul R. 1972. "The Politics of Ayurvedic Education: A Case Study of Revivalism and Modernization in India." In *Education and Politics in India: Studies in Organization, Society and Policy*, ed. Susanne Hoeber Rudolph and Lloyd I. Rudolph, 342–459. Delhi: Oxford University Press.

Bray, Francesca. 1997. *Technology and Gender: Fabrics of Power in Late Imperial China.* Berkeley: University of California Press.

Brumberg, Joan Jacobs. 1997. *The Body Project: An Intimate History of American Girls.* New York: Random House.

Buddhananda, Swami. 1996. *Moola Bandha: The Master Key.* Mungher, Bihar: Yoga Publications Trust.

Bullock, Alan and Stephen Trombley, eds. 1999. *The New Fontana Dictionary of Modern Thought.* New York: HarperCollins.

Chace, Charles. 1993. "Ghosts in the Machine." *European Journal of Oriental Medicine* 1, 1 (Spring): 26–32.

Chakrabarty, Dipesh. 1998. "Postcoloniality and the Artifice of History: Who Speaks for Indian Pasts." In *A Subaltern Studies Reader: 1986–1995*, ed. Ranajit Guha, 260–96. Delhi: Oxford University Press.

———. 2000. *Provincializing Europe: Poscolonial Thought and Historical Difference.* Princeton, N.J.: Princeton University Press.

Chang, Iris. 1995. *Thread of the Silkworm.* New York: Basic Books.

Charles, B. G. 1923, L/E/7/1156, India Office Library and Records, London, May 5.

Chatterjee, Partha. 1986. *Nationalist Thought and the Colonial World: A Derivative Discourse.* Minneapolis: University of Minnesota Press.

———. 1990. "The Nationalist Resolution of the Women's Question." In *Recasting Women: Essays in Indian Colonial History*, ed. Kumkum Sangari and Sudesh Vaid, 233–53. New Brunswick, N.J.: Rutgers University Press.

Chavannes, Édouard. 1903. "Le Voyage de Song Yün dans l'Udyana et le Gandhara." *Bulletin de l'École Française d'Extrême-Orient* 3: 379–441.

Chen, Hsiu-fen. 2002. "Medicine, Society and the Making of Madness in Imperial China." Ph.D. dissertation, School of Oriental and African Studies, London.

Chen, Nancy N. 1999. "Translating Psychiatry and Mental Health in Twentieth Century China." In *Tokens of Exchange: Problems of Translation in Global Circulation*, ed. Lydia Liu. Durham N.C.: Duke University Press.

———. 2003. *Breathing Spaces: Qigong, Psychiatry, and Healing in China.* Columbia University Press.

Cohen, Floris H. 1994. *The Scientific Revolution: A Historiographical Inquiry.* Chicago: University of Chicago Press.

Cohen, Paul A. 1997. *History in Three Keys: The Boxers as Event, Experience, and Myth.* New York: Columbia University Press.

Connor, Linda H. and Geoffrey Samuel. 2001. *Healing Powers and Modernity: Tra-*

ditional Medicine, Shamanism, and Science in Asian Societies. Westport, Conn.: Bergin and Garvey.

Coon, Carleton S., Stanley M. Garn, and Joseph B. Birdsell. 1950. *Races: A Study of the Problems of Race Formation in Man.* Springfield, Ill.: Charles C. Thomas.

Coward, Rosalind. 1989. *The Whole Truth: The Myth of Alternative Health.* London: Faber and Faber.

Crombie, A. C. 1994. *Styles of Scientific Thinking in the European Tradition: The History of Argument and Explanation Especially in the Mathematical and Biomedical Sciences and Arts.* 3 vols. London: Duckworth.

Crozier, Ralph C. 1968. *Traditional Medicine in Modern China: Science, Nationalism, and the Tensions of Cultural Change.* Cambridge, Mass.: Harvard University Press.

Cunningham, Andrew and Bridie Andrews, eds. 1997. *Western Medicine as Contested Knowledge.* Manchester: Manchester University Press.

Day, Graham. 2000. *Medicine in Cochin.* GFilm Productions.

Deadman, Peter, Mazin Al-Khafaji, and Kevin Baker. 1998. *A Manual of Acupuncture.* Hove: Journal of Chinese Medicine Publications.

Desai, C. B. 1991. "Acupuncture in Ancient India." In *Marma Chikitsa in Traditional Medicine,* ed. Vaidya V. Dharmalingam, Vaidya M. Radhika, and A. V. Balasubramanian, 61–75. Madras: Lok Swaasthya Parampara Samvardhan Samithi.

Dey, K. L. 1894. *Indian Pharmacology: A Review.* Calcutta.

Devasena, Laxman. 1981. *Some Traditional Sri Lankan Medical Techniques Related to Acupuncture: A Study of the Sugathadasa Samararatne Manuscript.* Colombo: Marga Institute.

Dharmalingam, Vaidya V., Vaidya M. Radhika, and A. V. Balasubramanian, eds. 1991. *Marma Chikitsa in Traditional Medicine.* Madras: Lok Swaasthya Parampara Samvardhan Samithi.

Director of Public Instruction Report, Bengal, 1864–65. National Archives of India, New Delhi.

Dirks, Nicholas B. 1998. *In Near Ruins: Cultural Theory at the End of the Century.* Minneapolis: University of Minnesota Press.

Duara, Prasenjit. 1995. *Rescuing History from the Nation: Questioning Narratives of Modern China.* Chicago: University of Chicago Press.

Dube, Siddharth. 2000. *Sex, Lies, and AIDS.* New Delhi: HarperCollins.

Eckman, Peter. 1996. *In the Footsteps of the Yellow Emperor: Tracing the History of Traditional Acupuncture.* San Francisco: Cypress.

Eliade, Mircea. 1990. *Yoga: Immortality and Freedom.* Princeton, N.J.: Princeton University Press.

Ernst, Waltraud, ed. 2002. *Plural Medicine, Tradition and Modernity, 1800–2000.* London: Routledge.

———. 2002. "Plural Medicine, Tradition and Modernity: Historical and Contemporary Perspectives: Views from Below and from Above." In *Plural Medicine, Tradition and Modernity, 1800–2000,* ed. Waltraud Ernst, 1–18. London: Routledge.

Ernst, Waltraud and Bernard Harris, eds. 1999. *Race, Science and Medicine, 1700–1960.* London: Routledge.

Esherick, Joseph W. 1987. *The Origins of the Boxer Uprising.* Berkeley: University of California Press.

Farquhar, Judith. 1992. "Time and Text: Approaching Chinese Medical Practice Through the Analysis of a Published Case." In *Paths to Asian Medical Knowl-*

edge, ed. Charles Leslie and Allan Young, 62–73. Berkeley: University of California Press.

———. 1994. Knowing Practice: *The Clinical Encounter of Chinese Medicine*. Boulder, Colo.: Westview Press.

Featherstone, Mike. 1990. "Global Culture: An Introduction." In *Global Culture: Nationalism, Globalization and Modernity*, ed. Mike Featherstone, 1–14. London: Sage.

Fernando, Felix and Leo Fernando. 1979. *Theory and Practice of Traditional Chinese Acupuncture*. Colombo: Lake House Investments.

Feuerstein, Georg. 1990. *Encyclopedic Dictionary of Yoga*. London: Unwin.

———. 2001. *The Yoga Tradition: Its History, Literature, Philosophy, and Practice*. Prescott, Ariz.: Hohm.

Feurtado, Gardel MacArthur. 1986. "Mao Tse-Tung and the Politics of Science in Communist China, 1949–1965." Ph.D. dissertation, Stanford University.

Filliozat, Jean. 1949. *The Classical Doctrine of Indian Medicine: Its Origins and Greek Parallels*. Delhi: Munshiram Manoharlal, 1964.

———. 1969. "Taoisme et yoga." *Journal Asiatique* 257: 41–87.

Fixler, Marian and Oran Kivity. 2000. "Japanese Acupuncture—A Review of Four Styles. *European Journal of Oriental Medicine* 3, no. 3: 4–16.

Fulder, S. J. and R. E. Munro. 1985. "Complementary Medicine in the United Kingdom: Patients, Practitioners, and Consultants." *Lancet* 326, no. 8454: 542–45.

Furth, Charlotte. 1998. *A Flourishing Yin: Gender in China's Medical History, 960–1665*. Berkeley: University of California Press.

Gala, Dhiren. n.d. *Be Your Own Doctor with Acupressure*. Ahmedabad: Navneet Publications.

Gandhi, Mohandas K. 1938. *Hind Swaraj*. Ahmedabad: Navajivan Press.

———. 1992. *Key to Health*. Ahmedabad: Navajivan Press.

Ghaffar, Abdul. n.d. *Hayat-i-Ajmal*. Aligarh: Anjuman Taraqqi-I-Urdu.

Gilada, I. S. 1997. "ASCI Bans Ads on 'AIDS Cure': IHO Requests Media to Cooperate with ASCI." Indian Health Organization (IHO) press release.

———. 1999. "Pres-ICAAP 5: Traditonal HIV/AIDS Care." In Sea-AIDS (Message 1984): www.hivnet.ch:8000/asia/sea-aids/viewR?1984.

Goel, Satish. 2000. *Acupressure and Acupuncture Therapy*. New Delhi: Diamond Pocket Books.

Goffman, Erving. 1974. *Frame Analysis: An Essay on the Organization of Experience*. New York: Harper and Row.

Griffin, H. M. 1972. "T. B. Macaulay and the Anglicist-Orientalist Controversy in Indian Education." Ph.D. dissertation, University of Pennsylvania.

Gusai, Yojna. 2001. "Ayurvedic Doctor Claims Cure for AIDS." *Statesman* (India), February 21.

Habib, S. Irfan. 2000. "Delhi Tibbiya College and Hakim Ajmal Khan's Crusade for Indigenous Medicine Systems in Late 19th and Early 20th Century India." In *Science in Islamic Civilization*, ed. Ekmeleddin Ihsanoglu and Feza Gunergun, 257–65. Istanbul: Research Center for Islamic History, Art, and Culture.

Habib, S. Irfan and Dhruv Raina. 1989. "Copernicus, Columbus, Colonialism, and the Role of Science in Nineteenth Century India." *Social Scientist* 17, 3–4: 51–66.

Hacking, Ian. 1999. *The Social Construction of What?* Cambridge, Mass.: Harvard University Press.

Haiken, Elizabeth. 1997. *Venus Envy: A History of Cosmetic Surgery*. Baltimore: Johns Hopkins University Press.

Hannerz, Ulf. 1990. "Cosmopolitans and Local in World Culture." In *Global Culture: Nationalism, Globalization and Modernity*, ed. Mike Featherstone, 237–51. London: Sage.

Harahap, Marwali. 1981. "Blepharoplasty." In *Cosmetic Plastic Surgery in Nonwhite Patients*, ed. Harold E Pierce, 77–97. New York: Gruen and Stratton.

Haraway, Donna J. 1997. *Modest_Witness@Second_Millennium.FemaleMan©_Meets_Onca Mouse*™: Feminism and Technoscience. New York: Routledge.

Hardey, Michael. 2002. "Health for Sale: Quackery, Consumerism and the Internet." In *Plural Medicine, Tradition and Modernity, 1800–2000*, ed. Waltraud Ernst, 204–17. New York: Routledge.

Harding, Susan. 1998. *Is Science Multicultural? Postcolonialisms, Feminisms, and Epistemologies*. Bloomington: Indiana University Press.

Harikumar, M. K. 2001. "One Man Fights AIDS." *Kaumudi* (Mumbai, India), October 28.

Harper, Donald John. 1998. *Early Chinese Medical Literature: The Mawangdui Medical Manuscripts*. New York: Kegan Paul.

Harrison, Mark. 1994. *Public Health in British India: Anglo-Indian Preventive Medicine, 1859–1914*. New Delhi: Cambridge University Press.

He, Zhiguo and Vivienne Lo. 1996. "The Channels: A Preliminary Examination of a Lacquered Figurine from the Western Han Period." *Early China* 21: 81–123.

Headrick, Daniel R. 1981. *The Tools of Empire: Technology and European Imperialism in the Nineteenth Century*. New York: Oxford University Press.

Henning, Stanley E. 2001. "China." In *Martial Arts of the World*, vol. 1, ed. Thomas A. Green, 65–71. Santa Barbara, Calif.: ABC/CLIO.

Hicks, Angela. 1997. "A Clear Case of Possession." In *Acupuncture in Practice: Case History Insights from the West*, ed. Hugh MacPherson and Ted Kaptchuk. New York: Churchill Livingston.

Hinrichs, T. J. 2003. "The Medical Transforming of Governance and Southern Customs in Song Dynasty China (960–1279 C.E.)." Ph.D. dissertation, Harvard University.

———. Forthcoming. "Song-Yuan (960–1368): A Renaissance? The Social Production of Medical Knowledge." *Instituto della Enciclopedia italiana: Storia della scienza*, vol. 3, *Science in China*. Rome: Istituto della Enciclopedia Italiana.

Hittleman, Richard. 1988. *Richard Hittleman's Yoga: 28 Day Exercise Plan*. New York: Bantam Books.

Home Office Records, National Archive of India, New Delhi.

Hsu, Elisabeth. 1999. *The Transmission of Chinese Medicine*. Cambridge: Cambridge University Press.

Hua, Shiping. 1995. *Scientism and Humanism: Two Cultures in Post-Mao China, 1978–1989*. Albany: SUNY Press.

I-Ching. 1896. *A Record of the Buddhist Religion as Practiced in India and the Malay Archipelago, AD 671–695*. Ed. and trans. J. Takakusus. Oxford. Reprint New Delhi: Munshiram Manoharlal, 1982.

Inden, Ronald. 2000. *Imagining India*. Bloomington: Indiana University Press.

Informal Classes. 2002. Course catalog prepared by the University of Texas at Austin on behalf of Texas Union Informal Classes, June-August.

International Health Board. 5/2/sp.report box 49, f. 304a. Rockefeller Archive Center, North Tarrytown, N.Y.

Jain, Kalpana. 2002. *Positive Lives: The Story of Ashok and Others with HIV*. New Delhi: Penguin.

Jambhekar, B. G. 1835. "Nosology of Madhau and Anatomy of Susrut." *Bombay Durpan*, January 9.

Jayasooriya, Anton and Felix Fernando. 1979. *Principles and Practices of Scientific Acupuncture.* Colombo: Lake House Investments.

Jiong Xin. 1994. "94 Chen Lili Jixing Gaazhao" (94, Chen Lili's Lucky Star Shines High). *Mingxing Bao* (Star News), date and place unknown.

Joshi, Pornima. 2001. "The World in a Teaspoon." *Hindustan Times* (New Delhi), July 7.

Julien, Stanislas and Huili Yanchong.1853. *Histoire de la vie de Hiouen-Thsang et de ses voyges dans l'inde, depuis l'an 629 jusquà l'an 645.* Paris: Imprimerie Impériale.

Kalinowski, Marc. 2002. "The Interaction Between Popular Religion and Shushu Culture in Dunhuang Manuscripts." In *Proceedings of the Third International Conference on Sinology*, 243–84. Taiwan: Academia Sinica.

Kaviraj, Sudipta. 1988. *Imaginary History.* Occasional Papers Series 7. New Delhi: Nehru Memorial Museum and Library.

Kelly, John D. 2002. "Alternative Modernities or an Alternative to 'Modernity': Getting Out of the Modernist Sublime." In *Critically Modern: Alterities, Alternatives, Anthropologies*, ed. Bruce Knauft, 258–86. Bloomington: Indiana University Press.

Kelly, John D. and Martha Kaplan. 2001. *Represented Communities: Fiji and World Decolonization.* Chicago: University of Chicago Press.

Keswani, N. H. 1974. *The Science of Medicine and Physiological Concepts in Ancient and Medieval India.* New Delhi: All India Institute of Medical Science.

Khan, Jamil. n.d. Sirat-I-Ajmal. Delhi: n.p.

Kleinman, Arthur. 1980. *Patients and Healers in the Context of Culture: An Exploration of the Borderland Between Anthropology, Medicine, and Psychiatry.* Berkeley: University of California Press.

Knoblock, John and Jeffreu Riegel. 2000. *The Annals of Lü Buwei: A Complete Translation and Study.* Stanford, Calif.: Stanford University Press.

Kopf, David. 1970. "The Brahmo Samaj Intelligentsia and the Bengali Renaissance: A Study of Revitalization and Modernization in 19th Century Bengal." In *Transition in South Asia*, ed. Robert I. Crane. Durham, N.C.: Duke University Press.

Kopytoff, Igor. 1986. "The Cultural Biography of Things: Commoditization as Process." In *The Social Life of Things: Commodities in Cultural Perspective*, ed. Arjun Appadurai, 64–91. Cambridge: Cambridge University Press, 1986.

Kulkarni, P. H. n.d. *Probable Links Between Ayurveda and Acupuncture.* Pune: Institute of Indian Medicine.

Kumar, Anil. 1998. *Medicine and the Raj: British Medical Policy, 1857–1905.* New Delhi: Sage.

Kumar, Deepak. 1991. *Science and Empire: Essays in Indian Context (1700–1947).* Delhi: Anamika Prakashan.

———. 1995. *Science and the Raj: 1857–1905.* Delhi: Oxford University Press.

———. 1997. "Unequal Contenders, Uneven Ground: Medical Encounters in British India, 1820–1920." In *Western Medicine as Contested Knowledge*, ed. Andrew Cunningham and Bridie Andrews, 172–90. Manchester: Manchester University Press.

———.1999. "Colony Under a Microscope." *Science, Technology and Society* 4, 2: 239–71.

———. 2001. *Disease and Medicine in India: A Historical Overview.* Delhi: Tulika Publishers.

Kuriyama, Shigehisa. 1999. *The Expressiveness of the Body and the Divergence of Greek and Chinese Medicine.* New York: Zone Books.

Kwok, Danny Wynn Ye. 1965. *Scientism in Chinese Thought, 1900–1950.* New Haven, Conn.: Yale University Press.

Lakoff, George and Mark Johnson. 1980. *Metaphors We Live By.* Chicago: University of Chicago Press.

Lal, Maneesha. 1994. "The Politics of Gender and Medicine in Colonial India: The Countess of Dufferin's Fund, 1885–1888." *Bulletin of the History of Medicine* 68, 1: 29–66.

Langford, Jean M. 2002. *Fluent Bodies: Ayurvedic Remedies for Postcolonial Imbalance.* Durham, N.C.: Duke University Press.

Lau, D. C. 1995. *Mengzi zhu zi suo yin* (A Concordance to the Mengzi). Hong Kong: Shangwu yinshu guan.

———. 1996. *Xunzi zhu suo yin* (A Concordance to the Xunzi). Hong Kong: Shangwu yinshu guan,

Lauw, G. M. 1987. *De Dokter Djawa School: De eerste Medische opleiding voor Inheemsen in Nederlands Oost-Indië 1850–1875.* Nijmegen.

Leslie, Charles. 1976. *Asian Medical Systems: A Comparative Study.* Berkeley: University of California Press.

———. 1992. "Interpretations of Illness: Syncretism in Modern Āyurveda." In *Paths to Asian Medical Knowledge,* ed. Charles Leslie and Allan Young, 177–208. Berkeley: University of California Press.

Leslie, Charles and Allan Young, eds. 1992. *Paths to Asian Medical Knowledge.* Berkeley: University of California Press.

Li, Jianmin. 1996. "Contagion and Its Consequences." In *Proceedings of the 20th, 21st, and 22nd International Symposium on the Comparative History of Medicine—East and West.* Taipei: Academia Sinica.

———. 2000. *Sisheng Zhi Yu (The Territory Between Life and Death).* Taipei: Academica Sinica.

Liu, Lydia. 1995. *Translingual Practice: Literature, National Culture and Translated Modernity—China, 1900–1937.* Stanford, Calif.: Stanford University Press.

Liu Shu. 1997. *Meirong Yixue: Hemian* (Esthetic Medicine: Faxillofacial Region). Shanghai: Shanghai Keji Jiaoyu Chubanshe.

Lo, V. 2000. "Crossing the Neiguan 'Inner Pass'—A Nei/Wai 'Inner/Outer' Distinction in Early Chinese Medicine?" *East Asian Science, Technology, and Medicine* 17: 39–60.

———. 2001. "Yellow Emperor's Toad Canon, part 2." *Asian Major* 14.

———. 2002. "Spirit of Stone: Technical Consideration in the Treatment of the Jade Body." *Bulletin of the School of Oriental and African Studies* 65, 1: 99–128.

Loewe, Michael, ed. 1993. *Early Chinese Texts: A Bibliographical Guide.* Berkeley: University of California, Society for the Study of Early China.

Lu, Gwei-djen and Joseph Needham. 1980. *Celestial Lancets: A History and Rationale of Acupuncture and Moxa.* Cambridge: Cambridge University Press.

Ludmerer, Kenneth M. 1999. *Time to Heal: American Medical Education from the Turn of the Century to the Era of Managed Care.* Oxford: Oxford University Press,.

Lurie, Alison. 2003. "God's Houses, Parts 1, 2." *New York Review of Books,* July 3, 30–32; July 7, 41–43.

Lyon, Margot. 1990. "Order and Healing: The Concept of Order and Its Importance in the Conceptualization of Healing." *Medical Anthropology* 12: 249–68.

MacAloon, John. 1992. "Sport, Science, and Intercultural Relations: Reflections on Recent Trends in Olympic Scientific Meetings." *Olympika* 1: 1–28.

———. 1995a. "Humanism as Political Necessity? Reflections on the Pathos of Anthropological Science in Pluricultural Contexts." In *The Conditions of Reciprocal Understanding*, ed. James Fernandez and Milton Singer, 206–35. Chicago: International House.

———. 1995b. "Interval Training." In Choreographing History, ed. Susan L. Foster, 32–53. Bloomington: Indiana University Press.

Maciocia, Giovanni. 1989. *The Foundations of Chinese Medicine.* Edinburgh: Churchill Livingstone.

———. 1994. *The Practice of Chinese Medicine.* Edinburgh: Churchill Livingstone.

MacLeod, Roy and Milton Lewis. 1988. *Disease, Medicine and Empire: Perspectives on Western Medicine and the Experience of European Expansion.* London: Routledge.

Majeed, T. A. 1996. "Magic Johnson Should Tell the Truth." Unpublished document, T. A. Majeed, Fair Pharma, Broadway, Ernakulum.

———. 2001. "My Ultimate Challenge." Flyer, T. A. Majeed, Fair Pharma, Broadway, Ernakulum.

———. 2002. "The Plight of Medicine for AIDS." Flyer, T. A. Majeed, Fair Pharma, Broadway, Ernakulum.

Martin, Emily. 1987. *The Woman in the Body: A Cultural Analysis of Reproduction.* Boston: Beacon Press.

Mathew, Akhel. 2001. " 'Cured' AIDS Patient Chitra Is Dead." *Gulf News,* July 21. www.gulf-news.com.

McCurdy, John A. 1990. *Cosmetic Surgery of the Asian Face.* New York: Thiem Medical Publishers.

Mehta, A. K. 1999. *Acupuncture for Everyone: A Home Guide.* New Delhi: B. Jain Publishers.

Memorandum on the Pharmaceutical and Chemical Research Institute at the Ayurvedic and Unani Tibbi College. 1916. Karol Bagh, Delhi.

Mesters, Han. J. L. 1996. "Hydrick in the Netherlands Indies: An American View of Dutch Public Health Policy." In *Health Care in Java: Past and Present,* ed. Peter Boomgaard, Rosalia Sciortino, and Ines A. Smith, 51–62. Leiden: KTLV Press.

Metcalf, Barbara. 1986. "Hakim Ajmal Kahn: Rais of Delhi and Muslim Leader." In *Delhi Through the Ages: Essays in Urban History, Culture and Society,* ed. R. E. Frykenberg, 299–315. Delhi: Oxford University Press.

Meulenbeld, Gerrit Jan. 2002. *A History of Sanskrit Medical Literature.* Groningen: Egbert Forsten.

Miles, M. and A. Huberman. 1994. *Qualitative Data Analysis: An Expanded Source Book.* London: Sage.

Mills, James and Satadru Sen. 2003. *Confronting the Body: The Politics of Physicality in Colonial and Post-Colonial India.* London: Anthem.

Miners, Scott E. 1996. "HIV/AIDS Hypothesis Questioned: But Ayurvedic Indian 'AIDS Curer' May Have Started a New Wave of Immuno-Supportive Treatments." *Well Being Journal,* North Bend, Wash. www.lightparty.com/Health/HIVQuestioned.htm.

Mooney, Richard M. 2001. "Boxing, Chinese Shaolin Styles." In *Martial Arts of the World: An Encyclopedia,* vol. 1, ed. Thomas A. Green, 32–44. Santa Barbara, Calif.: ABC/CLIO.

Mukhopadhyay, G. 1923. *History of Indian Medicine.* Vol. 2. Calcutta Delhi: Orient Books, 1974.

Nader, Laura. 1996. *Naked Science: Anthropological Inquiry into Boundaries, Power and Knowledge.* New York: Routledge.

Nair, K. Santosh. 2002. "Ayurvedic Exports from India in Jeopardy; UK Plan to Classify It as Ethnic Remedies." www.Pharmabiz.Com/Newsfeat/Alter233.-Asp, August 5.

Nandy, Ashis. 1983. The Intimate Enemy: Loss and Recovery of Self Under Colonialism. Delhi: Oxford University Press.

Naquin, Susan. 1976. Millenarian Rebellion in China: The Eight Trigrams Uprising of 1813. New Haven, Conn.: Yale University Press,

———. 1981. Shantung Rebellion: The Wang Lun Uprising of 1774. New Haven, Conn.: Yale University Press.

Needham, Joseph. 1962. Science and Civilisation in China. Vol. 2, History of Scientific Thought. Cambridge: Cambridge University Press.

———. 1965. Science and Civilization in China. Vol. 1, Introductory Orientations. Cambridge: Cambridge University Press.

Needham, Joseph, Lu Gwei-djen, and Nathan Sivin. 2000. Science and Civilization in China. Vol. 6, Biology and Biological Technology, Part VI, Medicine. Cambridge: Cambridge University Press.

Nizami, Zafar Ahmad. 1988. Hakim Ajmal Khan. New Delhi: Publications Division, Government of India.

Obeyesekere, Gananath. 1992. "Science, Experimentation, and Clinical Practice in Ayurveda." In Paths to Asian Medical Knowledge, ed. Charles Leslie and Allan Young, 160–76. Berkeley: University of California Press.

Palmier, L. H. 1962. Indonesia and the Dutch. London: Oxford University Press

Pandey, Gyanendra. 1990. The Construction of Communalism in Colonial North India. New Delhi: Oxford University Press.

Panikkar, K. N. 1992. "Indigenous Medicine and Cultural Hegemony: A Study of the Revitalization Movement in Keralum." Studies in History 2: 283–308.

Pati, Biswamoy and Mark Harrison. 2001. Health, Medicine and Empire: Perspectives on Colonial India. Hyderabad: Orient Longman.

Pearson, M. N. 1989. Towards Superiority: European and Indian Medicine, 1500–1700. Minneapolis: Associates of the James Ford Bell Library, University of Minnesota.

Petitjean, Patrick, Catherine Jami, and Anne Marie Moulin. 1992. Science and Empires: Historical Studies About Scientific Development and European Expansion. Dordrecht: Kluwer.

Pickering, Andrew. 1995. The Mangle of Practice: Time, Agency, and Science. Chicago: University of Chicago Press.

Pierce, Harold E. 1981. Cosmetic Plastic Surgery in Nonwhite Patients. New York: Gruen and Stratton.

Pietroni, Patrick. 1992. "Beyond the Boundaries: Relationship Between General Practice and Complementary Medicine." British Medical Journal 305: 564–66.

Pillai, Chidambarathanu. 1993. Varma Thiravul Kol Thirattu. Madras: International Institute of Thanuology.

Porkert, Manfred. 1974. The Theoretical Foundations of Chinese Medicine: Systems of Correspondence. Cambridge, Mass.: MIT Press.

Prakash, Gyan. 1999. Another Reason: Science and the Imagination of Modern India. Princeton, N.J.: Princeton University Press.

Prashad, Vijay. 2000. The Karma of Brown Folk. Minneapolis: University of Minnesota Press.

Premaratne, A. D. P. 1978. Principles and Practice of Modern Chinese Acupuncture. Colombo: Associated Publishing and Printing Company.

Qaiser, Neshat. 2000. "Colonial Politics of Medicine and Popular Unani Resistance." Indian Horizons (April-June): 29–42.

Raina, Dhruv. 1997a. "The Young P. C. Ray and the Inauguration of the Social History of Science in India." *Science, Technology and Society* 2, 1: 1–39.

———. 1997b. "Evolving Perspectives on Science and History: A Chronicle of Modern India's Scientific Enchantment and Disenchantment." *Social Epistemology* 11, 1: 3–24.

———. 2003. *Images and Contexts: The Historiography of Science and Modernity in India*. Delhi: Oxford University Press.

Raina, Dhruv and S. Irfan Habib. 1996. "The Moral Legitimation of Modern Science: Bhadralok Reflections on Theories of Evolution." *Social Studies of Science* 26: 9–42.

———. 1999. "The Missing Picture: The Non-Emergence of a Needhamian History of Science in India." In *Situating the History of Science: Dialogues with Joseph Needham*, ed. S. Irfan Habib and Dhruv Raina, 279–302. New Delhi: Oxford University Press.

Rajamony, S. 1988. *Siddha Maruthuvathil Varma Parikavarmum*. Madras: Tamil Nadu Siddha Medical Board.

Rao, S. Ganapathi 1977. "Dhanvantri Mahal." *Journal of the Tanjore Saraswati Mahal Library* 30: i–iv.

Rao, S. K. Ramachandra. 1987. *Encyclopedia of Indian Medicine*. Vol. 2, *Basic Concepts*. Bangalore: Parameshvara Charitable Trust.

Ray, P. C. 1902. *A History of Hindu Chemistry: From Earliest Times to the Middle of the 16th Century*. Calcutta: Chukervertty Chatterjee.

———. 1932. *Life and Experiences of a Bengali Chemist*. Calcutta: Chuckervertty Chatterjee.

Reed, Louis S. 1932. *The Healing Cult: A Study of Sectarian Medical Practice: Its Extent, Causes, and Control*. Chicago: University of Chicago Press.

Ros, Frank. 1995. *The Lost Secrets of Ayurvedic Acupuncture: An Ayurvedic Guide to Acupuncture*. Delhi: Motilal Banarsidass.

Ross R. 1898. Letter to P. Manson, June 28. Ross Papers, MSS 02/159, London School of Hygiene and Tropical Medicine.

Rosu, Arion. 1981. "Les Marman et les arts martiaux indiens." *Journal Asiatique* 259: 417–51.

Russell. 1908. *Nature*, December 24.

Sah, Ram Lal, Binod Kumar Joshi, and Geeta Joshi. 2002. *Vedic Health Care System: Clinical Practice of Sushrutokta Marm Chikitsa and Siravedhan*. Delhi: New Age Books.

Saich, Tony. 1989. *China's Science Policy in the 1980s*. Manchester: Manchester University Press.

Sarguro, Dr. 2001. "AIDS Drug." Islamic Voice 15–04, no. 172 (April). www.islamicvoice.com/april.2001/readers.htm

Sarkar, Sumit. 1975. "Rammohan Roy and the Break with the Past." In *Rammohan Roy and the Process of Modernization in India*, ed. V. C. Joshi, 46–68. New Delhi: Vikas.

Scheid, Volker. 2002. *Chinese Medicine in Contemporary China: Plurality and Synthesis*. Durham, N.C.: Duke University Press.

Scheper-Hughes, Nancy and Margaret Lock. 1987. "The Mindful Body: A Prolegomenon to Future Work in Medical Anthropology." *Medical Anthropology Quarterly* 1, 1: 6–41.

Schoute, Dirk. 1937. *Occidental Therapeutics in the Netherlands East Indies During Three Centuries of Netherlands Settlement (1600–1900)*. The Hague: Netherlands Indian Public Health Service.

Scott, Julien. 2002. "Lurking Evil: Changes That Happen When You Treat Children." *European Journal of Oriental Medicine* 3, 6: 11–12.

Seal, B. N. 1933. "Rammohan Roy: The Universal Man." In *Rammohan Roy and His Work*, ed. Amal Home, 104–8. Calcutta: Rammohan Roy Centenary Committee.

Shastri, S. V. Radhakrishna. 1964. *Sareera Marma Vigyanam*. Trichrapalli: Tamil Nadu Ayurveda Mahamandalam.

Shifrin, Ken. 1997. "Shouting for Sympathy." In *Acupuncture in Practice: Case History Insights from the West*, ed. Hugh MacPherson and Ted Kaptchuk. New York: Churchill Livingston.

Siddharth, Chitra. 2000. "Modern Medicine with an Open Mind." *Times of India*, January 31.

Singh, Attar. 1999. *Akyupreśur: Prakr̥tic Upchār*. Chandigarh: Acupressure Health Center.

Singh, Harjit. 1998. *Akyupreśur: Siddhānth āwn Cikitsā—Health and Divine Life Through Acupressure*. Chandigarh: Health Care Systems.

Sivin, Nathan. 1987. *Traditional Medicine in Contemporary China: A Partial Translation of Revised Outline of Chinese Medicine (1972) With an Introductory Study on Change in Present-Day and Early Medicine*. Ann Arbor: University of Michigan, Center for Chinese Studies.

———. 1993. "Huang-Ti Nei-Ching." In *Early Chinese Texts: A Bibliographic Guide*, ed. Michael Loewe. Berkeley: University of California, SEEC.

Slamet-Velsink, Ina E. 1996. "Some Reflections on the Sense and Nonsense of Traditional Health Care." In *Health Care in Java: Past and Present*, ed Peter Boomgaard, Rosalia Sciortino, and Ines A. Smith, 65–80. Leiden: KTLV Press.

Song Ruyao. 1987. "Woguo Zhengxing Waike Fazhande Lishi Huigu (A Look Back at the History of the Development of Our Nation's Plastic Surgery)." *Zhonghua Zhengxing Shaoshang Waike Zazhi* (Chinese Plastic and Burn Surgery Journal) 3, 4: 241–43.

Sontag, Susan. 1977. *Illness as Metaphor*. London: Penguin.

Soulie de Morant, G. 1994. *Chinese Acupuncture*. Brookline, Mass.: Paradigm Publications.

Spence, Jonathan D. 1996. *God's Chinese Son: The Taiping Heavenly Kingdom of Hong Xiuquan*. New York: W.W. Norton.

Subramanian, S. V. and V. R. Madhavan. 1983. *Heritage of the Tamils: Siddha Medicine*. Taramani, Tamil Nadu: International Institute of Tamil Studies, TTTI.

Tagore, Saumendranath. 1975. *Rammohan Roy: His Role in Indian Renaissance*. Calcutta: Asiatic Society.

Tambiah, Stanley. 1990. *Magic, Science, Religion, and the Scope of Rationality*. Cambridge: Cambridge University Press.

Tang, Xiaobing. 1996. *Global Space and the Nationalist Discourse of Modernity: The Historical Thinking of Liang Qichao*. Stanford, Calif.: Stanford University Press.

Taylor, Kim. 2000. "Medicine of Revolution: Chinese Medicine in Early Communist China, 1945–63." Ph.D. dissertation, University of Cambridge.

———. 2001. "A New Scientific and Unified Medicine: Civil War in China and the New Acumoxa 1945–49." In *Innovation in Chinese Medicine: Festschrift in Commemoration of Lu Gwei-Djen*, ed. Elizabeth Hsu, 136–243. Cambridge: Cambridge University Press.

Thatte, D. G. 1988. *Acupuncture Marma and Other Asian Therapeutic Techniques*. Varanasi: Chaukhamba Orientalia.

Thrasher, Alan R. 1980. "Foundations of Chinese Music: A Study of Ethics and Aesthetics." Ph.D. dissertation, Wesleyan University.

Tilak, Moses. 1982. *Kalaripayat and Marma Adi (Varmam)*. Madras: Neil Publication.

Trawick, Margaret. 1992. "An Ayurvedic Theory of Cancer." In *Anthropological Approaches to the Study of Ethnomedicine*, ed. Mark Nichter, 207–22. Philadelphia: Gordon and Breach.

Trivedi, Peeyush. 1998. *Acupressure*. Jaipur: Vidya Bhawan.

Turner, Bryan S. 1995. *Medical Power and Social Knowledge*. London: Sage.

Turner, Victor. 1974. *Dramas, Fields, and Metaphors: Symbolic Action in Human Society*. Ithaca, N.Y.: Cornell University Press.

———. 1982. *From Ritual to Theater: The Human Seriousness of Play*. New York: Performing Arts Journal Publications.

Tytler, John. 1935. *Centenary Volume of the Calcutta Medical College*. Calcutta:

Unschuld, Paul U. 1978. *Medical Ethics in Imperial China: A Study in Historical Anthropology*. Berkeley: University of California Press.

———. 1985. *Medicine in China: A History of Ideas*. Berkeley: University of California Press.

———. 1989. *Approaches to Traditional Chinese Medical Literature*. Dordrecht: Kluwer Academic.

———. 1992. "Epistemological Issues and Changing Legitimation: Traditional Chinese Medicine in the Twentieth Century." In *Paths to Asian Medical Knowledge*, ed. Charles Leslie and Allan Young, 44–61. Berkeley: University of California Press.

———. 1998. *Forgotten Traditions of Ancient Chinese Medicine*. Brookline, Mass.: Paradigm Publications.

Van der Knoef, Justus Maria. 1980. "Dutch Colonial Policy in Indonesia, 1900–1941." Ph.D. dissertation, University of Michigan.

Van der Veur, Paul. 1987. *Toward a Glorious Indonesia: Reminiscences and Observations of Dr. Soetomo*. Southeast Asia Series 81. Athens: Ohio University Center for International Studies.

Van Doorn, Jacobus. 1983. *A Divided Society: Segmentation and Mediation in Late Colonial Indonesia*. Rotterdam: Faculty of Social Sciences, Erasmus University.

Van Heteran, G. 1996. "Which Differences Will Have to Go: The Variety of Physiological Differentiations in the Colonial Context of Java 1860–1900," *In Health Care in Java: Past and Present*, ed Peter Boomgaard, Rosalia Sciortino, and Ines A. Smith, 5–19. Leiden: KTLV Press.

Van Hollen, Cecilia. 2003. *Birth on the Threshold: Childbirth and Modernity in South India*. Berkeley: University of California Press.

Verma, Rupalee. 1995. "Western Medicine, Indigenous Doctor and Colonial Medical Education." *Itinario* 3, 19: 130–41.

Vincent, Charles and Adrian Furnham. 1997. *Complementary Medicine*. Chichester: Wiley.

Visvanathan, Shiv. 1985. *Organizing for Science: The Making of an Industrial Research Laboratory*. New Delhi: Oxford University Press.

———. 1997. *The Carnival of Science*. New Delhi: Oxford University Press.

Waley, Arthur, trans. 1937. *The Book of Songs*. London: Allen and Unwin.

Waley-Cohen, Joanna. 1999. *The Sextants of Beijing: Global Currents in Chinese History*. New York: W.W. Norton.

Wang, Hui. 1995. "The Fate of 'Mr. Science" in China: The Concept of Science and Its Applications in Modern Chinese Thought." *Positions* 3(1): 1–68.

Wang Wei. 1979. "Chapter One: Corrective Surgery Definitions and Terms, Scope of Treatment and Future Developments." In *Zhengfu Waike Xue* (Corrective Surgery), ed. Zhang Disheng. Shanghai: Shanghai Science and Technology Press.

White, David Gordon. 1996. *The Alchemical Body: Siddha Traditions in Medieval India.* Chicago: University of Chicago Press.

———. 2000. *Tantra in Practice.* Princeton, N.J.: Princeton University Press.

Wittrock, Bjorn. 1998. "Early Modernities: Varieties and Transitions." *Daedalus* 127, 3: 19–40.

World Health Organization. 2002a. *WHO Traditional Medicine Strategy 2002–2005.* Geneva: WHO.

———. 2002b. "Traditional Medicine: Growing Needs and Potential." In *WHO Policy Perspectives on Medicine* 2. Geneva: WHO.

Worsley, J. R. 1990. *Traditional Chinese Acupuncture.* Wiltshire: Element Books.

Wujastyk, Dominik. 1998. *The Roots of Āyurveda: Selections from Sanskrit Medical Writings.* New York: Penguin.

———. Forthcoming. "Change and Creativity in Early Modern Indian Medical Thought." *Journal of Indian Philosophy.*

Young, Allan. 1997. *The Harmony of Illusions: Inventing Post-Traumatic Stress.* Princeton, N.J.: Princeton University Press.

Young, Jacqueline. 1997. "Headaches, Angels and Guiding Spirits." In *Acupuncture in Practice: Case History Insights from the West,* ed. Hugh MacPherson and Ted Kaptchuk. New York: Churchill Livingston.

Yu, Q. Y. 1999. *The Implementation of China's Science and Technology Policy.* Westport, Conn.: Quorum Books.

Zarrilli, Phillip. 1989. "Three Bodies of Practice in a Traditional South Indian Martial Art." *Social Science and Medicine* 28, 12: 1289–309.

———. 1995. The Kalarippayattu Martial Arts Master as Healer: Traditional Kerala Massage Therapies. *Journal of Asian Martial Arts* 4, 1: 67–83.

———. 1998. *When the Body Becomes All Eyes: Paradigms, Discourses and Practices of Power in Kalarippayattu, a South Indian Martial Art.* Delhi: Oxford University Press.

———. 2001a. "Kalarippayattu." In *Martial Arts of the World: An Encyclopedia,* vol. 1, ed. Thomas A. Green, 225–31. Santa Barbara, Calif.: ABC/CLIO.

———. 2001b. "Varma Ati." *In Martial Arts of the World: An Encyclopedia,* vol. 2, ed. Thomas A. Green, 647–51. Santa Barbara, Calif.: ABC/CLIO.

Zepp, Ira G., Jr. 1997. *The New Religious Image of Urban America: The Shopping Mall as Ceremonial Center.* Niwot: University Press of Colorado.

Zhang, Disheng, ed. 1979. *Zhengfu Waike Xue* (Corrective Surgery). Shanghai: Shanghai Science and Technology Press.

Zimmermann, Francis. 1992. "Gentle Purge: The Flower Power of Ayurveda." In *Paths to Asian Medical Knowledge,* ed. Charles Leslie and Allan Young, 209–23. Berkeley: University of California Press.

Zysk, Kenneth. 1991. *Asceticism and Healing in Ancient India: Medicine in the Buddhist Monastery.* New York: Oxford University Press.

———. 1993. "The Science of Respiration and the Doctrine of the Bodily Winds in Ancient India." *Journal of the American Oriental Society* 113: 198–213.

CONTRIBUTORS

Joseph S. Alter teaches in the anthropology department at the University of Pittsburgh. His research is in the field of medical anthropology and he has published on a range of topics including sports, sexuality, physical fitness, nationalism, health, and medicine in South Asia. Previous publications include *The Wrestlers Body: Identity and Ideology in North India, Knowing Dil Das: Stories of a Himalayan Hunter* (University of Pennsylvania Press, 2000), *Gandhi's Body: Sex, Diet and the Politics of Nationalism* (University of Pennsylvania Press, 2000), "Heaps of Health, Metaphysical Fitness: Ayurveda and the Ontology of Good Health in Medical Anthropology," and *Yoga in Modern India: The Body Between Science and Philosophy.*

Susan Brownell is Associate Professor of Anthropology at the University of Missouri, St. Louis. She is the author of *Training the Body for China: Sports in the Moral Order of the People's Republic* and coeditor of *Chinese Femininities/Chinese Masculinities: A Reader.* Her most recent research has dealt with cosmetic surgery, fashion models, and images of Chinese gender and national identity in global popular culture.

Nancy N. Chen is Associate Professor of Anthropology at the University of California, Santa Cruz. She is coeditor of *China Urban: Ethnographies of Contemporary Culture* and author of *Breathing Spaces: Qigong, Psychiatry, and Healing in China.*

S. Irfan Habib is a research scientist at the National Institute for Science, Technology and Development Studies, New Delhi. He is interested in cross-cultural exchanges of scientific knowledge between India and Central Asia, the institutionalization of the modern scientific and technological research system in late nineteenth- and twentieth-century India, and the cultural reception of modern science and the dialogue with other knowledge systems. With Dhruv Raina he has edited *Situating the History of Science: Dialogues with Joseph Needham.* He is also the author of *Ramchandra: A Popular Biography* (in Bengali), forthcoming. Among his most recent articles are "Reconciling Science with Islam in Nineteenth Century India," "Delhi Tibbiya College and Hakim Ajmal Khan's crusade for Indigenous Medicine Systems," in *Science in Islamic Civilization*, ed. Ekmelledin Ihsanoglu and Feza Gunergun, "Munshi Zakaullah and the Vernacularisation of Science in 19th century India," in *Uncharted Terrains: Essays on Science Popularisation in Pre-Independence India*, ed. N. Sehgal et al., "Sir Syed Ahmad Khan and Modernization: The Role of Aligarh Scientific Society in 19th Century India," in *Sir Syed Ahmad Khan: A Centenary Tribute*, ed. A. A. Ansari, and "Science and Cultural Diversity in a Post-Colonial Context,"in *Science and Cultural Diversity*, ed. J. J. Saldana.

Deepak Kumar teaches the history of science, society, and education at the Zakir Husain Centre for Education Studies, Jawaharlal Nehru University, New Delhi. Apart from contributing articles to various scholarly journals, he has authored *Science and the Raj: 1857–1905* and edited *Science and Empire: Essays in the Indian Context* and *Disease and Medicine in India: A Historical Overview.*

Vivienne Lo's research is on the history of Chinese medicine, in particular the history of acupuncture and moxibustion. Key publications include "'Crossing the Inner Pass' An Inner/Outer Distinction in Early Chinese Medicine," "The Influence of 'Nurturing Life Culture' on Early Chinese Medical Theory," in *Innovation in Chinese Medicine*, ed. Elisabeth Hsu, and "Survey of Research into the History and Rationale of Acupuncture and Moxa Since 1980" an introduction to the reprint of Lu and Needham, *Celestial Lancets.*

Dhruv Raina teaches at the Zakir Husain Centre for Education Studies, Jawaharlal Nehru University, New Delhi. With S. Irfan Habib he has edited *Situating the History of Science: Dialogues with Joseph Needham*. He is also the author of *Images and Contexts: The Historiography of Science and Modernity in India.*

Sylvia Schroer is an acupuncturist and herbalist specializing in the Japanese techniques of Toyohari (acupuncture) and Kanpo (herbal medicine). She works in a variety of settings in London which include specialist clinics, a GP surgery, and a hospital. She has a degree in psychology from University College London, and is currently completing an M.Sc. in complementary therapies at the University of Westminster.

Martha Ann Selby is Associate Professor of South Asian Studies at the University of Texas at Austin. Her specialties include Tamil, Sanskrit, and Prakrit poetry and poetics, as well as representations of women and gender dynamics in classical period texts. She is the author of *Grow Long, Blessed Night: Love Poems from Classical India*. A recent awardee of research fellowships from the National Endowment for the Humanities, the American Council of Learned Societies, and the Guggenheim Foundation, she is currently completing a manuscript titled *Sanskrit Gynecologies: The Semiotics of Gender and Femininity in Sanskrit Medical Texts*.

Cecilia Van Hollen teaches anthropology and South Asian studies at Syracuse University. Her scholarly interests are in critical medical anthropology, reproduction, gender, and South Asia studies. She is the author of *Birth on the Threshold: Childbirth and Modernity in India*. She has also published articles on theoretical approaches to the anthropology of birth, and on family planning, postpartum practices, and maternal and child health development projects in India. She is now working on a social-cultural study of AIDS in India.

Index

Abeyasekere, Susan, 86

Abeysinghe, P. M. P., 156 n. 42

acupuncture, 5; European, 61; exorcism, 45, 56; meridians, 80; Worsley style, 58, 59

Acupuncture for Everyone, 37

Acupuncture Marma and Other Asian Therapeutic Techniques, 36

Acupressure Health Center, 27

adangal, 155 nn. 35, 38. See also *marma*; *nila*

adangal therapy, 34

Adas, Michael, 68

AIDS, 18, 104

Akūpreśur: Prakṛtic Upchār, 27

Akūpreśur: Siddhānth āwñ Cikitsā, 27

Al-Khafaji, Mazin, 57

al-Qanunfi'l tibb, 70

alchemy, 17–19, 22, 40, 73, 74, 151 n. 4

alternative modernities, 19

alternative therapies, 64

All India Institute of Hygiene and Public Health, 85

All India Institute of Medical Science, 25

allopathic medicine, 68, 77, 97. *See also* biomedicine; Western medicine

Anagnost, Ann, 113

anatomy, 68

Andrews, Bridie, 78

antibody test, 99

Appadurai, Arjun, 12, 129, 142

Aristotle, 15

Arnold, David, 4, 159 nn. 5, 8

Arya Vaidya Sala, 75

Arya Vaidya Samajam Conference, 74

Atreya, 126

Āyurveda, 2, 3, 6–8, 10, 24, 71, 74, 120–31; and "accomplished women," 120; as brand, 127–29; classical, 125; and commodities, 129; and drug regulation, 159 n. 15; Euro-American representations of, 125–29; formal training in, 121; knowledge transmission of, 29; and nationalist identity, 89; and New Age spirituality, 17; as science, 74, 75, 100

Āyurvedic: cosmetics, 130; drug classification, 160 n. 31; epistemology, 99; literature, 12, 25, 29, 68, 122–25, 156 n. 41; medical practice, 69; skin care, 128; spa culture, 130

Āyurvedic and Unani Medical College, 69

Āyurvedic Healing for Women, 125

Ayuryoga, 11, 12, 122

AZT, 101

Bagchi, Asoke, K., 76

Baker, Kevin, 57

Bala, Poonam, 159 n. 5

Basham, A. L., 159 n. 10

beauty, 12, 148, 149; and cosmetic surgery, 138

Bernal, Martin, 67

Bhishagratna, Kaviraj Kunjalal, 123, 124

Bian Que, 56

Bikram Yoga, 130

biomedicine, 10, 12, 90, 91, 98, 132–36; categories, 17; and colonization, 90; as hegemonic, 100; and HIV/AIDS, 101; market monopoly of, 102; model, 64; and pharmaceutical companies, 103; as tool of imperialism, 92. *See also* allopathy; Western medicine

Bivins, Roberta E., 57

bloodletting, 5, 35, 36, 55, 153 n. 14, 154 n. 24, 156 n. 44

Bodde, Derk, 56

Bode, Maarten, 24, 91

body, 7; bodily practice, 150; boundaries of, 65; ecologic, 47; and environment, 51; and health, 15; image, 149; and

Acknowledgments

This volume is the direct result of support provided by the Asian Studies Center at the University of Pittsburgh. In particular, I would like to thank Bell Yung, the director of the Asian Studies Center, for his support and encouragement. I would also like to thank Dianne Dakis, Elizabeth Greene, and Doreen Hernandez for their hard work. The Asian Studies Center functions under the auspices of the University Center for International Studies, and I am grateful to this body for both intellectual and financial support. Additional very generous financial support was provided by the Dean of the Faculty of Arts and Sciences (now Arts and Sciences), through a Faculty Research and Scholarship Program Grant and by the Provost. My sincere thanks to Dean N. John Cooper and Provost James V. Maher. Smaller but significant contributions from the University Honors College, the Japan Council, and the Department of Anthropology were also very much appreciated.

Along with the contributing authors I would like to thank a group of scholars whose work contributed to the development of this volume: Anthony Barbieri-Low, Fred Clothey, Nicole Constable, Christopher Cullen, Jonathan Erlen, Waltraud Ernst, Paul Griffiths, Akiko Hashimoto, Sean Hsian-lin Lei, Katheryn Linduff, Evelyn Rawski, Ruth Rogaski, Richard Smetherst, Alec Stewart, Pamela Stewart, Andrew Strathern, C. Michele Thompson, and Bell Yung. A number of students played a vital role, for which I am grateful: Tina Phillips, Kara Pampanin, and the indefatigable Daisy Xia-hui Yang.